Rocky Mountain West

ROCKY MOUNTAIN WEST

Colorado, Wyoming, and Montana,
1859–1915

Duane A. Smith

Histories of the American Frontier
Ray Allen Billington, General Editor

Howard R. Lamar, Coeditor
Martin Ridge, Coeditor
David J. Weber, Coeditor

UNIVERSITY OF NEW MEXICO PRESS : Albuquerque

Dedicated to the memory
of a dear friend and fellow scholar
John Creighton

Library of Congress Cataloging-in-Publication Data
Smith, Duane A.
  Rocky Mountain West: Colorado, Wyoming, and
Montana, 1859–1915/Duane A. Smith—1st ed.
    p.   cm.—(Histories of the American frontier)
  Includes bibliographical references (p.   ) and
index.
  ISBN 0-8263-1339-6 (cl.).
  ISBN 0-8263-1340-X (pbk.)
  1. Rocky Mountain Region—History. 2. Colo-
rado—History. 3. Wyoming—History. 4. Montana—
History. I. Title. II. Series.
F721.S65 1992
978—dc20 91-41638
CIP

Design by Susan Gutnik

CONTENTS

FOREWORD

W hen the first argonauts in the Pike's gold rush of 1859 came to the area where Denver is today, they could not fail to see the central Rockies, usually snow-capped and shimmering in the western distance. And as Duane Smith observes in his fine new study, *Rocky Mountain West: Colorado, Wyoming, and Montana, 1859–1915*, the Rockies' vast overwhelming physical presence somehow conveyed to every viewer—whether explorer, goldseeker, or settler, the realization that more than a change in the landscape was occurring in their lives—that their very existence in these mountains would be a different, even unique, frontier experience.

As an expert on the history of the American West at Fort Lewis College, Durango, Professor Duane Smith is already nationally known for his excellent studies of Colorado's mining and urban past. But in *Rocky Mountain West* he has not only produced a general history of the first half century of the three northernmost mountain states, he has captured a sense of their regional uniqueness in scores of ways and at many levels. As he himself notes in his Preface, "no man or woman ever goes into those mountains and succeeds, except on the mountains' terms."

The story of the settlers' interaction with a powerful nature is only one of several major themes in this fresh, lively, and persuasive new synthesis. In addition to providing us with readable narrative histories of Colorado, Wyoming, and Montana between 1859 and 1915, he explains how they related to and affected one another—how, for example, a gold rush to Idaho or Montana could threaten Colorado's economic future; or later, how union labor leaders headquartered in Butte could affect the lives and fortunes of miners at Leadville or Cripple Creek as fully as absentee mine owners could.

Central to Smith's understanding of the Rocky Mountain West is his conviction that, unlike other western regions, the "frontier stage" there passed swiftly. It had disappeared, he writes, "within five years of the mining rushes into Colorado's eastern and western slopes and western Montana." Instead this region was characterized by instant settlement, the overnight rise of urban centers, the appearance of the twin economic forces of industrialization and capitalism, and the completion of an adequate transportation system. Moreover, the complex urban and industrial society that emerged did not resemble a frontier community so much as it did urban towns in the East. And where most observers would expect this to be a narrative of progress and modernization—which it is in many ways—Smith goes beyond to describe cycles of boom and bust, gripping scenes of economic hardship, examples of injustice to labor, and veritable sagas of cynical corporate exploitation of the resources of the Rockies. And perhaps most important of all, he notes that long after the frontier had been occupied and conquered, nature remained a central actor in human affairs there.

These larger themes are but part of an engaging and colorful narrative about the specific mineral rushes that occurred in each state. The story of Central City and Helena are here along with the up-again, down-again saga of Denver's and Butte's competition to be the "Queen City of the Rockies." We also learn about Helena's and Cripple Creek's fierce efforts to avoid becoming ghost towns like Virginia City, Montana. Smith's accounts of the fabulous gold boom at Cripple Creek and the way Montana's rival "Copper Kings" engineered a fantastic rise in copper production at the turn of the century are exceptionally fresh and clear. Nor does Smith neglect the roles of railroads, ranching, irrigated agriculture, immigrant labor, or the experiences of women and families.

One senses that he also understands exactly how settlers, miners, and mine owners felt about their plight in the depression-ridden 1890s and how strongly residents resented control by outside interests and the seemingly unfair rules about lands, forests, and water imposed by the federal government.

Writing from the inside, as it were, Smith constantly challenges our usual inclination to see a lingering *frontier* in the Rockies by explaining how urban, progress-oriented, and materialistic the settlers were and how they demanded the latest conveniences, whether they were new mining technologies, home comforts, or the current fashion in clothes. He clinches his argument with descriptions of the successful crusades for the vote for women, the election of progressive reform leaders to political office, and the Rocky Mountain public's enthusiasm for baseball and football. Smith even finds that an environmental crusade against the toxic fumes spewed forth by Butte's copper mills came many years before full national awareness of the dangers of industrial pollution.

Smith concludes his discerning study by noting how Rocky Mountain residents at the beginning of the twentieth century experienced a growing desire to recapture a lost frontier and wilderness by successfully advocating the creation of four national parks—Yellowstone, Mesa Verde, Glacier, and Rocky Mountain National—by 1915. In a moving closing passage he writes:

> These national parks preserved the vanishing frontier as nearly as anything could in 1915. The dream of 1859 had been transmuted into something strangely different from, and yet hauntingly similar to, the goals that a twentieth-century generation had set for itself. In preserving the past, the parks showed to the future that once there had been a Camelot in the Rocky Mountains. Women and men could still keep their dream in the midst of the progress that was transforming the world around them. The soul of the West lived on (p. 236).

When Ray Allen Billington, distinguished historian of the American West, founded the *The Histories of the American Frontier Series* in 1961, he envisaged the completion of a set of volumes devoted to the regional and topical histories of the frontier experience. In the early years of the Series, such fine volumes as W. J. Eccles's *The Canadian Frontier* and Rodman Paul's *The Mining Frontiers of the Far West* amply fulfilled Billington's hopes for scholarly but highly readable narrative syntheses about the frontier experience.

In 1973, however, Billington expanded the definition of his Series to embrace new topics and new approaches that would reflect interest in social, ethnic, and environmental history. Recent volumes such as David J. Weber's *The Mexican Frontier, 1821–1846: The American Southwest under Mexico*, Sandra L. Myres's *Westering Women and the Frontier Experience*, Robert M. Utley's *The Indian Frontier of the American West*, and Elliott West's *Growing Up with the Country: Childhood on the Far Western Frontier* have been fine examples of this expanded approach.

It has been the good fortune of the present editors of the Series to have enlisted Duane Smith as an author, for his highly readable *Rocky Mountain West* embraces both Ray Billington's older concept of frontier history, and the later approaches of regional, social, and environmental history. It is with genuine pleasure and pride that we introduce the reading public to this latest volume in the Histories of the Frontier Series.

Howard R. Lamar
Yale University

Martin Ridge
The Huntington Library

David J. Weber
Southern Methodist University

PREFACE : MAGIC OF THE MOUNTAINS

L ieutenant John Charles Fremont, resting upon the summit of what would be named Woodrow Wilson Peak in Wyoming's Wind River Range, waxed poetic when he observed a bumblebee:

> It was a strange place, the icy rock and the highest peak of the Rocky Mountains, for a lover of warm sunshine and flowers, and we pleased ourselves with the idea that he was the first of his species to cross the mountain barrier, a solitary pioneer to foretell the advance of civilization.

On that "sunny and bright" August 15, 1842, the bee became one of the victims of that advance. Fremont collected it and placed the high-flying pioneer between the "leaves of a large book."[1]

Carried away by the rugged climb and breathtaking view, and supported by the opinions of the "oldest traders of the country," the young officer believed there could be nothing higher. Fremont stood far removed from the highest peak in the Rocky Mountains, Mount Elbert, near where Leadville, Colorado, would be located one day. Still, he caught the spirit of the Rockies, as he romantically described them for his readers in reports of this and several later expeditions.

For over a generation, Americans had been reading about the "Stoney" mountains, as they had been dubbed earlier. Thirty-five years before, almost to the day, Meriwether Lewis had found himself upon a less rugged part of the Continental Divide on the boundary between the eventual states of Montana and Idaho. "I discovered immense ranges of high mountains still to the West of us with their tops partially covered with snow." Proceeding down the western side, he "first tasted the water of the great Columbia river." Coming back in July 1806, Lewis wrote of the "beautiful and extensive high plain" along the foothills.[2]

While Lewis and Clark went north, that inveterate westerner President Thomas Jefferson sent Major Zebulon Pike to explore the southern portion of the Louisiana Purchase. The hot, dry plains did not interest Pike, but he was captivated by the mountains, especially one that he called the "Grand Mountain" and attempted to climb in November 1806.

> The summit of the Grand Peak, which was entirely bare of vegetation and covered with snow, now appeared at the distance of 15 or 16 miles from us, and as high again as what we had ascended, and would have taken a whole day's march to have arrived at its base, when I believe no human being could have ascended to its pinnacle.

Only fourteen years later, on July 14, members of the Long expedition conquered that very peak; botanist Edwin James observed that "from the summit of the Peak, the view towards the north, west, and southwest, is diversified with innumerable mountains, all white with snow." The Rockies impressed him mightily, and he concluded that "the most prominent feature of the continent of North America is the great chain of the Rocky Mountains . . ."[3] For a brief while, that peak would be named after James, but Pike claimed the final honor.

These explorers painted a picture of a strikingly beautiful land that was, at the same time, very different from any other that American pioneers had already settled. This was a romantic land, and perchance a practical and profitable one as well, as Lewis and others had hinted. Several lifetimes and a tragic Civil War later, Katharine Lee Bates would paint it best in words. Captivated by the panorama from the top of Pike's Peak in 1893, she penned the verses to "America the Beautiful." Bates brought together the romantic view of nature, which Americans had inherited from Europe, and combined it with her generation's faith in progress. The "purple mountain majesties" symbolically stand at the heart of her vision.

Immense and rugged, this backbone of America served as a picket fence between plain and basin. Its foothills began somewhere immediately west of the "Great American Desert," as maps labeled the plains. Some maps had them starting in Kansas or Nebraska, but by the time of Fremont the location had become generally standard and accurate.

The forty-niners, in their haste to reach the golden streams of California, rushed right over the Rockies and through that rolling, natural gateway, South Pass. William Swain, fairly typically, commented, "We have looked forward to this pass with anxiety for weeks, as the spot where half our toils would be over." His party admired the Wind River Range at a distance and described central Wyoming as a "broken, rocky, mountainous country," which was also "sandy, gravelly, windy, and sage-filled"—hardly an appropriate characterization for a romantic land.[4]

The Rocky Mountains were all these things and more. They were part of the dream that pushed the settlement of the continent, the dream of new opportunities that awaited those who journeyed westward. The fur trappers had first tapped the Rockies for monetary rewards; they and the explorers had made them seem an adventuresome and romantic place. They seemed to harbor a rich treasury of natural resources and certainly provided vast acreages for those who dared to meet the mountains' challenge. The public read and pondered. This Rocky Mountain frontier seemed to hold potential for many of them, who hoped that they would be the pioneers who got there in time to get something for nothing—or, as some of the miners later explained it, "to get rich without working." What many of them never comprehended was that no man or woman ever goes into these mountains and succeeds, except on the mountains' terms.

For a brief moment more, this land would be a frontier, a little-explored, undeveloped, and unsettled land. At that point, it promised everything to everybody, epitomizing the promised land of milk and honey. Mining then turned it inside out with a speed that was only exceeded by the rush to California; it set the pace and direction of Rocky Mountain development. Materialism, urbanism, transportation, exploitation, industrialism, capitalism, society, and the inventions of the day overwhelmed the frontier. Within five years of the mining rushes into Colorado's eastern and western slopes and western Montana, the frontier was gone, except for isolated pockets. It took the railroad, mining, and ranching slightly longer than a decade to accomplish the same thing in western Wyoming. In the history of mankind, the frontier was that blink of an eye between wilderness and civilization.

But the frontier did not die; it would not die. The myth endured. In some ways, it had always been a myth—the freedom, the independence, that rugged individualism, the black-and-white simplicity of life, and western democracy and economic opportunity.[5] As surely as there lies somewhere in the myths of history a historical basis for the Arthurian legend and Camelot, there was once a frontier in the Rocky Mountains. Nevertheless, the mythic frontier has proven to be much more durable and significant than the physical frontier.

The frontier was, and is, a state of mind, the "gunsmoke and gallop west," a fleeting moment of time that generated an eternity of memories. It bequeathed to its descendants a hodgepodge of legacies that would be built upon, according to the old western saying, "with the calm confidence of a Christian holding four aces."[6]

In the final analysis, the story is man in awe of these mountains, man versus the mountains, and man adjusting to them. The millenniums-old Rocky Mountains have been relentless, uncompromising, and unforgiving adversaries of those puny individuals who have sought to challenge and conquer them during the past century and a half. Visitors and residents alike tended to be overawed by their breathtaking majesty and grandeur, calling them, for lack of something more original, "God's country." That description fit very well with the concept held by Americans of the late nineteenth century that they were the chosen people, the manifestation of God's destiny fulfilled. That the chosen people bowed to a golden calf in their scramble for property and profit did not seem to contradict that belief. They mixed the sacred and the profane with reckless abandon, from the East Coast to the West.

Over all of man's activities towered the Rocky Mountains. The ruggedness, the height, the loneliness, the larger-than-life environment, the natural wonders, the space, the abundant resources, the magic of the mountains—all came in for their share of discussion by nineteenth- and twentieth-century writers.[7] The Rockies had an impact, for better or worse, on those who came into contact with them. They molded, influenced, refined by adversity, fooled by success, and, quite frequently, defeated man, who has yet to conquer them. The Rocky Mountains remain the one constant focus throughout the story of how men and women have attempted to live and work in this vast network of foothills, valleys, canyons, and mountains that constitute the whole.

In the end, one could conclude that the Rocky Mountains are a timeless, natural place, the history of which encompasses both the realities of man and his culture, as they have attempted to match its high-country challenges. At the same time, there exists a state of mind about a mythic frontier, which is just as timeless. The mountains are eternal; the fate of man is unknown.

Pondering the mountains and their people, poet Thomas Hornsby

Ferril wrote these words in his hauntingly bittersweet and incisive poem, "Magenta":

> Once, up in Gilpin County, Colorado
> When a long blue afternoon was standing on end
> Like a tombstone sinking into the Rocky mountains,
> I found myself in a town where no one was,
>
> . . .
>
> The town was high and lonely in the mountains;
> There was nothing to listen to but the wasting of
> The glaciers and a wind that had no trees.
> And many houses were gone, only masonry
> Of stone foundations tilting over the canyon.

What follows in these chapters are the chronicles of scores of Gilpin counties and Central cities, from 1858 through 1915. Opening with the Pike's Peak gold rush, which brought permanent settlement, the story closes with the creation of Rocky Mountain National Park. Along with Yellowstone and Glacier national parks, it was designed to preserve the wilderness that the first settlers had tried so valiantly to conquer. The circle was complete.

Montana, Wyoming, and Colorado—from the sweeping Big Sky country through rolling South Pass, to the jagged San Juans—encompass this region, a region dominated by the Rocky Mountains, the backbone of the continent, the heart of the West. The mountains and the attempts to settle them are the focus of the story, but the sweep must also include the nearby high plains, which were so impacted by the settlement immediatley west of them. In examining the broad contours of regional history, a determined effort has been made to retain the uniqueness of the individual locales about which Ferril so movingly wrote.

In fifty-eight years, these three states evolved from wilderness through frontier and to permanent settlement. The opening three chapters recount the founding of these struggling territories and their interrelationships during the 1860s. The next five chapters trace their development to the watershed "silver crisis" of the 1890s; the last five chapters follow events through 1915, as the old West becomes the new. It is a geographic and historic region framed by a beautiful and varied land; a story of reality and legend, of success and failure; a potpourri of memories, of high moments and low.

Historians are supposed to untangle the past, give context to the present, and provide guidance for the future. I hope to have achieved these aims for the Rocky Mountain states, whose history is exciting, varied, and relevant.

One cannot write a book of this sweep without assuming deep debts of gratitude to many people and institutions. Research in preparation for this project was conducted in libraries and archives from the East Coast to the West. My sincere thanks go to all the librarians and archivists who were so considerate and professionally helpful. No work of this kind can be accomplished without relying on the research of other scholars. My obligation to them is apparent in the footnotes of each chapter.

The coeditors of the *Histories of the American Frontier* series—Howard Lamar, Martin Ridge, and David Weber—read the manuscript and provided most appreciated advice and direction. During research trips to the Huntington Library, I had the privilege of getting to know Ray Billington and to savor his love and enthusiasm for the American West. It is a special honor to be asked to write a book in the series that he established and nurtured through its early years.

As she has done for three decades, Gay Smith offered her fine sense of language and her sharp editing pen that is reflected on every page of this book. My thanks are also extended to David Holtby and the staff of the University of New Mexico Press, who did the final editing and guided the manuscript into becoming a book.

1 : COLORADO

G old! Gold in the Pike's Peak country! Another California! The mother lode of the Rocky Mountains had been discovered. In newspaper headlines and then in the excited voices of those hoping to strike it rich, news of a new gold field promised much to the adventurous American in fall of 1858. Those glorious days of 1848–49 had at last seemingly reemerged, when dreams became reality and reality seemed unreal in the golden streams of California. Now, much nearer to the states, gold had been found in the central Rockies.

Suddenly, the profit of the fur trade, the adventures of John C. Fremont, and the lure of the Rockies appeared to be within the grasp of the average American. Few, indeed, were those who had been presented with this opportunity before, and another one would be unlikely to come again within their lifetime.

Since the days of Spanish exploration, men had probed the inner depths of these mountains. The Spanish had been especially active in the far southwestern ranges, leaving behind names for the places in which they dug: La Plata, Animas, and San Juan. They also left legends of lost mines, along with scattered holes and log-ribbed portals, which gave later prospectors reason to ponder the fortunes of mining. Far-ranging trappers added a few more stories, but they were not interested in digging for gold.

Legends surfeited the armchair adventurer; facts buttressed those who had more determination and ambition to seek a fortune in the West. The American and Spanish governments unintentionally pro-

vided a reference point for the hardheaded realists who did not suc-
cumb to will-o'-the-wisp legends. In the hot summer of 1806, the Pike
expedition journeyed west to explore the southern portion of the recently acquired Louisiana Purchase. The expedition eventually trespassed onto Spanish Territory, where a patrol arrested the Americans
and took them to Santa Fe.

There, Pike encountered James Purcell, who "assured me" that he
had found gold "on the head of the La Platte," and had carried some
of the "virgin mineral in his pouch for months."[1] The gold did little
good for Purcell; the Spanish would not allow him to leave New Mexico,
and he refused to show them the gold-bearing site, which he believed
to be in American territory.

In the following years, a few more stories of gold came out of the
region, but not until 1849, when anything seemed possible, did interest
really begin to spark, if not to flame. California-bound immigrants
usually avoided the rugged, central Rockies, a barrier to be bypassed
at all costs, if speed and time held any importance. A few travelers,
however, sojourned briefly along the foothills; one of them, Oliver P.
Goodwin, claimed several years later to have toured the front range
in 1849, finding a few "good prospects."

The turning point came the next year on a quiet June day, when a
party of Cherokees, on their way from Indian Territory to intersect the
Oregon Trail, camped on what they called Ralston Creek, a few miles
from the future site of Denver. One of them kept a diary and noted
on the twenty-second, "Gold found." It was not enough to keep them
there, however; they were bound for the "banks of the Sacramento,"
where more than a few flakes awaited the lucky miner.[2]

In the remaining years of the 1850s, intriguing reports filtered back
to the border towns. The Lawrence, Kansas, *Herald of Freedom*, on May
26, 1855, reported "gold in great abundance" in the headwaters of the
Arkansas River. D. C. Hail, traveling to California, wrote a letter that
was reprinted in the Little Rock *True Democrat* of April 13, 1858, which
told of gold prospects on the upper waters of the Arkansas and Platte
rivers. Even as men prospected along the foothills, the Marysville *Daily
California Express* of July 21, 1858, reported "gold fever" raging in Kansas, the consequence of discoveries in the western part of the territory.[3]
The communications lag precludes this item referring to any events of
that summer, so the editor must have been alluding to an earlier rumor.
Although always eager to read about new discoveries, Californians did
not rush to the Pike's Peak excitement—they had their own Comstock
in neighboring Nevada.

The very same month that Marysvillites were reading about Kansas gold fever, gold had actually been discovered there by a party moving out of Georgia and Indian Territory. This group came because of the 1850 find. Under the leadership of an experienced Georgia and California miner, William Green Russell, a party of over one hundred traveled over the Santa Fe Trail, turned northwest at that relic of another era, Bent's Fort, and reached the site of future Denver in May. Prospecting Cherry Creek and nearby streams did not produce promising "color" in their pans. They panned mostly discouragement. Easily disillusioned, many of them turned dejectedly homeward. But not Russell, his two brothers, and a handful of friends, who stayed on and in early July found a small pocket of gold (maybe two to three hundred dollars worth) and continued to prospect.

Unknown to them, a second party was prospecting farther south near Pike's Peak. It had come from Lawrence, Kansas, enticed by gold that a Delaware Indian, Fall Leaf, had brought back in 1857, after serving as an army scout. Vague about where he had obtained the gold, Fall Leaf refused to lead the party. That refusal should have served as a warning. But the group came anyway and found no gold. These prospectors moved across the front range into the San Luis Valley and stopped at Fort Garland. Somehow, the news of the Russell discovery had reached there and they hurried northward.

The two parties joined and prospected with little more success. Up to now, however, their long months away from home and their hard work had produced only a few hundred dollars. Not much reward for so much trouble. Yet gold rushes have been built on far less, and the turning point was at hand. That mysterious mountain "telegraph" somehow spread the word of the prospecting both south and north, where trader John Cantrell heard about it at Fort Laramie. On his way back east, he detoured to see the "mines" and left with a small amount of placer gold. A vivid imagination and many miles of lonely prairie in which to let it flourish did the rest, as the Paul Revere of the Pike's Peak rush hied himself to the east.

By the time he reached "civilization," the magnitude of the discovery had become greatly inflated. On the basis of his story, the Kansas City *Journal of Commerce*, on August 26, was emblazoned with the headline, "The New El Dorado!!! Gold in Kansas Territory."[4]

From this beginning came the Pike's Peak gold rush. The first in time and size in the Rocky Mountains, it proved to be only the first of about two-score similar rushes in subsequent decades. The pattern would become familiar by the time of Butte in the 1870s or Cripple

Creek in the 1890s. Sometimes, the pattern was disturbingly similar, but always the hope persisted that just over the next mountain would be the mother lode of gold, silver, copper, even coal, not to mention lead, zinc, and other less glamorous minerals.

It took a chance discovery, grandiose rumors, and a footloose population that was willing to race for the "New El Dorado" to produce the proper explosive reaction. The Rocky Mountains would have a surplus of all these factors for the rest of the century. Mix with them those outsiders who wanted to make a quick profit, invest, or just "see the elephant," and the marriage between the region and its chief boom industry was consummated. Neither the industry nor the Rocky Mountains would ever be the same again.

Although excitement and adventure colored the days, make no mistake about it, greed drove the multitudes. From the idea of "getting rich without working" at the diggings to the phenomenon of "mining the miners," Americans moved to exploit the opportunities at hand. Some stayed home to write guidebooks and dream up all kinds of fancy gold machines and gadgets that every rusher needed to own. That perhaps illustrates best the ultimate exploitation—never leaving the East or Midwest to make money off the Rocky Mountains. Such philosophical points received little consideration, as exploitation came early and stayed late.

The word was gold. No time could be lost—those who arrived first stood to profit the most. They rushed to get there, stake a claim, make a fortune, and get back home, maybe before a season expired.

Americans read about all of it in their newspapers, those heralds of good fortune and bright prospects. Cantrell, then the papers, broadcast the news and inflated the wildest of stories. On September 20, the New York *Times,* crediting an interview from the St. Louis *Democrat,* reported that gold had been found at Cherry Creek, "in all places" prospected, and predicted that a "new gold fever" was plainly at hand. A few expressed doubt; the St. Louis *Republican,* on October 5, noted discouragingly that the latest accounts from the mines (note how the term *mines* was now accepted) were unfavorable. Evidence, both real and imagined, continued to accumulate, however. Finally, the editorial appeared on February 21, 1859, in the *Times,* which announced that there was "no longer room for doubt" about the discovery of "an important gold region."[5]

Doubt! Many Americans harbored no doubts whatsoever—they wanted to believe. For them, the Pike's Peak news came as a blessing.

Not only did it promise a better, an easier, life, but it also offered them the opportunity to get away from their own depressed conditions.

Times were not good in the Midwest, from which most of the fifty-niners would depart as soon as weather permitted. The depression of 1857 had hit this region and its agriculture particularly hard. The Rocky Mountain economic events would always be played out against the background of the national setting.[6] Further motivation for migration came from the debilitating fevers and ague, which left sufferers seeking a change of climate. Having read or heard about earlier accounts of the West's salubrious one, they suspected the mountains might be just the place to regain their health. Those perceptive enough to grasp the trend of the times saw the threatening clouds of sectionalism and slavery hovering on the horizon. It might be time to move west before the storm broke.

A rush seldom resulted from just a pull; there needed to be a push as well, to start large numbers of otherwise homeloving, stable people moving. The drifting crowd always stood ready for new excitement, but a mining frontier needed permanence, not the transience of those who were here today and gone tomorrow.

A few migrants became fifty-eighters, braving the undependable, late fall weather in their hurry to reach Pike's Peak. Much to the amazement of the Russell and Lawrence parties, these newcomers dropped into their camps with unbelievable stories of gold in the Pike's Peak country. With cold weather and winter storms fast approaching, cutting off the opportunity for the disillusioned to return east, they all set up winter quarters. Samuel Curtis was one who dug and decided that "it was very hard work and after I had washed one pan full I concluded it was here, but that I was not adapted to digging it." With time on their hands, the fifty-eighters turned to town planning and promoting, long-cherished frontier practices. Soon Denver, St. Charles, and Auraria competed on paper to be the destination of the fifty-niners.[7]

The early miners idled and dreamed the winter days away, abetted by a load of Taos Lightning, which "Uncle Dick" Wootten thoughtfully freighted up to the little settlements on Cherry Creek. During the winter, a few hardy prospectors ventured into the mountains in an attempt to find the places from which gold washed down into the streams.

During this time, thousands of Americans in the East dreamed of leaving for the "New El Dorado" in the spring. They read guidebooks, which foisted all kinds of information—and misinformation—on the unsuspecting public; they purchased special Pike's Peak mining equipment, money belts, and other items, all made especially for them. And they selected which "gateway," the shortest route to the mines, they planned to use and prepared to depart.

In the late winter and early spring, they came, perhaps as many as 100,000 (the exact number will never be known). They moved over all types of trails, using pitifully poor maps that showed nonexistent water holes. The common theme of all the guidebooks was how easy the trip would be. In the race to get rich without working, it seemed only right that the trip west would be a smooth one; both the authors and their readers assumed it would be so.

Most of the fifty-niners rode in wagons or on horseback, a few walked or pushed handcarts, and one dreamer lured a party aboard his wind wagon. Designed to be the ultimate in speed, ease, and comfort—a real prairie schooner, complete with sails—it sank forever when it encountered a gully not far from port. Still, they came—gullible, excited, in a hurry.

Perhaps fifty thousand persevered and reached Denver (by spring, Denver had become the generally acknowledged name, giving it a formidable jump on becoming the "Queen of the Mountains and Plains"). Probably half of those fifty thousand decamped after a few discouraging weeks of hard and cold prospecting work in the streams. Neither gold nor well-paying jobs met them, but the high cost of living relentlessly undercut everything they did.

Many of the early arrivals sampled the life, saw the reality, and returned—"pilgrims" and "go-backers," they would be called. Their tales of woe discouraged many along the trail, and soon, it seemed, the rush ebbed eastward as much as it flowed westward. Wrote one, "the Pike Peak Gold Diggings are all a humbug, a matter of speculation got up by men a doing business on the Mississora River . . ."

It was now being called a "humbug" in the same press that had hailed it as the "El Dorado" only three months earlier. D. C. Oakes, who wrote one of the dubious guidebooks, gained a certain degree of immortality when some sharp-witted person left a mock grave with this inscription on the wooden headboard: "Here lies the remains of D. C. Oakes, Who was the starter of this damned hoax." The angry Chicago *Press and Tribune* wrote on March 28, "We believe there is more gold to be dug out of every Illinois farm than the owners will ever produce by quitting the home diggings for those on the headwaters of the Arkansas and Platte."[8] This newspaper comment and others like it contained more truth than fiction. The 1859 rush had been predicated more upon imagination than upon fact.

The credibility of the Pike's Peak rush was preserved by several prospectors who went into the mountains. An experienced California miner, George Jackson, had discovered gold near future Idaho Springs in January 1859; he knew about human nature and gold and kept silent. The same month, a group out of the tiny settlement of Boulder, at the mouth of Boulder Canyon, found gold at what they named Gold Hill. They, too, kept quiet and waited for spring. Finally, in April, John Gregory, who also had California experience, opened the biggest discovery yet, between soon-to-be-established Central City and Black Hawk.

These three discoveries provided a firm foundation for the gold rush, but few people heard about them until late April and May. By then, it was too late for many fifty-niners. It was not too late for guidebook author, now newspaper editor, William Byers, whose *Rocky Mountain News* gave Denver an advantage unequaled by any of its rivals when it appeared in April. Byers barely beat out another rival, the ill-starred Oakes, whose *Cherry Creek Pioneer* lost the newspaper race by a matter of minutes and did not survive to publish a second issue. Wrote editor Byers, a booster from the start:

> Gold, in scale, exists in sufficient quantity to reward the
> working miner, over a large surface of the plain on the
> eastern slope of the mountain . . .
> If the richness and extent of the Gold Regions realize their
> present promise, a new State will be organized west of
> Kansas and Nebraska ere this year is closed, with a hundred
> thousand inhabitants. (April 23, 1859)

Attention now centered on Gregory's and Jackson's diggings, both called "poor man's diggings," where a pick, a shovel, and a strong back could produce a fortune. Among those who arrived to see the sights was none other than the famous New York publisher Horace Greeley, then on his way to California by stage. He detoured to check out the conflicting stories about the Pike's Peak country. "As to gold, Denver is crazy," he wrote.

Most of the farmers, storekeepers, tradesmen, teachers, and what have you—very few with any experience in mining—were not so lucky as Greeley, who happily found gold in the pan he worked (his might have been salted!). They found the work of mining backbreaking and not always as remunerative as promised. Even Greeley was wise enough to warn his *Tribune* readers that "a good farmer or mechanic will usually make money faster, and of course immeasurably easier, by sticking to his own business than by deserting it for gold diggings."

The real fifty-niners, in their search for placer, or free, gold claims, found that most of them yielded only busted hopes, rather than gold in the pan. Harry Faulkner knew that from firsthand experience; comments such as "hope fails" and "have done our best and failed" laced his diary over a period of some months. He remained undiscouraged, understanding that it happened all the time: "We find here many who have been to the mines and are returning, sick of gold-hunting, others are going up again and so it continues, a constant flow and ebb."[9]

Like their predecessors in California, the fifty-niners quickly advanced from slow, physical panning to rockers, which looked much like a baby's cradle, then on to sluice boxes and long toms. Each evolutionary step allowed more gravel to be worked at a quicker, more economical, and somewhat less labor-intensive pace. Hardly realizing what they were doing, the fifty-niners followed the primitive pattern of the industrial revolution and moved right into companies, only a step away from the corporation mining era.

At the moment, few saw any reason to be concerned about the disappearance of the poor man's diggings. In the rush to strike a bonanza, time considerations forced one to adapt. The theory upon which these processes were bedrocked was a simple one. Gold, one of the heaviest of minerals, would eventually sink to the bottom of the pan, rocker, or sluice. Then the miner simply added mercury, which has an affinity for gold, and easily separated the latter (in its free element) from surrounding materials, like the heavy black sand found with it. This became the basis of the amalgamation process that was long popular in Colorado milling.

As mining evolved, so did government. The Pike's Peak region had had no government at all, except what could be provided by far distant Kansas and Nebraska. In theory, those two territories split the Pike's Peak area between them, with Kansas claiming the lion's share. No organized basis for landownership existed in the mountains. Was this Indian land, government land, or theirs who claimed it? The Americans digging and prospecting did not have time to deal with those questions. They turned to the traditional answers—mining districts, miners' laws, and miners' courts. They had sufficed in California, and they would do so here.

These extralegal controls gave some semblance of order and exemplified frontier democracy at its most fundamental point. A meeting would be called (the first at Gregory Diggings was on June 8), a chairman elected, and opinions voiced about size of claims, water rights, and other problems. Before they were finished, these fifty-niners defined district boundaries, limited the number and size of claims a miner could hold, specified the amount of work necessary to hold a claim, and designated procedures for settling disputes. The election of a district secretary to record claims and call future meetings as needed gave a semblance of permanence to this up-to-now transitory frontier.[10]

Other districts were formed after Gregory's. Some elected more officers—constable and president, for example—and formulated more laws as needed. As a rule, all the miners wanted was something to guide their efforts and protect their claims. To them, the simplest and cheapest methods appeared to be the best.

They quickly learned that life would not be quite so simple; complaints and arguments over water rights led to further discussions. Water was required for all placer-mining methods; thus, the streams quickly resembled sewers of sand, mud, and debris, rather than the branches of a once pristine Clear Creek, along which most of the fifty-niners dug and sluiced. Soon, only the miners near the headwaters could drink sparkling mountain water and use it for working; and there was not enough water when the summer sun melted the banked snow and the rains failed to come. As soon as man arrived, he made his impact on the environment.

These problems eventually would force the formation of rudimentary water law; future Colorado would be a pioneer in this endeavor. For the moment, the miners tried to dig ditches to bring in water from outside sources. The most famous was the eleven-mile-long Consolidated Ditch, which conducted water into the Gregory District. Digging ditches in the mountains was difficult and costly work that required more than one person to accomplish successfully. Not many of these prospectors had expected to labor like this to get rich without working.[11] The fifty-niners were finding out about the hardships of mining in short order.

They were enlightened about many things that summer, not the least of which was the fact that the placer deposits failed to match those of California. Two trends resulted. One rested on the certainty that surely they were as extensive, if not as intensive, and prospectors scurried about in search of new discoveries. Their wanderings carried them north of Boulder, with no luck, and southwest into Clear Creek Valley in South Park, where they met with more success. By fall, some had even climbed over the Snowy Range and prospected on the isolated Western Slope before winter set in. This abiding faith in potential "El Dorados" that beckoned from over the next creek or mountain dominated Colorado mining for the next three decades.

Back in the established districts, the other trend emerged: the rapid disappearance of "poor man's diggings" and the rise of hard-rock mining and companies. The placer claims also required more capital and manpower than most individuals could muster. If several men cooperated, more profit could be made. Companies began to operate several claims by building large sluices and constructing short ditches to divert water. By 1860, primitive hydraulic mining made its appearance, shooting water under pressure through hoses and nozzles to wash more gravel down from stream banks into sluices.[12]

An unsightly mess ensued, but environmental concern did not prevent the fifty-niners or their descendants from using the procedure. Better control over water, more yards of gravel worked, and higher profits were the primary considerations, and hydraulicking promised all of them. California experience, not money, moved the Pike's Peak mines ahead. Colorado would be tied financially to the Midwest and East, not to the West Coast.

Even before the placers started to play out, men wise in mining realized that the gold had to come from quartz veins in the mountainsides. They followed "float" to its source—the "mother lode." Upon finding a likely outcropping, they removed the ore with pick and shovel, then panned to see what they had uncovered. They paused on the threshold of hard-rock or quartz mining, then quickly bridged the gap and began to dig. The technique created the need for blasting, timbering, shafts, and windlasses to bring the ore to the surface. All these demanded more money and skill, which were in short supply at that moment.

When the ore was brought to the surface, it had to be crushed before it could be worked by amalgamation. Primitive stone mortars, called *arrastras* by the Spaniards, were used first; they ground the ore between two large rocks. Slow, cumbersome, and not overly efficient, the *arrastras* did not provide the best solution.

Stamp mills, already in use in California, solved the problem. By late fall, several had banged into operation, as freight wagons were bringing more in. Heavy weights, run by water or steam power, hammered the ore into pulverized sand, which could be handled by introducing mercury. Milling, mining's supplementary industry, had arrived.[13] The two would dominate the industrial scene for the next generation and change the course of Rocky Mountain development.

The evolution from placer to hard-rock mining had happened with a rapidity not known in California; it had been accomplished in only one season. For a couple of years, the two mining methods would exist side by side, but the future belonged to hard-rock. Unlike California, in Colorado hard-rock mining would reign supreme.

Not everyone looked to mining for a living. Lacking self-sufficiency, the miners required nearby support bases from which to purchase supplies and to provide commercial relaxation. As a consequence, two waves of settlement advanced into the Rocky Mountains almost simultaneously—mining and, in its dust, urbanization.

Along the foothills, gateway supply towns mushroomed—Denver, Golden, Boulder, and a score of soon-forgotten rivals. They struggled for supremacy, but Denver, with its earlier start, its newspaper, its aggressive founders, and its advantageous location, surged to the fore within the year. Many communities dreamed of being banking, transportation, and commercial hubs; Denver was determined to succeed, and that bulldogged determination set it apart from its rivals' wishful dreaming. Each town eyed the others warily in the dog-eat-dog existence of mid-nineteenth-century America; each sought to exploit the slightest advantage that might give it the edge over a rival.

In the mountains, hardly a district did not contain at least one jerry-built camp; many had several. Befitting its revered number-one position, Gregory Diggings could claim Central City, Black Hawk, Missouri City, Nevada City, and Mountain City, with others not far away. Most of them grew like Topsy (having a passing knowledge of *Uncle Tom's Cabin*, these Americans understood that phrase), without guidance or plan. Their founding fathers delighted in attaching city to camp names, giving them an image of a respectable, established municipality.

These early pioneers did not relish living in what Americans would later describe as a frontier epic. They hoped to re-create quickly the life they had left behind in their former homes. That desire in itself showed a subtle change in attitudes. Most of these people had rushed westward to make their fortunes, planning to stay no longer than a season, or two at the longest. Now some of them decided to put down roots.

Pioneer life implied hard work, especially for the few families. Miner Harry Faulkner felt sympathy for women and children: "The hardest sight however is to behold four or five women with families of little children, washing and cooking in the boiling sun and obliged to gather and cut their own wood."[14] He did find some consolation in the fact that the trip west and the "salubrious air" endowed them with "excellent health."

Many of the early settlers moved out of the mountains when September brought an unmistakable hint of coming winter. A sizable percentage traveled all the way back to homes in the East and Midwest. Those who were forced to stay because of ill luck in 1859 settled in as best they could; others, like William Byers, had planned to make the Rocky Mountain West their home from the start. From this motley group of individuals and nondescript camps and villages arose permanent settlement in the Rocky Mountains, something no earlier frontier had accomplished to any significant degree.

These communities might not have looked like much to the outsider, but stature was in the beholder's eye. Harry Faulkner had passed through Auraria in May; he thought it "quite the place," with over one hundred houses. Humorist Artemus Ward later called Denver a "flourishing and beautiful city" and Colorado, the "queen of all the territories." Of the mining camps, businessman Robert Bradford could only warn a friend:

> It must be recollected however, that towns in mining districts, are like mushrooms. Houses spring up today & tomorrow a new & rich discovery is made, & away go Miners, Traders, Merchants & all, and perhaps the town is never heard of again.[15]

Abandoned sites and camps marked the advance of mining from 1859.

Along some of the streams and rivers—most notably the Arkansas and Platte rivers, and the lower Clear and Boulder creeks—agriculture took hold. Some of the would-be miners reverted to their original midwestern vocations, when they found the soil and climate conducive to farming. They also discovered a ready cash market in the mountain and foothill settlements. Maybe this was not, after all, the "Great American Desert" that they remembered from their geography books.

In the mountains, meanwhile, many were panning only disappointment. Unsuccessful Harry Faulkner spoke for those who stayed, when he confided in his diary on September 30, "Few can realize the trials of a miner here." Undaunted, he predicted:

> Thousands have left discouraged, thousands will do the same again. But next year will prove the truth of what I have said that the mines in the region equal any that have yet been found at this writing.[16]

The rush of 1859, after a winter's pause, spilled over into 1860. The immigrants kept coming. Auraria resident William Pierson knew why and wrote to a friend, "Next season will be the time to make money in the country"; there was "no humbug about it the mines are very rich."[17] The 1860 arrivals never warranted the newspaper or national attention of their 1859 brethren. Interest in Pike's Peak had waned and was diverted by a presidential election and threats of secession, which seemed more newsworthy than a rehash of Rocky Mountain mining items.

The 1860 rushers came to a much better defined area, one of known wealth and with a year's mining experience, a rudimentary road system packed down by a year's travel, an embryonic economy (supercharged by mining, at the moment), and struggling settlements with the trappings, if not the substance, of civilization. All these, amazingly enough, were acquired in a year, far more quickly than the farming frontier had managed to achieve them.

Some of the "old-timers" did not automatically roll out a welcome mat, wishing to keep this paradise for themselves, a feeling that many of their descendants have shared—the well-recognized "last settler syndrome." Erstwhile miner and longtime newspaper editor Ovando Hollister wrote:

> It does not seem very strange, either, that the old settlers—
> who had been in the mines a year!—were somewhat cold
> toward the immigrants. They felt that they had earned what
> they had got and there was chance enough for others to do
> likewise. . . . let them branch out and find mines for
> themselves, or if not, go back.[18]

There would not be so many exciting finds that year, with the best one California Gulch in the upper Arkansas River Valley. Thousands rushed to stake a claim, including those New Englanders, Horace and Augusta Tabor, who settled in Oro City. The mining frontier ebbed and flowed, just as it had done in 1859.

At the same time, some older districts were being deserted; all of them suffered some loss of population. Even California Gulch, by the end of the season, had declined; within a few years, it would be nearly forsaken. Only manmade relics littering the site served as reminders that man had passed that way in his search for wealth. The lack of steadfastness disgusted Samuel Mallory, ex-mayor of Danbury, Connecticut: "I am satisfied that many leave for want of 'pluck' and lack of energy, while others get awful homesick, and are ready to cry wolf when there is no wolf, for the sake of an excuse to go home."[19]

The next year brought the most improbable rush of all, the one to the isolated, rugged San Juan Mountains tucked way down in the southwestern corner of the new territory of Colorado. Charles Baker almost singlehandedly promoted this excitement, after completing his 1860 exploration of what became Baker's Park in the heart of the mountains. His enthusiastic letters to the *News* whetted mining appetites.

What the rushers discovered was not what they wanted or expected: difficulties in reaching the site (despite Baker's claim of a toll road), high mountains, shortages of supplies, little gold, an inhospitable climate, and angry Utes. Until now, the Pike's Peakers had been fortunate, because no Indians had laid serious claims to the land they overran. But the Utes were serious about their hunting domain and challenged intrusion. The miner struggled out, sadder but not noticeably wiser; gold fever addled the judgment of those who caught it.[20]

The El Dorados of 1862 included Buckskin Joe, across the mountains from Oro City, but the heyday of placer mining had passed. If Colorado held a future, it would have to be in hard-rock mining, a much different proposition from the glory days of placering only two years before.

Not all had journeyed to Colorado to mine. Some came to start a business, some as town boomers, others for the sheer adventure of it, or to escape from life back home. Then there were the aspiring politicians, who saw every new territory as the gateway to power, position, and prestige.

State-making and senator-electing were something of an American passion, and the Pike's Peakers fully understood the advantages to be gained from a political framework recognized by the federal government. This explains why (along with having time on their hands), in November 1858, the tiny population at Cherry Creek voted to send a delegate to Washington, D.C. to lobby for territorial status. Congress got busy, but no legislation ensued.

Washington having failed them, these determined pioneers moved to create their own territory, just as the great wave of the 1859 rush hit Denver. But gold, not politics, was on people's minds. It would not be until the fall that Jefferson Territory would finally be formed without any congressional authority. A constitution, counties, two-house legislature, a governor, and other elected officials gave it the trappings of authority and respectability. An election produced legislators, who met in session in November.

Playing politics required funds. When the legislators approved a tax bill, hundreds protested, and Jefferson Territory soon went the way of many western utopian dreams. It hung on for months, growing ever more impotent and unloved. At best, Jefferson Territory could have been only a stopgap measure, a chance for the politically ambitious to dabble in politics. Congress would have to make the ultimate decision.[21]

Congress could not decide, caught up as it was in the onrushing sectional debate and the presidential election. By whatever name, the potential territory learned a painful fact of life—it would never break its ties to the East or be separated from the issues that engulfed the rest of the country.

Would it be slave or free? Nothing could be accomplished until this fundamental question was resolved, not in the Rocky Mountains but in the halls of Congress. Pike's Peakers were not masters of their own destiny; they would be buffeted by that larger issue until it split the country asunder. By the time the secession movement reached its peak, only one thing seemed to be resolved, a name for the territory. "Colorado" won over such contenders as Columbus, Weapollao, Idahoe, San Juan, and Lula.

The secession of South Carolina and its sister slave states removed most of the opposition to new territories, and a bill to create Colorado Territory was introduced. After congressional approval, outgoing president James Buchanan signed Colorado's "birth certificate" on February 28, 1861. It would be up to Abraham Lincoln and the young Republican party to breathe life into that decree. They did their job splendidly from the political point of view, and Colorado would be a Republican stronghold for a generation. It had helped, of course, that the vast majority of the early settlers had come from Republican bastions in the Midwest and East. Indeed, some of the local politicians could trace their roots back to the founding of the party seven years before.

Despite this benchmark event, there would be no escaping the consequences of what was occurring "back in the states," as some Coloradans liked to refer to them. The Confederate States of America had been created, much to the disgust of most northerners and a few southerners. The shots that broke the silence of a still morning dawn at Charleston eventually jarred the new territory. Although Denverites lived over a thousand miles away from Fort Sumter and it took better than a week to get the news there, the war had come to the territory. Those who wanted to escape the pressures of a country seemingly gone mad found no haven in Colorado. The Rocky Mountains, for all their renowned benefits, could not shield their people from such overwhelming issues.

Lincoln selected William Gilpin, a verbose bachelor and ardent Republican, as governor. Having traveled through the region back in the

1840s, he later forecast a great future for the Pike's Peak country as the center of America. Coloradans could not imagine a better choice.

Greeted by the best welcoming reception Denver could provide when he arrived in May, Gilpin responded with one of his patented flights of oratory about the future. More relevant to present territorial concerns, he promptly set out on a tour of the mountains, authorized a census, and launched the process to elect a lower house. The council, judges, and other appointees all came from Washington. By September, a government organization had almost been accomplished, although Washington paid scant attention, caught up as it was in the throes of what appeared to be a losing war effort.[22]

Gilpin was caught up in that crisis, as well. Sometimes described as a worrier, he imagined that he saw southerners lurking behind nearly every rock and in every strange movement. It seemed to him that the Confederacy had especially marked out the territory for subversion because of its mining potential; he was right about one thing— it did need gold.

There was enough smoke to cause even a less nervous individual than Gilpin to worry about a major conflagration. A Confederate flag had been flown in Denver in April, some southerners in the territory had openly toasted the new Confederacy, and other more patriotic ones had left to join the army. When Gilpin became convinced that they planned to strip Colorado of most of its weapons, he reacted; a local arms race promptly benefited anyone who had weapons to sell.[23]

To make matters worse, federal troops marched east when the war started, leaving Colorado and its umbilical cords, the overland trails, unprotected. Vulnerable as never before, Colorado braced for trouble. Attacks by plains Indians, whom Gilpin and others feared were being courted by the Confederacy for its own diabolical purposes, seemed imminent. Threatened from within and without, the governor was determined to take action. Washington could offer no help. It seemed to have more than it could handle much nearer to home.

The determined and stubborn Gilpin turned his efforts to raising a volunteer regiment, which proved easy because most Coloradans remained loyal. Gathering a military staff, accepting volunteers, and equipping and training the First Colorado proved to be a simple chore compared to finding the funds to pay for everything. Never one to shrink when duty called, the nearly frantic governor issued some 375,000 dollars in drafts on the federal treasury, fully expecting them to be honored.

Merchants, tradesmen, and ordinary citizens were willing to go along with the preparedness campaign. It certainly boosted a territorial economy that had been suffering from the decline of placer mining. While the troops trained, Gilpin used the drafts to pay for supplies, arms, uniforms—everything to ready the regiment to defend Colorado. When the first drafts reached an astonished Treasury Department, the whole scheme came tumbling down. Unwilling to validate the governor's impetuous action, the treasury would not pay. Although he claimed to have received verbal authorization from Lincoln to issue the drafts, Gilpin found himself suddenly one of the most unpopular men in the territory.[24]

Colorado, with few local financial resources, found an alarming percentage of them tied up and possibly lost forever. The economy dipped and the governor's rating plummeted, finally forcing him to journey to Washington in the winter of 1861–62 to defend his actions.

In Colorado, a winter of despair loomed. Mining seemed to have peaked, and the question of draft payment remained unresolved. The First Colorado regiment trained, in the meantime, generally in camp maneuvers, but sometimes with forays into Denver, to the dismay of harassed merchants and townspeople. Coloradans nervously kept their eyes on neighboring New Mexico. A Confederate force under General Henry Sibley was driving northward from El Paso up the Rio Grande Valley; his goal was the Colorado gold fields, just as Gilpin had predicted earlier.

Ordered south to join Colonel Edward Canby's troops at Fort Union, the First Colorado helped rout Sibley's forces in March engagements at Apache Canyon and Glorieta Pass. Coloradans played conspicuous roles in the campaign, later to be called the "Gettysburg of the West." By eastern standards, it had been a minor affair, but it represented Colorado's major military contribution to the war and redeemed Gilpin's extralegal issuing of those drafts.[25]

Alas, the victory did not save the governor's job. The Lincoln administration removed Gilpin and sent another ardent Republican, the scholarly doctor John Evans, to Colorado. The drafts would eventually be paid, and Gilpin would return to Denver, where he would dabble in real estate and other promotions and be honored as one of the state's founders. Coloradans ultimately came to realize that they might have some impact on their own political destiny, even though the final say came from Washington. A growing number saw statehood as the answer to their troubled position.

Evans brought the needed measure of stability and serenity to the territory, helped by the withdrawal of Sibley's forces.[26] In the spring of 1862, Coloradans could return to more traditional pursuits—farming, mining, town promoting—and read about the war back east, which stretched on, not going well for the Union cause.

Nor were things going very well for Colorado mining. No new Gregory Diggings, California Gulch, or San Juan discoveries brightened that spring. Placer mining slumped, and trouble hammered the hard-rockers. Despite encouraging early returns from the gold mines of Gilpin County (the old Gregory Diggings), the miners quickly passed through the easily worked surface ore zone. At a depth from sixty to a hundred feet, miners found themselves with ore that assayed well, only to find the mills unable to save enough gold to produce a profit. They termed it refractory ore, meaning that it resisted amalgamation. Some mills saved only 15 percent of assayed value; whatever silver and copper might have been present flowed onto the dump or into the stream with the tailings.

Miners blamed the millmen and millmen blamed the ore, leaving everyone unsatisfied. The inexperienced miners and millmen were mystified about just what was going wrong. One writer commented: "Somehow the mills as a general thing do not save the gold; why, it is hard to tell."[27] That "why" had to be resolved, and Coloradans without much money, resources, or experience set out to do it.

The milling movement was generated in Colorado's most famous gold district, Gilpin County, the crown jewel of the territory. The population of Black Hawk, Central City, and Nevada City surpassed even that of Denver, which relied strongly on trade with this region to maintain its business prosperity, as did the farmers who planted their spring crops in the river bottoms to the east. If mining prospered, so did the whole territory.

The outlying districts could provide little help. California Gulch no longer attracted attention, and last year's phenomenon, Buckskin Joe, withered when easily worked surface ore pinched out. The miners found that the deeper the mining, the higher the cost, the more complex the ore, and the lower the grade. Well known by California miners, these mining facts were faced by Coloradans for the first time.

The pattern unfolding in the territory discouraged all concerned and, sooner or later, would affect nearly every Coloradan. Eager to pull out, some tried to sell their claims or mines to outside investors. These new owners, in theory, would be able to furnish the needed financial transfusion, which would, it was assumed, magically solve the milling problems, produce the needed equipment, such as pumps and engines, and hire the skilled hard-rock miners. Then Colorado would prosper again with quartz mining, as it had done with placer mining in those golden days of 1859.

It looked so easy—and so familiar to anyone who had studied earlier American mining development. The elixir of mining life, the investor and his money, would ride to the rescue. While searching for these individuals, Coloradans continued to develop their territory in the image of the life and communities they had left behind.

Culture and maturity came to the gold towns, at least in the form that their residents assumed would furnish the ingredients for successful urbanization. Denver's preeminent position put it far ahead in that department. William Pierson had clearly seen the future when he had written in 1860:

> There is no doubt that Denver will always be the great city
> under the Rocky Mountains. There will be many other good
> and healthy towns but Denver will always be the
> headquarters. Here the wholesale trade of this country will
> be located.[28]

Denver's tents and rude log cabins had given way to frame and brick construction and architecture that emulated, as nearly as possible, the world back east. Its movers and shakers aspired to make their community the transportation, political, cultural, banking, and business heart of the territory. Scattered about town were churches, schools, theaters, and other signs of maturity. While Denverites were enthusiastically planning and opening a seminary to bring higher education to the mountains, they should have been paying more attention to more worldly matters. The wind-dried buildings crowded into the central business district were a fire awaiting the spark. On April 19, 1863, Denver paid for its negligence; seventy buildings and nearly 200,000 dollars worth of supplies fell to a fire. The owners rebuilt and restocked, and the community pushed ahead.[29]

Social climbers already promenaded the streets of Denver, their activities chronicled by the newspapers. Only Central City, Nevada City, and Black Hawk could rival the prospective capital, a designation Golden and Denver alternately shared. Their rivalry produced the inevitable jealousy: "There is one feature of the people, with whom I have come in contact since my arrival here [Denver] with which we are not very familiar in Mo. They are decidedly the *closest* stingiest set of Blue Bellied Yankees on the Western Continent."[30]

Denverites looked with pride on the progress their city had made in a few short years; so, in their own way, did the residents of Buckskin

Joe, Idaho Springs, and Boulder. Urbanization had come to Colorado, and with it improved transportation and economic development. At some unnoticed point, the frontier had ended for Denver, Central City, and their contemporaries, giving way to the beginnings of a settled, middle-class way of life. Individualism yielded to cooperation, isolation to togetherness, unfettered democracy to political organization, and unbounded economic potential to interdependent economic development.

Mining gave clear evidence of the changes. The free-wheeling placer days had been replaced by cooperation, companies, and onrushing industrialization. The troubles did not go away, however. The problem of refractory ore did not yield to the simple solutions of the school of hard knocks, nor to the lack of milling experience, machinery, and capital available in the mountains.

Coloradans thought they had found the answer to escaping the mining doldrums. By the fall of 1863, with the tide of battle turning in the North's favor, the wartime economy booming, and the specter of inflated paper money haunting investors, northerners were primed to invest. Nothing appeared to them safer than a gold mine. Gold held a known value and was there to be mined when needed. Coloradans had plenty to offer, and the winter of 1863–64 saw a scramble of sellers and buyers. The classic case of greed and prosperity overcoming caution and investigation unfolded.

Claims were filed, mines reopened, and mining companies incorporated at a record pace, as promoters raced furiously to the East to catch the peak of investment fever. For a brief time, Coloradans enjoyed national attention; they were the hit of the stock market. During the winter of 1863–64, easterners saw too much outgo of money to build mills, develop mines, pay officials and miners, and buy supplies, and too little return of profits and dividends. Spring would tell the tale.[31]

The mining frontier moved on all the while; Idaho was now beckoning Coloradans. Then, to make matters worse, a new Rocky Mountain rival had arisen. What would soon be called Montana was being heralded as the new California, the poor man's bonanza. Coloradans had already left for those promising gold fields, and others were preparing for the trip.

The cycle was complete in five years, from the new California to a "has been" mining region. Byers and others tried heroically to stem the tide, but it ran against Colorado. In the fast-paced mining life, the pattern was typical.

As Grant prepared to take his army south to attack Lee along Virginia's bloodied Rappahannock River, perhaps to win the war, Coloradans saw little to cheer about at home. They sensed that the opportunity they had come to exploit was gone. Colorado did not seem so promising nor so exuberant as in the days of 1859.

Despite the discouragements, Coloradans could be justly proud of their accomplishments in so short a time. The wildnerness had been replaced by the mining frontier, which was evolving into something much more permanent. Although stagnation had beset mining, it still held promise—and not just in precious metals; rudimentary coal mines had been opened and oil found. Oil, though, awaited a general commercial use before Coloradans would get very excited about it. Corporation control already dominated Colorado's principal mining district, and absentee owners held many of the best properties. Central City's evolution foreshadowed the trend of the next generation throughout the Rockies.

In the mountain valleys and along the foothills, urbanization had quickly taken root, and agriculture was plowing the river valleys with some success. Embryonic home industries were being established and nascent tourism was looming, despite the discomfort of stagecoach travel across the plains. Communications isolation disappeared in the click of a telegraph, when lines reached Julesburg in 1863. A branch line soon crossed the sage hills to Denver and continued up Clear Creek Valley to Central City.[32] Colorado set the pace; the rest of the region would follow.

Publicity, both good and bad, and investment had come to Colorado. Coloradans had also quickly fallen into the habit of looking to Washington for any and all help. There, they sowed the wind. Already, too, a legend had been born, that of the frontier days of 1859. Some people yearned for that simpler, more romantic time, when opportunity beckoned over every hill.

The slow growth and development of neighboring New Mexico (two centuries had not brought it as far as Colorado had leaped in five years), or even a midwestern farming state (Illinois' first generation, for example), accentuates the importance of the lure of mining to Colorado. That lure and the fascination with the Rocky Mountains pointed to a promising future for Colorado.

All the progress in Colorado was perceived with mixed feelings by easterners. Emma Teller Tyler wrote that her mother's wedding was like a funeral, "for no one expected her to return from far away Colorado." E. H. N. Patterson wrote a letter to his children explaining to them where he was going:

> I am soon going over a great big river, and then away off to a
> place where there aint any people living. There are no
> houses there, only tents that are made out of cloth, and look
> a little like a house and keep out the rain. That is the place
> they call Pike's Peak.[33]

Emma's mother found Colorado to be a wonderful new home, and
Patterson stayed to become a newspaperman. Others were not so fortunate, but through good and bad, Colorado persevered.

2 : MONTANA

Although Montana sat in the northern rather than the southern Rockies, its early history closely paralleled Colorado's. Gold brought the rush of pioneers, and placer deposits lured them onward. The jerry-built camps blossomed overnight, with some disappearing almost as quickly, and mining would bedrock its early history. Coloradans actually helped to stimulate the Montana excitement and get their sister Rocky Mountain territory off and running.

Unlike Colorado, gold had been rumored to be in the region only since the early 1850s. Isolation and the great distance from the Oregon Trail and other transcontinental routes had kept visitors to a minimum, except fur trappers and fur-company employees. A few scattered posts and missions forged only weak links to the westward-moving frontier.

Former California miners James and Granville Stuart, who first appeared in the region in the winter of 1857–58, discovered gold in May 1858, in what became known as Gold Creek. The paucity of the deposit, the hostility of the Blackfeet, and the isolation effectively discouraged them and they left; no rush ensued.[1] The Stuarts returned in 1860 and prospected, without noticeable success, for two years.

The Idaho placer mines, which so distressed Denver's William Byers because they threatened his beloved Colorado, burst on the scene about the same time. Coloradans were enticed to travel northwest; one party, led by John White, wintered in Montana in 1861–62 and made a major strike there the next July. The Grasshopper Creek diggings became Bannack; Montana had uncovered its first gold of any consequence.

The Stuarts, who were working what seemed to be a promising strike, hurried over to the diggings that appeared to be even better. So did others from Colorado and Idaho—once more the mysterious mountain "telegraph" had spread the word. This fever was described "Bannack on the brain."

The gold was first dug from the grassroots, or as these early Montanans were wont to say, they panned it "out of the sagebrush," which blanketed the site. Bannack flourished for a season before it declined. James Stuart and others set out in 1863 on a prospecting tour, which eventually resulted in the discovery of an even more significant district, Alder Gulch, where Virginia City would soon take root. Roughly seventy-five miles apart, the twin attractions of early Montana mining invited all to come.

The next year, Last Chance Gulch (where Helena would be), Butte, and Confederate and Emigrant gulches kept the fever high, as the boys stampeded to the latest bonanza. Astute observer Rossiter Raymond later observed that their "exploitation seems to travel in a circle."[2] One gulch would be abandoned in the race to find a more promising one elsewhere. Upon reexamination, however, repentant old-timers would sometimes reconsider the gold they left behind, returning to it themselves and luring newcomers.

The exhilaration, the fast-paced life, and the constant movement resembled life in earlier California or Colorado. Both areas contributed their share of former residents, with their knowledge, experience, and equipment. Californians generally came in through Idaho, rather than directly from home. California, the mother lode of western mining, was ranked as the greatest placer region in the United States. Colorado had failed to equal its production, but now Montana was seriously challenging it.

As it evolved through discovery, rush, mining-district organization, and camp development, each district hailed itself as the richest "poorman's diggings" in the Rocky Mountains. Then followed disappointment for the latecomers or the unlucky, who were led away by rumors of an even greater strike over the next mountain or up another nameless creek. The cycle, with variations, then moved through stabilization and eventual decline.

When the news of the Montana discoveries reached the wartorn states, particularly Missouri, the hotbed of internecine warfare, it created an instant yearning to go west to escape the horror and suffering. Some came by covered wagon; others innovated and traveled by steamboat up the Missouri River. For the only time in Rocky Mountain history, a river played a major role in transporting men and supplies to a major mining rush. During high water, the boats could reach Fort Benton, as they had done since the days of the fur trade. There, the goods were loaded into wagons, and they reached their destinations with an ease seldom equaled prior to the appearance of the railroad. The only limiting factor, besides the basic treachery of the Missouri (nicknamed "the harlot" because it changed its bed so often), was the seasonal nature of river travel. Low water during the fall and winter freezes closed this artery until spring.

So they came to Montana while the war dragged on—from the Mississippi Valley and from western territories and states. They came with all the familiar expectations: to get rich as quickly as possible and return home to live the life of the well-to-do. Few had any intention of staying beyond the allotted time it took to put enough gold in their pouches to make their dream come true.

That dream was as old as Coronado's 1540 expedition or the Jamestown, Virginia, settlers' fruitless search for gold in 1607; and it was as new as yesterday's rumor and tomorrow's hope. The hopeful rushed to a land full of mining promise, the same kind that had brought them earlier to California, Nevada, Colorado, and Idaho.

These pioneers discovered (some already knew it through experience) that maintaining a mining frontier demanded a great deal of work and worry. It meant creating a transportation network and communities with urban amenities and rudimentary government, and establishing primitive agriculture and lumbering to support the miners while they dug, panned, and sluiced. They had always to be on the lookout for nearby Indians, who resented these pioneers who trespassed on and dug up their hunting grounds. Nor could one ever escape the nagging fear that there could be someone in the district who planned to gain his stake by robbing those who had already acquired one. Until the mines produced, money was in short supply, as were women and news of the outside world. The mining frontier was an urban frontier, and it came in step with the miners in Montana, just as it had in Colorado. The townsite of Virginia City, for example, was laid out on June 6, the same day the first rushers arrived. The men inhabited dugouts, wagons, tents, caves, and wickiups—or simply slept outdoors wrapped in their blankets Those who took time from placering could find abundant timber nearby to cut for logs, but in the rush to riches, logging seemed to them to be time wasted. Log buildings eventually appeared, however, followed by that sure sign of progress, frame buildings. The nearest sawmill at Bannack later did ship lumber, but at a cost of 250 dollars per thousand feet.[3]

The mining area grew until it dipped and curved seventeen miles along Alder Gulch, at its zenith appearing to be one long shoestring of settlements. Nevada City emerged as the only one of the smaller camps that had a chance of rivaling its neighbor, Virginia City. The post office encountered some confusion, because other Virginia and Nevada cities existed elsewhere in the West. Miners could be original in their selection of names, but there was a certain comfort in using familiar ones for camps and mines.

Into this world of Bannack and Virginia City and their satellites raced the waves of prospectors, drawn by the magnetic news of a new El Dorado. Close behind them came those who would make their money off the miners by providing the necessary business, entertainment, and legal base to allow mining to continue and to expand. This fast-paced urbanization created the major uniqueness that characterized the mining frontier, when compared to the other waves of settlement in the trans-Mississippi West. Except in the brief life of the cattle towns, and in the few weeks of town-booming fever that would come later to some areas of the agricultural West, nothing would equal it. It brewed a flavor, a character, a sense of place and time, and opportunities that intrigued westerners and easterners alike. A good living, even a fortune, could be made even more easily on a dusty Main Street than it could with backbreaking digging and sluicing in the gulches.

Contrasting with the pattern of Rocky Mountain settlement was Zeandale, Kansas, which had so discouraged Horace Tabor. This farming community, organized in 1855, grew slowly. A church was established three years later and a school in 1859, but in 1870 it had only 373 residents. Job opportunities, except for farming, remained almost nonexistent, and farming required many mortgaged years before it could be expected to return a reliable profit. The chance to move to Colorado or Montana, where money could be made quickly, was irresistible. That pattern was a typical one for the pioneer, for it had become a part of western development. Only the Mormons' initial movement to their promised land equaled in numbers of people the Rocky Mountain mining rushes.

Bannack and Virginia City exemplified the zenith of 1862–64 urbanization. The residents generally saw only progress and a growing community, while the first impressions of people just arriving varied. One member of N. H. Webster's party from Central City, Colorado, upon seeing Bannack, called back to his friends, "Here is your famous mining camp you have traveled one thousand miles to see. Look at it. Only a few log cabins and not a person to be seen." Webster himself concluded after a tour that it "isn't much of anything," a "desolate place indeed." Another 1863 visitor described his impression of the first mining camp he had ever seen, "If there is such a place as hell, this must be the back door to it"; and an unidentified immigrant called it the "sink hole of creation."[4]

These were indeed strong words. On the other hand, Mary Edgerton, the wife of the first territorial governor, pictured Bannack "very quiet and orderly . . . much more so than I expected to find it." Lucia Park, who came west with the Edgerton party, believed that Bannack and its mines held great possibilities and their newness made them attractive. She did not disagree, however, with the opinion of another member of the party, five-year-old Jimmie Sanders, who expected so much of his new home but, upon seeing it, called out with childish insight, "Bangup is a humbug."[5]

Virginia City, with richer deposits, created a somewhat better appearance. F. W. Patten arrived early in August 1863, when it was in full swing, with a mushrooming population "living in all manner of ways." A year later, a Wisconsin visitor was surprised to see an "orderly village of neat log and frame buildings nestled in a sheltered basin," instead of a sprawling town of shacks. Mary Ronan, who came with her wanderlusting father from Colorado, knew no other life, "I took quite for granted as the way of all places in which little girls lived." To her, Nevada City, Central City, and Denver, Colorado, as well as Virginia City, were "much alike." Sarah Raymond's comment on seeing the territorial capital in September 1865 was simply, "It is the shabbiest town I ever saw, not a really good house in it.[6]

Mining camps always seemed to astonish the uninitiated, while appearing quite ordinary to their residents and to veterans of the mining frontier. Right from the start of Rocky Mountain settlement, these islands of urbanization, in an otherwise unsettled wilderness, colored the public's impression of the region. To the west, where mining held sway, the urbanization produced similar results. People were surprised by how quickly civilization came to the mines and their camps.

In the transitory, rushed life of the mining community, money could be made and lost overnight. Simply selecting the right business location required foresight and some degree of luck. The main business district was usually not the product of town planning. The Stuarts showed how success could be achieved by converting a Bannack butcher shop and the trading of merchandise into a three-thousand-dollar profit in six months. Then, they went to Virginia City to open a store and a blacksmith shop and profited again. Granville Stuart, however, made a mistake when he ordered six hundred pairs of heavy boots that proved to be unpopular with the miners. Thomas Conrad confessed to his wife that competition ran so high that he did not get "as big profits as anticipated." A merchant had to understand his customers and be able to gauge tomorrow's business conditions, if he or she hoped to survive. The rush to riches did not assure equal prizes. Like many others, however, Conrad was not discouraged. He expected to make money if he did not get burned out, a common fate in the crowded, tinder-dry, wooden mining camps.

Male-dominated as they were, mining camps still provided a home for families and women, who helped give it a degree of gentility not found in outlying parts of the district. Women such as Mary Edgerton tried to re-create in the Rocky Mountains the life they had left behind, a recurring theme over the next generation. Her letters from Bannack and, later, Virginia City reveal concerns about the West not being as formal, the need for "practical clothes," pregnancy, lack of interest in Sunday School, the health of her family, and finally, the summation, "I do not get much time to do anything but housework . . ." Her contemporary, Emily Meredith, complained of high prices and that people had not yet "made their pile." Most seemed to be getting along all right, however, and very few "were discouraged." She observed that "anyone who is shrewd & has money can make money."

Being governor, Mary's husband did not have to worry about making a living from mining, although his salary proved none too liberal, considering the high cost of living. One of the major problems she faced was raising her children in this environment. With no schools at first, they studied at home. This, in itself, appeared almost to be a blessing, because, had her sons gone to school, "they would [have learned] so many *bad things* that would injure them more than all the good they would learn." Most of the boys, she concluded, "swear as soon as they talk." Her fourteen-year-old daughter, Mattie, presented her with other problems. With the shortage of women, she was already being invited to balls. Her mother refused to let her attend: "I should be the last one to be willing to have her associate with the 'set' that generally attend them." From Mattie's point of view, there were few other parties or amusements of any kind for diversion.[7] These children, the first truly western generation, would help to shape their own world in the Rocky Mountains.

Entertainment created no problems for the miners; the camps existed, in part, to provide it. The loneliness of the miners' lives was alleviated somewhat by the bright lights and attractions of the saloons, gambling halls, theaters, hurdy-gurdy houses, and the "fair but frail" who worked out of the cribs and parlor houses. Sporting events came almost as quickly. Con Orem arrived from Colorado, already hailed as a boxing champion, and baseball was not far behind. The *Montana Post* on May 26, 1866, happily announced the "organizing of a base ball club, the national game," which was "calculated to brace the nerves and to promote a healthy circulation." More to the point, both boxing and baseball provided opportunities for gambling, a popular pastime in a land where gambling fever innately infected people who, as Horace Greeley pointed out, had come west to make a fortune in mining.[8]

Business, entertainment, society—the camps had them all, as well as a variety of clubs, fraternal organizations, and churches. Nothing pleased the editors of the *Helena Herald* more than the July 1867 organization of an Independent Order of Odd Fellows (IOOF) Lodge, whose growth and "new and very pretty Hall" proved the town's maturity. That was not quite true, however. Although the finished product of urbanization was evolving and bestowing a potpourri of benefits upon locals, it still displayed some rough edges.

The church, Protestant and Catholic, faced trying times. Sometimes the enthusiasm to raise a building engendered more support than the struggle to maintain a congregation. While it was an important symbol of middle-class respectability, the church sometimes generated costs that seemed to outweigh benefits. The *Montana Post* of September 15, 1866, sadly made note of the sale of the Union Church to discharge creditors' claims. The church confronted another challenge in its attempt to lift people above the materialism of the era. Sunday was a wide-open day, probably the best business day of the week, and the only day the miners generally stopped working. Thomas Conrad did not like "the Sabbath breaking habit of this country—Yet I have hopes of it being speedily stopped." That would not happen, and he conceded to open on Sunday just like the rest.[9]

Since many people planned to stay only until they made their "pile," they did not consider it worthwhile to strive for or support improvements such as schools, water systems, and municipal government, with their corresponding taxes. Jails and courts seemed unnecessary when there also existed miners' districts, with rudimentary laws and low costs. Nor did these people come to know their neighbors in much more than a cursory manner. When these factors were taken together, and the lack of territorial organization in 1862–63 was also considered, it became evident that the bonds that usually stabilized a community were weak. A few of the pioneers did not travel west to become miners or farmers, for they found lawlessness and freedom from all social responsibility appealing. The lawless, drifting element, always attracted by the potential for easy money, found a bonanza waiting to be seized.

The West displayed numerous examples of lawlessness over the years, none worse than in the Montana outbreak of 1863. Anyone who traveled in the Bannack–Virginia City region risked his life—more than a hundred people disappeared or were murdered. The unsettled transitory life allowed these things to happen without repercussions until the end of the year. Following the California expedient, men in Virginia City, Nevada City, and Bannack secretly met to organize a vigilance committee.

Once organized, the committee acted quickly and decisively, with supreme confidence in its members. In the next weeks, they tracked down and hung twenty-four men and, by threats and intimidation, forced other undesirables to take their leave. Mary Edgerton expressed what must have been a general sense of relief when she wrote her sister, "I hope the Committee will not have to hang anymore here for I do not like such excitement, but I shall feel that Mr. Edgerton will go much more safely now . . ." Astoundingly, the elected sheriff, Henry Plummer, organized the murderous gang. The Dr. Jekyll and Mr. Hyde of western outlaws, the handsome Plummer had charmed the public, been honestly elected, and appeared to be carrying out his duties with dispatch. Unfortunately, a final "dispatch" was often the reward for those who trusted him with confidential information.

The secret activities of the vigilantes will never be completely unveiled, nor will the debate ever be resolved over the real need for their actions. Men who were involved or knowledgeable about the times defended their work, and even Plummer has his defenders.[10] No other Rocky Mountain territories would experience the problem to this extent, nor would they react with such total finality. Montana's situation was not unique, but the magnitude of the criminal element and the lack of organized restraints were. Easterners would have been more alarmed by western lawlessness if the Civil War had not diverted their attention to matters closer to home.

Fortunately for Montana's future reputation, these events would be forgotten; but Montanans in the years ahead would occasionally rely on vigilantism, with less justification. Helena's *Montana Radiator* warned on April 7, 1866, "TO THE PEOPLE OF MONTANA. The ends of justice shall be carried out in the FUTURE as in the PAST. VIGILANCE COMMITTEE." By then, with regular law enforcement and a government in place, the need for extralegal action was vanishing.

Life in the mining camps offered temptations, which were never as exciting, however, as staking a claim in a new bonanza district. Montana's placer days were filled with discoveries and stampedes that impelled the drifting crowd, as well as more permanent folks, to rush off to the newest El Dorado. Granville Stuart called it a "stampede craze" in January 1864, when, in the midst of a cold winter with local mining frozen to a stop, rumors surfaced about new finds. The boys raced off to the Gallatin River ("no one seemed to know exactly where they were going") and later to Wisconsin Creek, where one could "just shovel up the gold." Neither area panned out, but both of them stimulated business and raised the price of horses. Some prospectors became addicted to mining wanderlust and would spend the rest of their lives following the will-o'-the-wisp lure to new diggings.

Founded on placer mining, Montana proved to be more fortunate than Colorado in having a longer succession of discoveries, from Bannack to Virginia City, to Last Chance Gulch, to Butte and beyond, as latecomers spread out to find their own bonanzas. The familiar western pattern unfolded here, too: the poor-man's diggings, using pan and shovel, evolved into sluices, long toms, and companies. Some men prospected for mineral outcroppings, and lode mining eventually superseded placer.

Like the early prospectors elsewhere, they had come to get rich without working, but they never worked so hard in their lives. As one observer noted, "labor is worship." They also found that poor-man's diggings did not last very long, and soon those with capital, equipment, and hired laborers gained the advantage. And quartz mining meant that someone had to buy or build stamp mills to crush the ore to separate the gold from the gangue. Those demanded more investment and equipment, which, just as in Colorado, came from the East rather than from California.[11]

Hard work, investment, new discoveries, the decline in older districts, and the need for technology—all were time-honored components of western mining. Placer diggings everywhere sowed the seeds for industrialization and eventual corporation dominance. Easterners might have had their own romantic views of the mining West, but Montanans were not fooled. Dejected over his lack of success, one man bemoaned to the Chicago *Tribune* that "claim gambling is almost equal to gambling with cards." Astute Emily Meredith, writing her father from Bannack in April 1863, summed up the situation:

> I never would advise anyone to come to a new mining country because there is a great deal to risk & a great deal to endure, nevertheless many persons undoubtedly will come here this summer & make more than they could in years at home. And they ought to, a person ought to make money pretty fast here to pay them for living in such a place.[12]

Far to the south, Denver editor William Byers had seen it all, but he could not stop himself from worrying about Coloradans, suffering from "quartz on the brain," being lured to the "bonanza" discoveries. By 1863–64, the agitated editor saw a crisis developing: Coloradans, like Californians before them, had succumbed to an irresistible urge to try a new, more promising district. The historical precedent did not ease Byers's anxiety. Colorado was losing population and failing to attract sufficient newcomers; in this grow-or-die nineteenth-century world, that deficiency could be fatal.

Byers would have been delighted with the reaction of N. H. Webster and his friend to their arrival in cold, snowy Bannack in October 1863, two months after leaving Central City: "I feel like Jim; I want to go home too, but there is no use in wishing, am for it now and will do the best I can." That Webster did not instantly return to Colorado would have dismayed the editor. Blacksmith George Aux would have eased Byers's fears. In 1864, he took his family to Montana; disappointed after trying Bannack and Alder Gulch, he returned to Colorado.

Despite the competition, Montana's connection to Colorado became strong and profitable. The Pike's Peakers brought to Montana mining skills and knowledge and the determination to establish businesses.[13] Though it was no consolation to Byers, Nevada, Idaho, and California also lost population to Montana, but the numbers were fewer, except for those involved in the early rush from the Idaho diggings to Bannack.

As the spring of 1864 warmed the valleys and creeks of Montana and propelled the prospectors over the landscape (also, it was hoped, promising a better season for Colorado), both territories became permanently established. While the war raged back in the states, the frontier continued to expand. A few men came west to dodge the draft, but more simply wanted to escape the horrors of war. Most of the immigrants, however, continued to come west in the age-old quest for a fresh start in life.

Both territories experienced the familiar problems of local versus national politics. Isolated from Washington, each had by necessity and in the frontier tradition initially experimented with extralegal organizations, until federal control was exerted. In Montana's case, that came formally in May 1864, when a busy wartime Congress managed to find enough time to create another western territory. A former Ohio congressman and more recently a judge in this previous piece of Idaho Territory, Sidney Edgerton, was appointed governor. One major difference between Colorado and Montana was the latter's unusual (at least for the Rockies) Democratic leanings. One Republican complained that "the defeat and overthrow of the left wing of Price's army in Missouri in '63 sent a horde of rebels over the border into Kansas who evidently disposed to peace, sought employment as ox-drivers in trains crossing the plains for Montana." Where else in these superheated emotional times did Confederate Gulch, Jeff Davis Gulch, and the village of Dixie come from? Joined eventually by other southerners and immigrants, the so-called rebels bolstered the local Democratic party, which became the majority party, much to the discomfort of the Republican administration in Washington.[14]

Democratic on one wing and Republican on the other, Rocky Mountain politics took root. Each territory would have troubles with Washington, regardless of its political affiliation; federal appointees—governors, judges, secretaries— did not measure up to local standards. Nor did rule by faraway Congress—where the territory was represented by only a nonvoting delegate—meet with approval. But politicians had come west with the miners, seeking their own promised land, and they maneuvered to carve out a following and create a name for themselves just as if they had campaigned back east. Power and prestige rewarded the skilled or the lucky. As a result, political contests over legislative seats and the site for the all-important capital erupted as soon as territorial organization was accomplished. Once more, there emerged a pattern familiar to westerners of earlier frontiers.

Likewise commonplace was the attitude toward the people who already lived on and hunted over the land that these newcomers now called home. The pioneers had passed through the dominion of the daunting plains Indians on their way west. Fortunately for Coloradans and Montanans, neither had initially confronted powerful tribes where they mined and settled. Decimated by smallpox a generation before, the Blackfeet offered no resistance, thereby facilitating Montana settlement. The Utes in Colorado stayed largely on the Western Slope, only occasionally hunting on the eastern side.

Men and women moved West with deeply ingrained conceptions

and misconceptions of Indians; most were stereotyped and negative. Typically, neither side understood the other's culture, its way of life, or its attitudes toward such diverse topics as landownership and war. The result had been America's longest running civil war, which stretched back several centuries; the two peoples and their "armies" had been fighting as early as the seventeenth century for their chosen homeland.

Comments like those in the Denver *Weekly Commonwealth* of December 18, 1862, attested to the prevailing attitudes: "They [Indians] simply perpetrate murder and robbery. None of the laws of war govern them. No quarter or kindness or liberality is shown by them. They simply kill and steal." Mary Edgerton, during an 1865 Indian "scare," expressed an unequivocal opinion: "*I do want to have* the Indians killed." She favored a military solution, the stationing of soldiers along the river and on the plains. The *Montana Post*, while favoring well-guarded reservations, rebutted those easterners who sympathized with the Indians: "Christianize him sir, is whispered by the ignorant philanthropist of the day. A wolf knows no better and he is shot and tamed. It is all nonsense thus to drivel." Denverite Susan Ashley was no admirer of "Poor Lo" (as Americans sometimes called the Indians) and lived in fear that they would invade her home. She insisted that a fence be built around the house, having been assured that Indians "are too lazy to open a gate." That expedient failed, and she found Cheyenne and Arapaho peering in her windows.[15]

Both territories suffered more from the threat to their vital overland trails (Montana's Bozeman Trail, for example) than from any immediate danger to settlements. Even steamboats on the Missouri River were not immune from attack. Indian raids disrupted the flow of supplies and settlers, raised the cost of living, painted the image of a wild frontier, and even caused potential investors to shy away, none of which could be tolerated.

Coloradans had been around long enough to have learned to discriminate among the Indian tribes. The more isolated, therefore less threatening, Utes seemed peaceful, even friendly, to the few prospectors who traversed their country. For the moment, there was little desire for their land. The plains-dwelling Cheyenne and Arapaho represented the other side of the problem, for they had been in the way since 1858. Although the Pike's Peakers sought to settle their lands, the overland trails shot right through them. Then came the disruption caused by the Civil War, the rumored arming of Indians by Confederate sympathizers, and the Sioux outbreak in Minnesota, all of which sent disgruntled bands west to join their cousins. To make matters worse, farmers were creeping out onto the plains, where, vulnerable to attack and isolated from the foothill settlements, they provided badly needed agricultural products. The year 1863 saw a startling increase in raids and disruption along the trails. Angered Coloradans demanded action, but little resulted.[16]

In the spring of 1864, when plains warfare resumed after a winter's hiatus, tension reached the breaking point. The killing of the Hungate family in June, combined with the storefront display of their mutilated bodies, caused the *Weekly Commonwealth* of June 15 to demand that "those that perpetrate such unnatural, brutal butchery as this ought to be hunted to the farthest bounds of these broad plains and burned to the stake alive . . ." Hysteria swept Denver and spread to the surrounding settlements. Governor Evans tried frantically to get military help as the overland trails were closed, stage stations were attacked, and telegraph wires were pulled down by frolicking war parties. Supplies and equipment languished at the river gateways, the cost of living rose, and mail had to be delivered via San Francisco. Locked into the brutal campaigns of Grant and Sherman and trying to win a three-year-old war, Washington could provide no help, but it did agree to the raising of a regiment of volunteers. Governor Evans promptly began to recruit what became the Third Colorado. At the same time, he tried to defuse the tension peacefully, but a conference failed.[17]

Coloradans, in no mood for compromise, wanted the issue resolved. Everything seemed to be moving in slow motion: government response to their complaints, recruitment of the volunteers, and removal of the Indians. As long as the overland roads continued to be seasonally threatened, settlement would be endangered. By late fall, the Third, short of equipment, weapons, and training, was nevertheless committed to a campaign. Its commander, John Chivington, the hero of Glorieta Pass, had to deal with the predicament of commanding hundred-day volunteers whose enlistments were coming to an end. To complicate matters further, Chivington and Evans both had political aspirations, should Colorado achieve statehood. They could ill afford to raise volunteers, then allow their enlistments to expire without action of some sort.

Meanwhile, on the plains, cold and snow settled in, and the Cheyenne and Arapaho went into winter camps. They also had complaints: treaty agreements had not been fulfilled, settlers crisscrossed their lands, and they saw only more whites coming. Their leaders understood only too well the emerging pattern. Some of them wanted warfare, while others sought peace. The latter included Black Kettle, who took his people to a camp on Sand Creek, apparently assuming he had satisfied Evans's earlier peace proposal, which directed "friendly Indians" to designated campsites where they would be safe. Evans had hoped to separate friendlies from hostiles, but nothing had been accomplished to this point.

Chivington led his troops on a winter campaign, arriving at Fort Lyon on the Arkansas River. From there, he ordered a night march, and on a crisp November 29 morning, with bugles blowing, his men attacked Black Kettle's village. The officers lost control of their men; two years' worth of pent-up emotions burst forth, flooding the field of battle. From that point, controversy surrounds nearly everything that happened that day—mutilations, the numbers of dead, the responsibility. Sand Creek would reverberate down through the years.[18]

Congress would investigate, charges would be hurled, lies would be told under oath (charitably called forgetfulness), and careers would be besmirched. The fallout included Evans's removal, Chivington's resignation, and Colorado's reputation suffering another setback. Easterners were beginning to wonder about this territory. Coloradans had reacted toward a crisis much like Montanans had with their earlier vigilante activities—directly and abruptly. Now they planned to turn their attention to other pressing issues.

The tragedy of Sand Creek masked the fact that in the Rocky Mountains the Indian "barrier" dissolved rapidly. The tribes primarily hunted and summered in the mountains, retreating to lower elevations before winter's storms settled in. The Indians were neither numerous nor strong and, except for the plains tribes that hindered transportation, posed no long-term threat to the miners, who settled in urban clusters. This circumstance provides a sharp contrast to Texas, Kansas, Arizona, and New Mexico, where isolated farmers and small hamlets confronted much more warlike and hostile neighbors for years.

The year 1864 had not been a good one for Colorado; earlier in April, that most encouraging Gilpin County gold-mining marvel had "busted." It had lasted a little over six months before the continual westward flow of money, combined with infinitesimal returns, raised questions and pricked the stock bubble. Investment, desperately needed to continue and expand mining and milling, disappeared almost overnight. Easterners shunned Colorado stocks, and they became a pariah on the market. Affluent northerners quickly looked elsewhere to invest.[19]

Colorado and Montana had evolved quickly from poor-man's placer diggings to hard-rock mining, which meant that the simple gave way to the complex. That complexity, in all its variations, demanded money for development, money that the territories did not have. Easterners and Europeans who held the potential to supply it were avidly courted; the Rocky Mountains moved lightheartedly toward outside control of their economy.

Among the required skills for hard-rock, or underground, mining were timbering, blasting, draining, and hoisting, which called for experienced miners and machines. It also cost more to develop the mines than the placer claims; hence the need for investors right from the start. The ore taken from the mine had to be worked to separate the gold and silver from the waste rock. Smelters, with their varied processes, fulfilled this need, but they demanded technological and chemical skills far beyond those of the average western miner. Finally, year-round transportation was essential to lowering the cost of living, mining, and smelting, and to bringing the investor to the district with an ease and comfort unknown to other frontiers. This the railroad provided best at the least expense.

Everything fit neatly together; as long as mining yielded the profits, the rest would come. In this way, the Rocky Mountains would be developed and the entrepreneurs and investors would acquire the wealth they sought. The American dream of success had arrived in the Rockies.

Both Colorado and Montana required outside investment, the former more urgently because its refractory ore resisted the milling methods then in use. Assayers sampled good ore, but mill men could not save the gold in it, much to the miners' dismay. Something had to be done if the territory expected to have a mining future.

A variety of ill-starred attempts to separate gold from gangue had been made, but Coloradans had been unable to come up with a successful process; they tried everything from sagebrush to "chemically-combined gold." The answer eventually came from a most unexpected source, a thirty-two-year-old professor of chemistry from Brown University, Nathaniel Hill. Hill, who considered the West "the most favored section of our country," traveled to Colorado in 1864 on behalf of a group of Providence investors and visited Boulder and Gilpin counties and the San Luis Valley. Racing the oncoming winter, he returned east, his life irrevocably changed.

Intrigued by the milling problems and captivated by Colorado's business potential, Hill resigned his university position and returned to Central City to tackle the seemingly insoluble smelting riddle that depressed the industry. Relying on his scientific training, rather than on the popular "school of hard knocks," Hill spent two years in experimenting. In 1866 he traveled to world-famous Swansea, Wales, to study its smelting process and to confer with several authorities on nonferrous metallurgy. Convinced that the answer to Colorado's problems lay there, he returned home and purchased seventy tons of ore to send to Swansea.[20]

Shipped by wagon across the plains, then by boat down the Mississippi River, and finally by ship to England, the ore arrived along with Nathaniel. The process worked well, but the shipping expenses created a four-hundred-dollar loss for Hill and his partners. Hill, who had been considering starting a smelter of his own, sailed back to the United States to raise the necessary capital.

Convincing a few investors of this smelter's potential, Hill acquired the funds; early in 1867, the Boston and Colorado Smelting Company was organized. Central City's neighbor, Black Hawk, was chosen as the site for it, much to the joy of its townspeople. Hill, however, knew what a smelter did to the environment. He called Swansea "a filthy, crowded, smoky dingy town," where sulfurous fumes choked every bit of nearby vegetation and smoke hung like a pall over the district.

The plant began commercial operations in February 1868. More experimentation would be required before everything was completely worked out, but Hill, assisted by European-trained metallurgists, had found the answer. The complex process roasted the ore to reduce the sulfur content, then fired it in a furnace to a molten liquid, which further separated the precious and base metals from the slag that floated to the top. A variety of ores was used as flux to ensure that the process worked correctly; consequently, smelter operations produced smells and smoke that blanketed their surroundings. Eventually, Hill installed the final process for refining the gold and silver from the matte that emerged from the smelting process. This innovation involved more heat and created a chemical reaction, for example, to separate copper, lead, gold, and silver. Black Hawk became the center of Colorado, then Rocky Mountain, smelting.[21]

Colorado mining needed every bit of encouragement it could muster. Despite cheery forecasts—it "looms up as the giant of the West," for example—territorial gold mining languished. Mining awaited the milling solution and a new influx of capital to get it moving again. Silver discoveries at Georgetown and across the snowy range on the Western Slope looked promising, but little more. Silver miners needed a successful smelter, too, and money for development. Easterners had no interest. The whirlwind generated by the bursting of the "gold bubble" portended no good for Coloradans; investors remembered.[22]

Montana enjoyed several more years of placer bonanza before decline set in. New discoveries kept the prospectors rushing and panning uncounted streams along unnamed gulches. However, one-time California miner Steffen Aggens was lured out of the territory in 1865 to British Columbia, despite the fact that "times were not at all that bad near Virginia City and I would just as soon have stayed there." Some prospects turned out like Emigrant Gulch in 1864–65, where the claims proved to be poor or complete failures. Poor Aggens experienced that disappointment in 1867, when he raced off to Willow Creek: "The general opinion was that the whole episode had been dreamed up by the store keepers in Deer Lodge River who made quite a bit of money because the trailhead left from their site."

The placer-mining frontier seesawed, leaving a legacy of lost hopes and mined-out bonanzas. Virginia City's James Polk Miller took a ride along Alder Gulch on a pleasant April day in 1867. Observing the abandoned cabins, sluice boxes, and other evidence of a spent rush, he commented on "all the result of toil for gold, looking as if thrown up in some wallowing 'sports' which had taken place. All is deserted and still but speaking with voices louder than ever could be made by the miners were they there."[23]

As in Colorado, the future belonged to quartz mining rather than to placer. Men were already digging into the hillsides of the Butte, Bannack, and other districts, where they encountered problems similar to those of their contemporaries farther south—water, milling difficulties, lack of experience and the lack of specialized knowledge, little equipment, and a scarcity of capital to pay for it all. Already, money was being spent on "new" mills, which promised wonders but crushed hopes in Montana. In Colorado, new metals beckoned: copper, coal, iron, and even oil. Montana had some of these as well as silver. Both touted "fabulous" assays, then brought heartache to dismayed miners when their milling processes failed.[24]

By the late 1860s, both territories were bemoaning the trend of people moving on to more alluring prospects. Placer mining's days were over; yet it left behind more than a legacy of disappointment and ghost towns and the legends of poor-man's diggings. Although the Colorado and Montana rushes never equaled California's, they did create territories, initiate politics, generate promotion, stimulate development, and pave the way for more permanent hard-rock mining. Mining would be the economic cornerstone for both the remainder of the nineteenth century and a decade into the new one.[25]

In place now were overland and Missouri River transportation routes and territorial roads that reached out to the most isolated mining districts. All that remained to complete the ultimate nineteenth-century framework were the laying of rails and the arrival of the train. Business centers, such as Denver and Helena, Virginia City and Central City, were emerging and, at least in Denver's case, displaying blatant intentions to dominate the whole region. Denver and Central City were already caught up in a nasty little urban spat over business "empires," political spoils, and social pretensions. Dominance and power would reward the victors. The fight was a harbinger of things to come.

In both territories, agriculture developed in response to the needs of the miners. Some pioneers quickly realized they were not cut out to be miners and saw great agricultural potential in the valleys that surrounded the diggings or lay along the river bottoms that extended eastward from the mountains. When all goods had to be shipped in over hundreds of miles, and transportation costs raised prices to levels that shocked visitors, local farmers found a profitable market for their produce in the 1860s. The virgin land which they plowed and planted yielded astonishing abundance, even though the length of the growing season had not been accurately determined by these newcomers.

Agriculture's potential, like mining's, seemed limitless. F. M. Thompson, Montana's commissioner of immigration, wrote in July 1865 that the territory as a farming region could "hardly be excelled in any country." Sidney Edgerton, in his first annual message, called on his fellow Montanans to become self-sustaining "as soon as possible," and predicted that agriculture "must form the enduring basis of our prosperity." Editor Wiliam Byers had been advocating those same ideas for six years.

Farming would not be that easy. Franklin Kirkaldie wrote in August 1866 that "farmers have had such times last year & this with grasshoppers." He, in fact, failed in his first two seasons. Early and late frosts plagued others. Difficulties in transporting goods to market and occasional spot surpluses gave these pioneering farmers grief, and the transitory nature of the mining frontier did not provide the stability required for the dependent agricultural districts. Ranching, which had existed in Montana to a small degree before the gold rush and which came to Colorado soon after the Pike's Peak rush, also profited from the mining market. With the coming of the miner and the farmer, the Rocky Mountains had made a wholesale commitment to enterprise for the sake of enterprise. These westerners, bewitched by the facade of economic progress, were planting the seeds for future trouble.[26]

By 1868 settlement had taken hold in both territories, evident in the coming and going of placer mining. Already a visitor to Helena,

Andrew Fisk, could call it the "busiest place I ever saw"; perhaps not so large as he imagined, it nevertheless had a "good many fine buildings." Virginia City's James Miller paid over one hundred dollars for a suit of clothes and accessories in order to accept an invitation to a ball. He also attended a boxing match on January 1, 1866, in which the noted Con Orem came out the winner. Orem brought professional sports to both territories, while Jack Langrishe was bringing professional theater to each. Langrishe and his wife escaped the odium that sometimes trailed actors and actresses and were honored as pioneers and outstanding individuals.

World traveler and mining engineer Louis Simonin paid a visit to Colorado and complimented Denver highly as a well-built city with attractive houses, wide streets, and the "movement of life everywhere." Coloradans glowed with pride when he praised their society.

> Comfort, the habits of domestic life, the 'home,' cherished
> alike by Americans and Englishmen was quickly revived, re-
> established by the Colorado pioneers, and today you would
> be amazed to meet so much refinement and well being in the
> midst of these regions.

Not forgetting the women, Simonin lavished praise on those he had seen, "whom New York or Boston would envy or regret losing."[27] Coloradans were well on their way to re-creating the life they had left behind.

Years later, Mary Ronan penned her impressions of growing up in Colorado and Montana. She remembered how the men had always been kind to her and the "good women" and "fancy ladies." Young girls matured quickly in this male-dominated society. Because her father was a freighter, her family "always ate a good table," better, she thought, than might seem possible in a remote mining camp. Culture, civilization, and business all arrived in the wake of mining.

Amelia Buss confided to her diary that hard work and loneliness characterized the life of a farm wife near future Fort Collins. From the time she arrived to find that the renters of "our place" had left it in shambles, she determinedly set to work to tidy things up. She pioneered in the process of raising her young daughter, in being a housewife, in confronting "that old homesick feeling," and in "not getting suddenly *rich*." The complaints and self-doubts aside, she could write after the first year, "Now I have settled down with the belief that here I shall end my days & the sooner I make it home the better. My prospects look brighter today than they did one year ago."

New bride Elizabeth Fisk wrote to her sister about Montana in July 1867. Discounting the fact that she strived to put the best face forward, she had much to say about her adopted home and the aspirations of a pioneering generation:

> I like the place much; it is not like home, but there is a wide field for usefulness here, and entering upon the work earnestly and prayerfully we need never to be lonely or disheartened. There is *room* here for every one to win a name and an influence that shall be widespread and shall ever be for good on all those around.[28]

She stayed, as did many of the others, disdaining the "go-backers," who gave up before giving the territories a real chance.

Already, though, easterners were projecting their own impressions of this frontier and its people. Newspaperman Alexander McClure praised Rocky Mountain mining life and its "charms," which to "most men are stronger than the love of home or family." The urbanity of the region provoked repeated comments. These communities, with their caesarean births and aborted careers, their fast-paced life, "lawlessness," red-light districts, and instant success stories, seemed so different from their contemporary farming cousins. A Chicago *Tribune* correspondent disparaged Montana: "Avarice is everywhere hard, withered and grasping. But it is dreadful here." At the same time, writers rhapsodized about the beauty, majesty, and richness of the Rocky Mountains and their salubrious climate.[29] Nature's benefits and man's degradation stood in sharp contrast.

Coloradans and Montanans read about themselves and their region. Some of them inevitably tried to live up to their literary and journalistic reputations. A "live" mining community was forced to provide the attractions that were becoming accepted as the norm for a Rocky Mountain or a western camp. Whether they stabilized the community, it seemed best to acquire these trappings of a "real" mining camp. While the West was shaping visitors' impressions, the visitors were shaping the West, more than they could possibly realize.

The past eight years had been, in the words of that popular author of the day, Charles Dickens, "the best of times and the worst of times." The "Star of Empire," as newspaper editors were fond of saying, appeared to have come to rest over the Rocky Mountains. There might be problems today, but tomorrow looked more promising than yesterday had ever been.

3 : WYOMING

The persistent westering of pioneers, who were chasing elusive rainbows seeking their pots of wealth, moved from Colorado and Montana into Wyoming. Variations were inevitable, though, because this land between the mining rushes differed from its sister territories. For many years it had served as the gateway to the far West over gentle South Pass. Now, it would have its own rush.

Whereas gold was the primary lure to Pike's Peak and Alder Gulch, three elements would give birth to Wyoming and shape Rocky Mountain settlement for generations: transportation, investment, and urbanization. Transportation laid the foundation. It was the railroad—the ultimate nineteenth-century achievement in transportation—that brought in the people who would settle this territory permanently.

Some powerful incentive would have to entice settlement, because, overall, the region did not offer as attractive inducements as its neighbors. To start with, no bonanza gold deposits glittered. Oregon- and California-bound immigrants had hurried through, jotting down some acerb thoughts in their journals. Two of the era's most popular humorists passed through the region in the early 1860s; neither was able to find much of interest to tell his readers. In bleak February 1864, Artemus Ward, then at the peak of his fame, made his way east by stage and sleigh. Ward entertained Abraham Lincoln and others, but he could find nothing in Wyoming to laugh about: "The most wretched [country] I ever saw." A couple of years earlier, Samuel Clemens had hustled west to avoid the Civil War. His similar reaction used the phrase "monotonous execrableness" to describe one stretch of countryside; the "loneliest land for a grave," another called it. He was impressed, however, by the "mountain vistas."[1]

Settlement was limited to a few forts and stage stations, such as one described by Clemens (soon to be better known as Mark Twain). "South Pass City" consisted of four log cabins, one unfinished. "The hotelkeeper, the postmaster, the blacksmith, the mayor, the constable, the city marshal and the principal citizen and property holder, all came out and greeted us cheerily, and we gave him a good day." This gentleman was "the chiefest of the ten citizens of the place."[2]

The powerful incentive that would bring development to the region materialized in the form of the railroad. Since the days of the 1849 California gold rush, ideas of a transcontinental railroad had excited promoters and been bandied through the halls of Congress. Besides construction problems, the major obstacle had been where the railroad would start and where it would go. All plans ran smack into the widening North–South sectional controversy and were left to languish.

The time for debate came to an end when Fort Sumter was attacked in the Charleston harbor. The failure of the ballot would now yield to resolution by the bullet. For the first time, but certainly not the last, Wyoming settlement would be heavily impacted by events in the eastern United States.

Suddenly, the logjam over many issues, including railroad building, was broken in favor of the North. As surely as the war would doom slavery, secession would leave the once powerful South in a secondary position for decades to come. Southern leaders might not have understood what was happening, but when they marched out of Washington, northern business and industrial dominance marched in to replace them. One significant result of their departure came in 1862, when Congress chartered the Union Pacific and the Central Pacific railroads to build from the East and the West over the central route. The Midwest stood to gain from this designation. As surely as the war gave birth to the railroad, Wyoming was the grandson of that national trauma.

Enthusiasm outraced the laying of the track. The federal government had given each railroad company ten alternate sections of land for each mile of track it laid and the right to take building materials from the public domain. In addition to those benefits, Uncle Sam chose to ease the financial burden even more by granting loans that ranged from sixteen thousand to forty-eight thousand dollars a mile, depending on the terrain (the highest figure was reserved for the more challenging Rockies and Sierras). Nevertheless, construction sputtered for a number of reasons. In stark contrast to earlier efforts in the East, the railroads would be building through unsettled and undeveloped territory. Few eastern investors were interested in a proposal that promised them no appreciable returns for years. The government came to the rescue in 1864 by doubling the land grant per mile and sweetening the financial arrangements.[3]

By giving away minerals to the miners and land to the railroads, Washington encouraged Rocky Mountain settlement as decisively as it hammered at the Confederate armies. The public domain would be available for all who had the fortitude or the opportunity to tap it. Even as they arrived, westerners bellied up to the federal trough. Finding it fulfilling. they stayed rooted to it as much as possible throughout their pioneering days, though not without some reservations and appropriate grumbling when odious regulations came along with Washington largess.

The Central Pacific raced off to a fast start, ran into the granite Sierras, and soon slowed down. Meanwhile, the Union Pacific, with nothing before it but miles of prairie land, encountered financing difficulties, as well as labor and materials shortages, in the war-burdened nation. Only forty miles of track extended west beyond Omaha, when the guns fell silent. When the war ended, an abundance of workers descended, some well trained, thanks to war-related railroad construction. War-enriched northern investors eagerly anticipated profitable investment opportunities.

With all these incentives, the Union Pacific had dashed 305 miles west of Omaha by July 1866, aiming straight toward the Great Divide Basin. Coloradans, hoping a route through their Rockies would be chosen, were gravely disappointed when the less arduous and less expensive route was logically selected. Only tiny Julesburg, way up in the isolated northeastern corner of the territory, would receive any direct benefits. That little burg needed all the help it could get, if Twain's description of it can be trusted.[4] Like the rest of eastern Colorado, it served only as a pass-through point on the route to the mountains and mines.

Urbanization and the railroad moved forward together across the prairie. Each profited from the other and each needed the other. Not needed were the "hell-on-wheels" construction towns, which migrated with the laying of the track; permanent villages for settlers, trade, and investment were the primary goals.

Shocked and dismayed by the selection of the Bridger's Pass and

Cheyenne Pass route, Coloradans fumed. A few even opposed the idea of creating a new territory of Wyoming, fearful that it would hamper their own renewed bid for statehood, which had been turned down earlier. Wyoming would win that one. What especially frightened Denverites was the selection by the Union Pacific of Cheyenne as a division point for the railroad in July 1867, four months ahead of the onrushing tracklayers. Located slightly over one hundred miles north of Denver, Cheyenne was instantly acquiring the railroad connections that Denver had craved for so long. The UP had immediately created an urban rivalry. In hastily laid-out Cheyenne, settlers huddled in tents and shanties, borrowed Denver's city ordinances, and elected a city government. To add to their blessings, the army located Fort D. A. Russell nearby, providing further government contracts and profits.

Within a year, President Andrew Johnson signed the organic act that created Wyoming Territory. With railroad workers, lumberjacks, freighters, coal miners, settlers, and hangers-on crowding into the new territory, its population approached twenty thousand in that summer of 1868. Denverites could hardly believe the luck of their rival—and their own misfortune. The Rocky Mountain region promptly witnessed its first urban struggle for dominance of trade and travel.

Denver seethed while Wyoming prospered. As the Union Pacific moved west, Laramie, Rawlins, Rock Springs, Green River, and Evanston grew where Twain, Ward, and others had seen only desolation. Short-lived Benton, Bryan, and Bear River City added an element of wildness, before succumbing to the passing of the construction gangs. The years 1867–69 brought exciting times to Wyoming, perhaps unmatched in any period since.[5]

Territorial governor John A. Campbell caught the significance of the events in his inaugural address to the first Wyoming legislature in 1869:

> For the first time in the history of our country, the organization of a territorial government was rendered unnecessary by the building of a railroad. Heretofore the railroad has been the follower instead of the pioneer of civilization.[6]

Campbell, appointed by President U. S. Grant after the Senate failed to confirm Johnson's earlier selection, came to a territory that was calming down after a turbulent beginning. The railroad helped bring this blessing, as well; the worst lawlessness had moved west into Utah with the construction camps.

Cheyenne soon experienced typical frontier problems. Off to such an auspicious start, it quickly attracted the undesirable drifting crowd along with the sought-after respectable residents. For the moment, their juxtaposition did not seem to matter, for Cheyenne was a town full of exuberance and promise. French mining engineer Louis Simonin visited the community in November 1867. He heard the sound of the saw and hammer everywhere, as wooden houses replaced the earlier tent city. Amazed by the "already so alive, so animated" community only a few months old, he expressed the fear that Colorado might be depopulated by "this city of compelling attractions." The future looked rosy for "the magic city, the wonder of the desert," as its residents proudly called Cheyenne.[7]

A newspaper was soon trumpeting its virtues, and, with the arrival of the railroad in November, the population soared toward six thousand. "Cheyenne Folks can keep pace with even those of Eastern Cities in style and taste," boasted the brand-new *Cheyenne Leader*. By January 1868, city officials had been elected, with the Democrats winning the day. Like its counterparts elsewhere, the community acquired those other unattractive trappings of urban America—crime, corruption, and discrimination—as easily as it acquired respectability. The maintenance of law and order created a major headache before and after the arrival of the Union Pacific. Without established territorial government, or courts, Cheyenne's founding fathers turned to a familiar expedient in early 1868, vigilantism. Warnings, followed by rounding up and expelling five particularly troublesome individuals—and a couple of hangings—eliminated the worst offenders. As visiting Chicagoan James Chisholm observed, "When people speak of seeing *life* out here, I think they must allow a wide latitude in the interpretation of the phrase."[8]

While Cheyenne struggled with its birth pangs, Denver looked on with unsuppressed jealousy. Once it had been called the "magic city," and now it aspired to be the "queen" of the region. Upstart Cheyenne boldly challenged its older neighbor for the title. The *Cheyenne Leader* of September 24, 1867 unblushingly claimed that "total business asphyxia" has not struck Denver yet, but the city was "too near Cheyenne to ever amount to much." The decided advantage of railroad connections gave Cheyenne the potential for making that boast a fact. Denver's "movers and shakers" had to react rapidly and furiously to head off disaster. Cheyenne had hardly burst on the scene in the summer of 1867, when some Denver merchants decided to migrate to the rival, assuming that the Wyoming town would become the dominant metropolis of the region. That inaugurated a period of trouble.

Despite the supreme disappointment of being bypassed, the leaders of Denver announced that they had no intention of giving up on their community and would stay put. Now the supreme test loomed: they had to secure railroad connections. It was promptly announced that negotiations had opened with the Union Pacific for a line from Denver to Cheyenne, a humbling experience in itself for the so-called queen. Then came encouragement, with the news that the Kansas Pacific would push construction into Denver. Those hopes were quickly dashed when that railroad ran into financial difficulties.

With grim determination, the resourceful leaders formed, in November 1867, a Board of Trade. Like similar boards of trade in midwestern and eastern cities, its purpose was to make crucial decisions for Denver and be responsible for implementing them. The first project, of course, would be a railroad to Cheyenne. Ex-governor John Evans, who had confidently predicted that the Union Pacific would run through Denver, spearheaded a campaign of desperation. Speeches, promises, arm twisting, and fund raising occupied 1868. Success and failure dogged the efforts; eastern investors and Congress initially rebuffed Denver's pleas, until at last fortune smiled. The Kansas Pacific raised funds to build into Denver, and Congress agreed to a 900,000-acre grant for the homegrown Denver Pacific to connect with Cheyenne. The Day of Jubilee came at long last on June 24, 1870, with the hammering of a silver spike, the arrival of the Denver Pacific, and a time of ceremony and celebration. Denver had its railroad connection. "Three times three and a Tiger!" hailed the *Rocky Mountain News* and devoted four front-page columns to the great event.[9]

When a Kansas Pacific locomotive steamed into town in August, Denver's future was assured. A group of capable, determined men had pooled their talents and resources and gone to extraordinary lengths to save their city. They had turned back the first, and in some ways the most serious, challenge to Denver's dominance. Denver stood ready to become the prevailing force in the Rocky Mountains. The gateway to the mountains had become the gateway to the world, only days away from both the East and West coasts.

The threat had been real, though maybe not quite so dire as Denverites had imagined. Once the construction crews moved on, Cheyenne settled down and then began to lose population. The town did not have the economic hinterland, the developable natural resources, or the scenic attractions to sustain the boom beyond 1867–68. Its compelling railroad advantage had been matched by its southern rival, which possessed all the advantages that Cheyenne lacked.

Cheyenne experienced more than enough trouble from rivals to the west. By 1868, Laramie was luring its residents away, especially after the UP decided to locate its main shops there. Cheyenne's population boom busted, and the fate of earlier boom towns was all too evident immediately to the east. Fortunately, no rival Wyoming town offered more than Cheyenne; most offered much less. The railroad, ranching, Fort Russell, and the forwarding business (sending freight to Colorado and elsewhere) stabilized the local economy as the boom ended.[10]

When the Union Pacific moved on, it showed little concern for the fate of some of the struggling villages it had nurtured. A visitor described one of the most infamous hell-on-wheels towns, Benton, as lacking "ordinary comforts, and there was not a green tree, shrub or patch of grass." Ten months later, nothing of it remained, not a house "to be seen." That kind of callousness did not always rule, especially when the railroad reached one of its primary Wyoming goals—the coal fields, which stretched from west of Cheyenne to Utah. Profit and property have been called the "passion at the core of the Western adventure," a true statement in the case of this railroad. By mid-1868, the UP had formed the Wyoming Coal and Mining Company. As it breathed life into Cheyenne, it looked even more longingly to Carbon, a few miles southwest of Medicine Bow, where coal mines were being opened. Here, the railroad obtained needed fuel and a commodity to transport and sell. Other camps soon followed, and western Wyoming had its first major industry; long before the cowboy rode the range, miners had been digging underground in the dark depths of coal mines.[11]

Coal neither stirred men's imaginations nor fueled a mining rush; only gold and silver awakened those instincts. In those exhilarating days of 1867–68, however, Wyoming caught a measure of mining fever, when it experienced a gold rush to South Pass. Since the 1840s, gold rumors had been swirling around this well-traveled pass. Isolation, Indians, and insignificant rewards doomed earlier efforts. In 1865, determined prospectors organized a mining district and continued to look for the precious metal. Their efforts finally paid off with the discovery, in June 1867, of a rich outcropping of gold. Greatly exaggerated news of this discovery (the Carissa Mine) brought on the rush to the Sweetwater, or South Pass, mines. A little mining camp, optimistically called South Pass City, soon served the needs of the miners.[12] Neighboring Colorado and Montana, both momentarily in the mining doldrums, watched unhappily as attention shifted to the upstart in the middle.

They had reason to be worried; miners from both territories, as well as from Utah, Nevada, and California, rushed to the newest El

Dorado. Following the generation-old instinct to exploit newly available western mineral resources, they left the declining and the known for the unknown and promising. Since nature could not provide everything, some came for speculation and entrepreneurial prospects. Wyoming would be no different from its neighbors.[13]

Salt Lake, Omaha, and Chicago papers were publishing news of rich diggings in July 1867. By the next March, the local newspaper, the *Sweetwater Mines*, was predicting a population of ten thousand by July 4 in an area of richness "unsurpassed . . . by any gold region on the continent." Cheyenne predicted twenty thousand, but the *Nevada Reveille* cautioned its readers about "highly colored accounts." To gain reliable information, the Chicago *Tribune* sent out correspondent James Chisholm to this new western wonder in 1868.

He came to a mining district in full flower; the local newspaper even published the "commercial South Pass market report"! Not one, but three mining camps greeted him, all overrun with prospectors and miners. Chisholm was intrigued, yet realistic, in his assessment. South Pass City had fifty to sixty residents, and the greater part of the dwellings were "either forsaken or never inhabited." Interestingly, he commented that the mining camps furnished a pleasant contrast to the "tumult, uproar and din" of the railroad towns he had just visited. The miners, a "quiet industrious class of men," were mostly former Californians; however, the principal ledge they worked, which stretched for eight miles, made Chisholm wonder about their experience. "But the truth is the rock, so far as they have gone, is barren, or at best such a poor prospect as will not pay to work."

He praised the few women he encountered—"it must be a brave soul" who, accustomed to the refinements of life, would "voluntarily front the hardship and perils of a mining camp"—but western life held little attraction for him. Hardship and privation seemed to be the lot of the men Chisholm interviewed; "a dog's life," one described it, only rarely compensated by riches. The hope of making a big strike kept them going, as did an unwillingness to admit failure and return east.[14]

South Pass was already declining by the time Chisholm left. The *Sweetwater Mines* tried to allay some of the fears: "notwithstanding the false reports and wilful misrepresentations which have been circulating concerning our mines in this Sweetwater country, they fully come up to the expectations of all sensible and experienced men who have come here." With a flourish, the editor concluded, "We coincide with hundreds of others in predicting a brilliant future for Sweetwater . . ." The hyperbole failed to stem the flow of prospectors moving elsewhere to look for their personal fortune. Despite one more very small rush in 1869, South Pass's day proved short and its significance minor. The perceptive mining reporter Rossiter Raymond said that fifteen hundred lodes had been discovered, a "great number necessarily worthless." Isolation, Indians, low-grade ore, high costs, and limited capital doomed the district. By 1872 both the placer and hard-rock mines had been mostly worked out.[15]

Before it passed into history, however, South Pass made a contribution to western legend. It helped give those women whom Chisholm so admired the right to vote, with Wyoming being the first territory or state to do so.

That territorial legislature to which Governor Campbell had spoken so enthusiastically had granted women the vote and the right to hold office. It also adopted a school law, which provided for employment of teachers with no salary discrimination when all applicants, regardless of sex, were equally qualified. It also approved an "act to protect Married Women." Such progressiveness, hailed nationally by woman's suffrage supporters, contributed to the Rocky Mountain region's liberal image in the realm of women's rights. The reasons for this new territory's unexpected surge to the forefront of this long, hotly debated issue were complex.

Several woman-suffrage lecturers made presentations before the legislative session in Cheyenne, and the subject had been discussed in the local newspaper, though no suffrage campaign had been undertaken. Neither had the opposition organized. The cause had not suddenly sprung on the scene without reason, however. Like its neighbors, Wyoming experienced a shortage of women, and the legislators may have hoped that their actions would attract more of them. The issue also generated desperately needed publicity for the territory in the East, where Montana and Colorado were still much better known. Perhaps a bit of partisan politics was also involved, as the two infant parties jockeyed for political control of the territory. Some cynical males may have believed that too few women lived there to have any influence at the polls, and some may have voted out of a sincere concern for women's rights. For whatever combination of reasons, Wyoming passed the act rather easily and stood alone for years to come in granting women these rights.[16]

Campbell, who happened to be an ardent suffragist, appointed three women justices of the peace. Only South Pass City's Esther Morris qualified. The "first woman judge in the world" had come west with her second husband, where he had opened a saloon in the remote mining camp. She served nine months (filling out the term of a man who had resigned), handled twenty-six cases, and retired in November 1870. Her brief career as justice of the peace gave her the distinction of being the only woman in public life in the twenty years of Wyoming Territory's history, and she was South Pass City's greatest claim to fame. Despite the brevity of her career, she achieved a small step toward enfranchising women by proving that a woman could successfully manage what had previously been considered a male prerogative. The debate continued, still far from being settled; nonetheless, women now had the opportunity to participate in Wyoming's municipal and political decisions.[17]

The Sweetwater district gave Wyoming another brief mining frenzy, then faded. But prospectors would not give up on Wyoming so easily. Just because South Pass did not meet expectations did not dampen enthusiasm. By the end of the decade, rumors of gold and silver discoveries in the Seminole Mountains and in the Yellowstone region in the northwest corner were urging the hopeful. Although the Yellowstone Basin was considered terra incognita, a perception reinforced by reports of "grand and wonderful phenomena" that included geysers and petrified forests, there persisted a "deep-seated conviction among miners that it [contained] rich placers."[18] Prospecting parties ventured there to look for gold, not geysers.

Colorado and Montana mining was languishing all the while, yet slowly evolving toward a better tomorrow. Montana's placer production, which ranked it second only to California in gold production, rapidly withered in the decade's last years. Hydraulic mining, with ditches and high-pressure hoses and nozzles, revived Bannack somewhat and had the potential for reworking other older, "exhausted" districts. With that method, a few miners could work larger areas with smaller returns and still make a profit; regrettably, the environmental damage increased alarmingly. Few stopped to consider the depredations in the rush to wealth; they were too busy "leveling hills, day and night."

Hard-rock mining offered promise in all three territories; patience and perseverance would be needed, however. Unionville, near Helena, was the best developed Montana district; it produced half the territory's quartz and supported over eight hundred people. Quartz mining failed, for the time being, to take up the slack because of the old familiar complex milling–smelting problems, high costs of machinery, transportation difficulties, and lack of investment capital. The smelting problem was similar to Colorado's; Montana needed experience, investment, and methods that worked. The school of hard knocks, and desperation, did not produce a winner. Montana's first gold boom had collapsed by 1870, and only the promise of a better tomorrow kept the prospector-miners going. Montana pessimists remembered well those optimistic days when the cry had been "Montana or Bust"; now it seemed that "busted by God" was more appropriate.[19]

Colorado still suffered from the aftermath of the infamous "gold bubble" and its "humbug lodes," in addition to those frustrating re-fractory-ore problems. Investment and outside interest in its mines evaporated. Fortunately, the persistent Nathaniel Hill held out some hope for the future. His mill at Black Hawk could successfully work the refractory ore, but the smelting expenses continued to limit his process to high-grade ore. Most of the mines still operating produced lower-grade ores, which piled up, awaiting a cheaper reduction process and better transportation facilities.[20]

Lower transportation costs would unquestionably benefit the major mining territories. Colorado secured railroad connections; Montana hoped for them, while continuing to rely on wagons and steamboats. The shorter distance from the railroad to its mining districts promised speedier delivery than the wagon could provide across the plains.

Despite all the problems, expectations of a better life kept miners going. The miner today "may be the employer tomorrow." A fortunate discovery could turn someone's world around. It also helped to un-derstand that it was largely the "discontented and ambitious portion of the American population" who sought the frontier. There one gained "self-respect and the spirit of independence." The average miner was "far superior in both natural intelligence and acquired knowledge to laborers in the older states."[21] A legend was being woven around west-erners; they came to cherish it and relished living up to the pioneering image.

Agriculture also continued its slow growth along the river valleys in both Colorado and Montana. Although neither territory would be self-reliant for years to come, progress was steady. Publicity about outstanding yields or some unusual crop declined. Ranches and farms produced foodstuffs and animals that gave the necessary support for permanent settlement. The homegrown wheat, barley, oats, and veg-etables amply supplemented the supplies transported into the territory. No less important for the future were the fledgling industrial estab-lishments. The foundries and machine shops, though small compared to their eastern counterparts, could make repairs and even build quartz mills. An infant economy was emerging in the Rocky Mountains.[22]

An infant economy, yet a highly specialized, exploitive one—almost a "one-crop" economy—developed. It all depended on mining, which still searched for its own savior. The Rocky Mountain residents begged for eastern capital, technology, and organizational know-how. They went out of their way to ask for an eastern economic "dictatorship," and they got it; the colonialism they despised came primarily as a result of their own desires and needs.[23]

The onrushing railroads promised to be both a help and a hindrance to agriculture and industry. The smoky engines promised faster service and lower rates and brought the industrial revolution to the Rockies. But, at the same time, they opened what had been a cloistered market to outside competition. Railroads also would bring more settlers, which meant more customers, and also more home industry and agriculture to challenge the pioneers.

Those rails and trains served as harbingers of the future and rang the death knell of the pioneering frontier, as surely as they bisected the mountains and prairie. In their enthusiasm to gain those iron connections, these pioneers gave little thought to the total ramifications that would follow.

A mystique was growing up around the developments of the past decade, even before the 1860s became history. Rossiter Raymond had this to say about the Sweetwater miner, while his dream was turning sour:

> Indeed, the pioneers of Sweetwater may be proud of the
> result of their labors, and the whole country may rejoice and
> thank him for having reclaimed such a valuable portion of
> the vast wilderness of the great West to civilization and
> industry.[24]

It was Americans' "manifest destiny" to open this "land of milk and honey."

In return for that duty, they expected their federal government to protect them from "Indian outrages," allow them to develop the natural resources freely and privately, and to provide, as Raymond wrote, "such general aid to them as is consistent with the institutions and laws of a democratic republic." Intentionally or not, they re-created the life they had left behind. That they lived in what later generations would consider an epoch-age concerned them little or not at all.

The people and their government marched hand in hand. Already, there were signs of a love–hate relationship. Westerners needed Uncle Sam, but not his federal rules and restraints. In spite of the image of the rugged individualist conquering all that stood in the way, the western settler never walked entirely alone. Washington had been, was, and would be his ever-present partner. No more dominant theme emerged from the pioneering days of the opening of the Rocky Mountain West.

These pioneers had migrated westward, fueled by the desire for self-improvement. Many had not intended to stay, wanting only to make their fortune and go back home. When they set out, the problems of living in the West appeared to be less troublesome than the ones they had left behind. Now they could not go back, because they had not acquired what they considered to be their fair share of what the Rocky Mountains had to offer. Failure to achieve their individual manifest destiny seemed to them a personal tragedy that many could not confront or accept. That they had miscalculated the economic truth of western pioneering before they set out for the promised land was a hard fact to acknowledge. The West offered the opportunity to succeed or to fail. Talent and hard work did not always guarantee success. So they continued their search for fulfillment for another season, and yet another, and in so doing laid the basis for permanent development of the Rocky Mountain region in the decades ahead.

TOP: *A Ute camp near Denver. They were here first, but the rush to the Rockies overwhelmed them. (Courtesy: Center of Southwest Studies)*
BOTTOM: *Isolation was a problem that came with the first mining rush. Wagon trains, such as this one in Helena, kept the supplies coming. (Courtesy: Montana Historical Society)*

TOP: *The stage was the fastest way to reach most of the Rocky Mountain settlements in the 1860s. Main Street, Helena, 1866. (Courtesy: Montana Historical Society)*
BOTTOM: *The ultimate mode of nineteenth-century transportation, the railroad. A Union Pacific supply train, 1869. (Courtesy: American Heritage Center, University of Wyoming)*

TOP: *Urbanization came with mining, but every community needed a railroad. Cheyenne, 1868, was a child of the Union Pacific. (Courtesy: American Heritage Center, University of Wyoming)*
BOTTOM: *Miners, such as these at the Nancy Hanks Mine, Garnet, Montana, opened the region for settlement and development. (Courtesy: Montana Historical Society)*

TOP: *South Pass City was Wyoming's major mining camp in the 1860s, although it was well past its prime by 1893. (Courtesy: American Heritage Center, University of Wyoming)*
BOTTOM: *The pioneers strived to recreate the life they left behind; Caribou, Colorado's brass band helped to do that. (Courtesy: Duane A. Smith)*

Denver's Tabor Grand Opera House illustrated how far this city had traveled.
(Courtesy: Henry E. Huntington Library)

TOP: *Women worked hard to make the region one where they could raise their children and put down roots. Gold Hill, Colorado. (Courtesy: Boulder Daily Camera)*
BOTTOM: *Fire companies filled practical and social needs in communities such as Telluride, Colorado. (Courtesy: Homer E. Reid)*

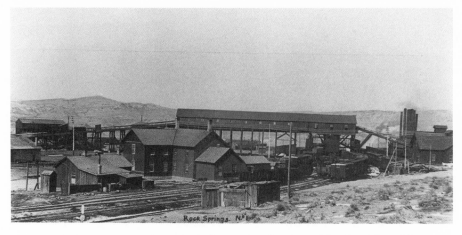

TOP: *Yellowstone was the nation's first national park, and by the 1890s visitors were coming in increasingly greater numbers. (Courtesy: American Heritage Center, University of Wyoming)*

BOTTOM: *Less romantic than gold and silver mining, coal mining was a regional mainstay. Union Pacific Coal Mine #1. (Courtesy: American Heritage Center, University of Wyoming)*

TOP: *The miner came and so did the farmer to tap that market. Farming in Montana's Horse Plains Valley. (Courtesy: Montana Historical Society)*
BOTTOM: *Ranching, railroading, and a little mining stimulated growth in Dillon, Montana. (Courtesy: Montana Historical Society)*

TOP: *A Chinese New Year's Celebration in Rock Springs, 1896. (Courtesy: Wyoming State Archives)*
BOTTOM: *"Promote or die," the Hall of Mines and Mining at the Chicago World's Fair. Montana's exhibit was the "renowned silver statue of Justice," which cost nearly $300,000. (Courtesy: Duane A. Smith)*

4 : UNCLE SAM IN THE ROCKIES

The decades of the 1870s and 1880s brought both progress and despair to the Rocky Mountain region. Looking at the early years of the seventies, a casual observer might not have seen too much promise.

Precious-metal mining stayed in the doldrums, with few fresh discoveries to energize newspaper reporters or generate publicity. When the Comstock roared into its "big bonanza," and other districts flourished in Nevada and Utah, investors diverted their attention from the Rocky Mountains. The rush of settlement seemed to have passed them by, with only agriculture maintaining its slow but steady growth. Population statistics sagged as the drifting crowd, and some bona-fide residents as well, moved on. The advent of the railroad did not bring its promised millennium. While local boosters bemoaned their fate, they were redoubling their efforts to promote their territories and, in effect, their own future. Out of the gloom and economic stagnation emerged several trends, which came to dominate the region for the next generation. They also gave a hint of what the Rocky Mountains would become a century or more hence. Urbanization, tourism, environment, and federal government involvement in the West were not generally topics for serious discussion, with the exception of the last. Nonetheless, in subtle and sometimes blatant ways, the issues arose, forcing themselves on unsuspecting and unprepared westerners.

The relationship with Washington was the most sensitive and volatile. Following the traditional pattern, federal appointees filled most positions in all three territories, starting with the governor and judges and reaching down to minor appointments. A few of these men proved to be poor choices, more were excellent selections, and most proved to be average. Because they started with a male population of five thousand, each territory could elect its own legislature and a nonvoting delegate to Congress. Sometime in the future, when sufficient population could be proved (sixty thousand inhabitants), statehood and equality with the older states would end the territorial period. Then the freedom to select who would govern and the authority to throw the rascals out would belong to the local populace.

In the meantime, these Rocky Mountain territories reacted ambiguously to domination by the federal government, berating it for the quality of its appointees while profiting from the advantages it bestowed. A similar pattern emerged for each territory, with an allowance for local variations and conditions; few would have called these the best of times.

All three territories suffered through turbulent years with their governors: Montana in the 1860s and Colorado and Wyoming in the 1870s. The stately Ohioan Sidney Edgerton had gotten Montana off to a good start, but then that Irish revolutionary, the mercurial Thomas Francis Meagher, injected chaos during his temporary appointment. It was left to Civil War veteran Green Clay Smith to restore order. Discouraged with the political factionalism, financial problems, and general turmoil, he soon left for Washington, never to return, leaving two years of his administration to an acting governor. President Grant's 1869 appointment of James Ashley proved particularly unfortunate. This intolerant, radical Republican found himself up against an overwhelmingly Democratic legislature. Confrontation and stalemate preceded Grant's sudden recall of Ashley, an action that closed Montana's decade of controversy.

With the exception of the individualistic, strong-willed Democratic legislature, and some powerful prosouthern sentiment, the problems faced by the Montana governors were the same as those in Colorado. The stresses and strains of the Civil War and Reconstruction years, against a background of federal neglect, left Colorado and Montana to languish in the political backwater, unattractive to aspiring politicians. The slumping condition of the local economies only added to the governors' woes.[1]

In startling contrast to earlier years, the 1870s in Montana were tranquil. The appointment of Ohioan Benjamin Potts, a highly praised Civil War veteran, gave nearly thirteen years of capable administration and bestowed a belated political maturity. Considering Montana as more than just a temporary, sight-seeing appointment, Potts worked with both parties and managed to stabilize territorial finances. He benefited greatly from the rebound of the economy.[2] Potts's administration spanned more than half of Montana's territorial period; neither Colorado nor Wyoming had a governor to match him in tenure or significance during this time.

President Grant's appointments hurt Montana to some degree, but by and large, the territory benefited from them. The same cannot be said for Colorado, where they did more harm than good. Paralleling what was happening on the national scene, the repercussions of Grant's inattention and naivete were reaching far out into the Rocky Mountains.

Colorado evolved into a carpetbagger's kingdom after the war; two governors came and went after much bickering and local disruption. So bad did the situation become that it unquestionably helped to stimulate several statehood movements, each of which failed. They failed because of insufficient population, local opposition, Washington's Reconstruction politics, and conflicts and jealousy among local politicians. Conditions did not improve when Grant became president in 1869. He quickly moved to employ the patronage of territorial offices to reward his supporters, the traditional practice.

Edward McCook, a fifty-niner and Civil War veteran, looked at first to be a strong appointment. Unfortunately, he turned to playing the customary game of spoils with the local appointments, while also enriching his own pocketbook. Within a few years, the governor had managed to alienate a large portion of Colorado's political community. The anti-McCook faction undertook an investigation and uncovered some scandals. Territorial delegate and longtime political leader Jerome Chaffee announced the results in Washington, which, along with Colorado petitions, pressured Grant into removing McCook. Samuel Elbert was named governor in 1873.

Not one to go down without a fight, McCook hurried off to Washington with his own accusations and charges of corruption. The harassed president, convinced of his friend's innocence, removed Elbert in 1874 and restored McCook to the office. The vacillating in Washington angered Coloradans beyond their limits of endurance, and for the first time they elected a Democratic territorial delegate. Infuriated local Republican leaders promptly launched an all-out campaign to remove the unpopular governor.

Again, Grant bowed to pressure; McCook was sent packing within a year, along with most of the rest of the territorial officials. So much federal indecision and confusion rekindled the smoldering desire for statehood. Grant finally found a man who could calm the turbulence and govern: Kentucky-born, Illinois-reared John Routt. One of the great strengths of this war veteran was his ability to reconcile disputes. He needed that virtue, along with his reputation for honesty, in his dealings with irate Coloradans.[3] They had had enough of federal appointees, federal neglect, and federal insensitivity to local wishes. There would be no stopping the statehood movement now.

Wyoming, too, endured the whims of Reconstruction and Grant. The unpopular and impeachment-enmeshed Andrew Johnson never had his nominees confirmed. Grant nominated thirty-three-year-old, Civil War veteran John Campbell, who received quick confirmation. Campbell survived legislative battles and local factionalism that involved an anti-Campbell protest movement in Washington until 1875. The territorial Republican party split over the governor's actions and other issues, including local party control, duplicating the predicament of its neighbor to the south. Grant's next appointment, John M. Thayer, proved to be a strong governor. Having lived in and been senator from Nebraska, he understood both western and national politics. Much like Routt, he adroitly restored Republican unity and dealt effectively with the independent legislators.[4] Wyoming began a decade of relative political tranquility under Thayer, although he would not be around to see the end of it.

While some of the appointees helped and others hindered, a pattern is evident. Men with midwestern and southern border backgrounds, and Civil War service, predominated. Each territory was affected adversely by the tribulations of Reconstruction and the instability of the Grant administration, although the hero of Vicksburg and Appomattox finally, in each case, found the right man to govern. By 1876, stability and a semblance of political order prevailed throughout the Rocky Mountains. Two of the three territories remained locked under federal control by its appointive system. But not Colorado, which was about to become the thirty-eighth state.

By this time, another interesting trend had become evident. Despite the fervent wishes of the Republican party, which controlled the legislative and executive branches, these three western territories had not come united into the party fold. They represented a cross-section of western political individualism. Montana was strongly Democratic, with Colorado just as ardently Republican; Wyoming harbored a vocal Democratic element within a Republican territory. No doubt, Colorado's political leanings enhanced its chances for statehood. Its improved status harmed somewhat the aspirations of the other two, neither of which had anywhere near the required population level.

The disparities created tensions and a we–they atmosphere. The *Helena Herald* (of February 2, 1872) editorialized on the plight of Montana's congressional delegate: "He has no vote—nothing to sell, and in consequence can buy nothing." Wyoming and Montana would remain political colonies for another decade, captive to the vagaries of Washington and the dominant political party.

Montana's Democratic leanings can be easily traced back to its earlier wartime immigration. The heavy border-state, mid-Atlantic migration, plus the Irish miners, favored the Democrats, who were strengthened by the Republican party's and Washington's mishandling of the Montana situation. The Republican appointees failed to come to terms with the self-reliant, utilitarian Montana Democrats, a political fact exacerbated by the radical Republican views of several governors. The anger boiled until Potts tempered it in the 1870s. By then, Montana's Democratic leanings were well established, much to the horror of the local and national Republican leaders.[5]

Colorado Republicans had a little more time to build a political base before wartime emergencies left them on their own. Their territory had not experienced a mining and war-spurred migration wave from the border states; Colorado emerged with a solidly midwestern heritage. As a result, the party firmly controlled the territory during the war and, except for the Grant-related problems, did not surrender that dominance before statehood. Almost without exception, the territorial leaders were Republicans, while the Democrats wandered in the wilderness for the proverbial forty years. The breach of that Republican fortress was what so upset politically astute Chaffee, Henry Teller, and the others when the McCook debacle produced a backlash that resulted in the election of a Democrat. Only a major Washington blunder or local Republican infighting could produce that type of defeat in rock-ribbed Republican Colorado.[6]

Last on the scene, Wyoming avoided some of the earlier problems. Needing the federal government and its subsidies more than the other two, Wyoming's Republican political leaders fought among themselves and less with Washington. Party factionalism, however, gave the Democrats more local power than they might have enjoyed otherwise. It even helped to produce overwhelmingly Democratic legislatures in 1875 and 1877. Fortunately, Governor Thayer worked effectively with the legislature; unlike his predecessors, who confronted Democratic majorities with little success, he got along famously.[7]

In each territory, as it matured, political leaders came forth to represent local views and to divide what political plums became available to them. These men dominated territorial politics in a way that reflected the national scene and spoke clearly to the question of western popular democracy. With the emergence in post–Civil War America of Boss Tweed and his Tammany Hall, and political powerbrokers such as James G. Blaine and Roscoe Conkling, it was understandable that western politicians would duplicate the eastern precedent, adding to it their own blend of politics.

Kentucky-born Democrat Samuel Hauser came to be Montana's kingmaker and string-puller par excellence and, coincidentally, he had excellent Washington connections. The shrewd, serious Hauser came to the Bannack diggings in 1862 and rapidly built up large holdings in mining, milling, banking, and transportation. In working for the creation of the territory, he established agreeable relations with the governors, especially Potts. Toiling behind the scenes, Hauser wielded political power and manipulated the economy and politicians with aplomb for twenty years. Always willing to fight to enhance his own, and what he believed to be the territory's, interest, Hauser primarily represented mining. That the industry benefited, in turn, from his activities was not surprising. Indeed, the idea of individual political leaders or interest groups reaping rewards from their activities was not out of line with the prevailing national attitudes of interlocking relationships between business and politics.[8]

In Colorado, Republicans Henry Teller and Jerome Chaffee served in the same way. Colorado's consummate politician of his era, Chaffee arrived in 1860 and turned successfully to milling, banking, and mining investment. Unlike Hauser, he ran for territorial office, serving in the legislature and as the territorial delegate. A close friend of Denver's leadership (and father-in-law of Grant's son), Chaffee represented that city's interests. Already Denver was assuming the role that it was destined to keep as the political heart of Colorado, and this created instant envy and mounting opposition from the mountain mining towns. Their spokesman, New York–born Henry Teller, came to Central City and became one of the territory's outstanding lawyers, as well as its "best known public speaker." Working behind the scenes, Teller, who was also a master politician, fought against Denver for political patronage and successfully opposed it in one of the statehood fights. Although both Teller and Chaffee favored statehood, Teller feared initially that Denver would gain everything at the expense of the mountain communities. Not until the 1870s and the Grant misadventures did the two reach a political truce and join to promote statehood, which then finally moved forward with vigor.[9]

Unlike its two neighbors, Wyoming was shaped from the start by a corporation, the Union Pacific Railroad. The railroad had given birth and early substance to the territory, but interestingly, it played a less significant long-range political role. Part of the reason had been that economic promises had failed to materialize in the 1870s. Wyomingites felt abused by the management of the UP because of its high freight and passenger rates, high coal prices, resistance to local taxation, and its town-lot policies. Railroad bashing became a popular sport. For instance, the *Cheyenne Leader* of June 18, 1873, called the railroad "a curse to the community." The why of it all was not hard to determine— its "outrageous and discriminating freight and passenger tariffs west of the city." Politics, meanwhile, became personalities rather than issues, as factions formed around men. Governor Campbell and his friends coalesced into one group and the opposition into another, as the Republicans went to war with themselves for most of the early seventies. Out of this turmoil emerged one Wyoming politician of note, Joseph M. Carey, who was appointed U.S. attorney for the newly organized territory. Ranching and real-estate investments gave this young lawyer an economic base, and he quickly became embroiled in local politics as a leader of the Campbell faction. The capable, calculating Carey would be a power for the next generation.[10]

Aiding these leaders in promotion and decision making were what would be termed *lobbyists* today. For Montana and Colorado, the major voice was mining, for Wyoming the railroad, with ranching emerging as a factor to be reckoned with as the day of the cattleman dawned.

Despite what appears to be the emergence of a ruggedly independent brand of Rocky Mountain politics, in truth it never removed itself very far from Uncle Sam. As long as they remained territories, Colorado, Wyoming, and Montana would be tied closely to Washington, political colonies in the fast-changing Rocky Mountains. Certainly, the primary reason that statehood advocates sought self-determination was to gain control of both their destiny and those cherished "loaves and fishes" to divide without federal help.

Wyoming exemplified the classic confrontation between Washington and westerners. New York lawyer William Peck wangled an appointment as a territorial associate justice. He came west in 1877, highly recommended, and was assigned to the district that encompassed the western counties. Almost instantly, a clash of personalities and judicial heritages clouded his court; he seemed to be unable to adapt to western conditions. For people used to having court business wrapped up in a hurry, his deliberateness and fastidiousness seemed wasteful and costly. His fines and appointments also stepped on local political toes, and as one of his supporters even admitted, he was "a little too old fogyish and puritanic for this latitude." His unpopularity gave birth to a movement to prevent Peck's confirmation, since he had been appointed during a Senate recess. Peck unwittingly became the symbol of the battle between territorial and national control. Confirmed against Wyoming's wishes, he was promptly redistricted by the angry legislators into two as yet unorganized northeastern counties. After failing to persuade Congress to disallow the redistricting act, Peck showed spunk by staying put and serving out his term. With time on his hands, he wrote almost all the Wyoming Supreme Court opinions. A Senate move to punish Wyoming was blocked by Henry Teller, among others, who stoutly defended the territory and its rights.[11]

Montana and Colorado also had difficulties with their territorial benches. Obstructed by limited funds, unfamiliarity with mining law, judges who were sometimes too inflexible to act effectively, and antagonism toward "foreign" officials, the judiciary struggled to establish law. Furthermore, Congress, with its appropriation and appointive powers, often failed to weigh the territorial needs on their own merits or to recognize the changes that needed to be accommodated. The Rocky Mountains crested far from Washington and seemed of little significance under the pressure of national matters.[12]

Westerners also continued to be wary of lawyers. The hostility toward them might not have been as flagrant as in the days when some mining districts prohibited them from owning claims, let alone practicing; but the feelings of antipathy were abroad in the land. This acid comment about the coming of a lawyer to a new town called him someone "who immediately runs as a candidate for county offices, foments grievances, and shows every man how he can get the better of his neighbor."[13] Lawyers were not very popular in the nineteenth century.

The law giveth, the law taketh away, and so did the federal government. Wyoming reaped the most benefits from Washington. In a sparsely populated region, the federal government dispensed subsidies through a variety of agents. Most important were the traditional territorial appropriations: generous grants of land and natural resources and the garrisoning of troops to protect the settlements. The census takers in 1870, for example, counted more than 1,800 militiamen in Wyoming's population of 9,118.[14] These posts represented contracts, jobs, and profits. Montana was the recipient of the second greatest largess. Colorado, facing less Indian danger and having the most well-developed economy, benefited the least.

The two mining territories had the most to gain, however, when Congress finally got around to adopting a national mining law. Following the examples of California and Nevada, miners had simply created their own extralegal mining districts, law, and government in the early days of the unorganized Rocky Mountain regions. These districts fulfilled the requirement for a practical and economical expedient but created problems of their own. Rossiter Raymond complained that Montana's 1867 placer law possessed no practical bearings. Nothing, he concluded, could be more confused and uncertain than mining rules in force in various gulches. Nevada, meanwhile, had been pushing for national legislation, and in 1866 (for lode claims) and 1870 (for placer claims), Congress gave legal status to the industry. These actions were followed in 1872 by a Federal Mining Law, which reflected both the strengths and shortcomings of its local western precedents.

The industry achieved legal status when, in fact, it had developed without authorization on the public domain. "Local laws, customs, and rules of miners" shaped Congress's deliberations. The resulting 1872 law wisely defined how claims should be marked and their size specified, determined how much assessment work had to be done annually on unpatented claims to avoid forfeiture, explained the procedure for obtaining United States patents on mining claims (a patent conveys title to the ground, with no further assessment work necessary), and described what information local records should contain. At the same time, Congress ruled that surface boundaries should embrace the apex (the top) of the vein. *Apex* appeared to be an unambiguous term, but in fact, it led to expensive and time-consuming litigation, as contestants defended their contradictory definitions of what constituted the apex. That geological uncertainty led to famous legal cases and lawsuits and exorbitant lawyer and witness fees that could bankrupt all parties.[15] Regrettably, no means were provided to enforce the law continuously and honestly.

With its actions, Congress had heartily endorsed western mining interests and their customary law, thereby allowing the rapid and thorough development of mineral resources with minimal federal regulation and fees. Mining spokesmen could ask for little more justification of their policies, even if some bones of contention still existed. A growing body of territorial, then state, legislation and judicial interpretation supplemented the basic 1872 stipulations, which remained in effect throughout the decades that followed.

Uncle Sam had been most generous to these pioneering miners and their industrial descendants, as well as to lawyers, expert witnesses, and mining engineers, all of whom made a living off the apex cases. Uncle Sam had been most benevolent to those who opened the Rocky Mountains, though they did not always appreciate those kindnesses. The love–hate relationship continued, as it did elsewhere during the westering process.

These Rocky Mountain westerners, like their neighbors, ardently desired that Washington deal, and deal quickly, with the long-festering question of the future of the Indians who already lived in the mountains or on nearby plains. The tragedy of Sand Creek had led to a major Indian war in 1865, which spilled over into Wyoming and Montana. Attention focused on the Bozeman Trail, Montana's shortest link to the overland routes. After some false starts and military setbacks, government negotiators produced a temporary truce there, and army columns were posted elsewhere. Colorado benefited the most, as its eastern plains Indians were removed by the late 1860s.

The remaining Indians still aggravated officials and settlers alike. The settlers too often carried a bias against them, which flared all the hotter once gold was discovered on Indian land or when the overland routes were threatened. James Rayner expressed their attitudes clearly, even from never-threatened Colorado Springs, in declaring that "people here would sooner kill Indians than not. I tell you the Indians are not the noble redmen you read about." The conflict raged on, as old as the oldest settlement and as new as the most recent one. The solution was not as simple as newspaper items led readers to believe.

Virginia City's *Montana Post* recommended in 1865, "More powder and less ink . . . if they would not stay on the reservations." Two years later, however, it observed that "the policy of indiscriminate and immediate extermination of 300,000 human beings, for they are human, is barbarous and inconsistent with our advanced civilization." The editor recommended killing the buffalo, ending the Indian department, making no treaties, and letting the territories take care of their neighbors. The *Sweetwater Miner* disagreed; it wanted government protection, at the same time ending the feeding, clothing, and arming of "vagabond Indians." The *South Pass News* of April 9, 1870, demonstrated the issue's emotional potential when it headlined the "Indian Outrage" upon "Our peaceable citizens." The mining camp of Ouray,

Colorado, named after the famous Ute leader, still insisted that "The Utes Must Go," praising the admirable Ouray all the while. Whites could use the land better, the editor argued. The reservation lay only a couple of miles north of the camp, and the government needed to act before war broke out. No recommendation was made about where the Utes should be deposited. By the time of this 1879 editorial, the West was filling up, and no one wanted bands of Indians suddenly dumped in the neighborhood.[16]

One has to feel sympathy for all concerned. The government was ensnared, trapped in an impossible position between two groups of people who coveted the land. Add to them the eastern taxpayers, who did not want much money spent on any solution, military or reservation, and Congress found itself pressured from all sides. The result proved predictable: a classic, tragic conflict between cultures and races. During the 1870s, this confrontation unfolded in the Rocky Mountains, with victory going to the more populous and technologically advanced group. Washington, caught between irate western voters and treaty-guaranteed Indian rights, vacillated between peace and war, experiencing the predictable complaints and failures. It was a no-win situation.

Mining relentlessly forced the issue in two major encounters, one in the Black Hills and another on Colorado's Western Slope. Rumors in 1873–74 of gold "from the grass roots" in the Black Hills enticed miners from Wyoming, Montana, and elsewhere, and their invasion infuriated the Sioux, who considered this region sacred and theirs by virtue of treaty. The United States' attempts to purchase the land failed and war came in 1876. That placed George Armstrong Custer in Montana's valley of the Little Big Horn on June 25; he and five companies of the Seventh Cavalry never rode out. The Sioux and their allies won the battle, only to lose the war. Congress and its constituents were so embarrassed by this military debacle and disrespect to the nation's centennial that they marshaled resources and manpower to conduct a sweeping campaign. Within a year, the Sioux, Cheyenne, and Arapaho found themselves herded onto reservations. This action ended, for all practical purposes, the Indian problem in Montana and Wyoming and left the losers huddled on land out of the way of settlers and miners.[17]

An equally swift and classic confrontation occurred when the Western Slope was opened. The Utes had been friendly for the most part, largely because settlement had not yet reached their land beyond the Continental Divide in the 1860s. Then came the early 1870s mining rush into the rugged, isolated San Juan Mountains, the heart of Ute country. Washington barely avoided trouble when it persuaded the Utes to sign the Brunot agreement that opened the mountain area to mining. This expedient did not provide a permanent solution. The San Juaners had Indians on three sides of them, a position they found decidedly uncomfortable. Demands that the Utes be relocated grew as the seasons passed, as did the number of settlers crowding in adjacent to the reservation and in the nearby Gunnison country. It was an Indian war just looking for a place to start. That spark came when the well-intentioned, stubbornly uncompromising, and naive White River Ute agent Nathan Meeker attempted to force his wishes on the Utes. When they rebelled, he and eleven other men were killed at the agency in September 1879. An army relief column, after being attacked and pinned down by furious Utes, arrived too late to help. Through the efforts of the peaceful Ouray, a general war was averted. Ouray's efforts came too late to save the Utes; Coloradans angrily called for their removal.

The problem of where to put them was resolved when Utah was selected. The Mormons were not in good graces with Washington at that time, so a reservation was carved out of the eastern part of the territory. By late summer 1881, the Utes were gone from their longtime western Colorado home.[18] When mining ran into an Indian barrier, the speed and finality of the solution was alarming to easterners, who wished for a less brutal result. Westerners wished only that Uncle Sam would act more quickly.

A third development drew attention to Indians in the Rocky Mountain region—the stirring campaign of the Nez Percé as they fled Idaho difficulties and tried to reach Canada. Their journey took them through Yellowstone National Park, panicking visitors there, and then into Montana, where temporary forts were built and Butte militia companies volunteered to assist the frustrated army. As one Bitterroot Valley resident exclaimed, "Indian excitement running high." When the danger had passed, the *Butte Miner,* on August 14, 1877, observed, "Time in Butte has been very dull since the Indian—what shall we call it?" It had been a frightening time for western Montana, before the army finally ran down the Nez Percé short of their goal. Montana's Indian wars came to an end.[19]

Now the tribes became tourist curiosities, trapped on small portions of what was once their homeland, with their nomadic way of life stamped out. Eventually, more westerners would come to perceive them as human beings, not simply as obstacles in the path of settlement. Mary Ronan, whose husband Peter served as Flathead agent, had been in the Rockies since 1861. She overcame her early prejudices and learned to appreciate and like her Flathead neighbors; she trusted them, a trust "never betrayed, not even in small matters."[20] Until the clear majority of her western contemporaries concurred, racism would be a part of the Indians' life, and reservations would separate them from their past and any reasonable future.

All these people, both Indians and whites, had come as immigrants to this new land. The Indians' "mistake" had been getting there first and being numerically fewer.

Then, from the viewpoint of these Johnny-come-lately westerners, a strange thing happened back East. They were not receptive to the emerging eastern opinion of the Indian, which focused concern on Indian rights and showed appreciation for Indian culture. Helen Hunt Jackson had helped to arouse sympathies with her books *Century of Dishonor* and *Ramona*. Her husband, William, harmonized more with the prevailing attitudes when he wrote a friend who had questioned him about the Indians:

> I take no New York papers & our dailies do not say much on
> the Indian subject just now. So you see your Eastern
> "sentimental" friends that are constantly looking outside of
> their homes, their towns & their state for some wrong to
> correct, must keep you posted on that question.[21]

Western settlers much preferred to read editorials like the one that appeared in the *Helena Independent* on September 25, 1885, praising the people of Montana, who had labored to "redeem a savage wilderness." The editorial opined that the subjugation of the Indian was considered a crowning achievement of the Rocky Mountain West over the past twenty years.

Even of more long-range significance had been the gaining of statehood. No more clearly was the love–hate relationship between Uncle Sam and his children shown then, as the three territories struggled toward this goal. Washington both helped and hindered.

Coloradans were the first to achieve statehood, after a decade-long struggle with bureaucratic Washington. The problems of the Grant administration and colonial status had been too oppressive. By 1875 local politicians were united toward that goal, united as they had never been before. Fortuitously, the national situation played right into their hands. The Grant administration scandals besmirched the Republican party, whose leaders feared the outcome of next year's presidential election. A new, solidly Republican state, with its three electoral college votes, would be a most welcome addition. Except for that single, brief aberration, Colorado met all the requirements.

Thus, Colorado was given another chance for admission to the Union. Territorial leaders proceeded to set in motion the necessary steps in the procedure. First, thirty-nine delegates were elected to a constitutional convention, which met in Denver in December. After eighty-seven days of work, on March 14, 1876, the constitution makers adjourned. They produced a traditional, conservative constitution, based to a large degree on earlier ones from Illinois and other midwestern states. As might be expected, the Colorado document accepted the existing American political ideas and forms.

Only three controversial questions came before the convention. The one that involved whether there should be a specific reference to God was compromised by acknowledging a "profound reverence for the Supreme Ruler of the Universe." With regard to the woman-suffrage question, which threatened to cripple the chances for ratification and statehood, the delegates, mostly lawyers, decided to forgo heroism. Choosing not to follow Wyoming's example, they gave women only a token victory: "no person shall be denied the right to vote at any school district election, nor to hold any school district office, on account of sex." They left everything else to the first General Assembly to decide. The location of the state capital created more controversy. The logical choice, Denver, stirred animosity, so the delegates again skirted the issue by leaving it to the General Assembly and the "qualified electors of the State" to decide at a later date. To let passions cool, that "later date" would be after 1879.[22]

It was now up to the voters to ratify statehood. Editor Byers was not concerned: "It requires no prophet to foretell what the verdict of the people will be." He was right, for on July 1, the voters approved it, exceeding a three-to-one majority. "Three Cheers for the State of Colorado," roared the *News*.

> Another star is added to Columbia's galaxy, and that Colorado is the Centennial State in good earnest. A sovereign state, mistress of herself and her destinies, Colorado will now conquering and to conquer, pursue the path of prosperity.[23]

It was a time to parade local pride. When Grant issued the proclamation of statehood on August 1, Coloradans celebrated wildly. Their enthusiasm was not unanimous throughout the country, however. A Pennsylvania editor growled: "Colorado consists of Denver, the Kansas Pacific

Railway, and scenery. The mineral resources of Colorado exist in the imagination. The agricultural resources do not exist at all." Byers and the others easily refuted heresy such as this, which said more about the editor's bias toward the West than his grasp of reality.

In this year of the centennial of the Declaration of Independence, the new Centennial State contained a population of approximately 180,000, with Denver as its urban keystone. The state had railroads, churches, schools, colleges, theaters, hospitals, and the other trappings that Victorian Americans deemed to be essential parts of modern American civilization. In an understandable outburst of boosterism, author Frank Fossett exclaimed, "Colorado has a population unsurpassed for intelligence, enterprise, thrift and energy; and this population is now of a settled and permanent character." Praising the law-abiding nature of the people, he concluded, "No state ever entered the Union with a people possessing an equal degree of culture, refinement and wealth." Less flamboyantly, agriculture had progressed markedly throughout the past seven years, drawing closer to fulfilling the needs of the local markets. Fossett's chauvinism carried him too far, though, when he claimed that Colorado flour was the best in America. Mining might have been depressed during the centennial year, but the expectation was still alive that it was just a matter of time before a new bonanza would be discovered.[24]

Even before official statehood, Coloradans proudly exhibited their wares at the Centennial Exposition at Philadelphia. Gold, silver, and other minerals were displayed and brought home eleven medals. The respected *Engineering and Mining Journal* called the display "in many respects, the most wonderful collection of gold ores in the Exhibition," and the "handsomest" silver.[25] Coloradans basked in the glory, and so did the Republicans, when they triumphed in the heatedly contested presidential election. Rutherford Hayes won the 1876 election by one electoral college vote. Colorado's three had made the difference in the closest presidential contest in American history. Not only was the East making an impact on the Rocky Mountains, but the high country was also beginning to have its impact on the rest of the nation.

Wyoming and Montana did not make that kind of a splash in the center of a hotly contested presidential election and a national centennial. They did, however, later join Colorado and entered the Union. Montana came first in November 1889. Both local parties supported statehood and also gained the active support of Colorado's congressional delegation. Because Montana Republicans had made strong gains during the decade, when immigration swung away from traditional

Democratic strongholds, the national GOP leaders smiled favorably on statehood. Leadership came from Butte and Helena, the mining and business centers, with the mining men predominating. Territorial government had improved over the years, as more competent men filled elective and appointive offices, but that did not deter Montanans' desire for statehood. It was no surprise that mining interests dominated agriculture at the constitutional convention. The debate over parceling out state institutions brought the small and large counties eyeball to eyeball and, as in Colorado, the decision was finally left to the legislature.

Montana could have been the first state to give women the right to vote, an honor it declined, overriding the wishes of some delegates who sought to "give women the right to exercise influence of good in the government of our cities and villages." Conservative and parochial opposition killed the proposition, but a compromise allowed women (who were taxpayers and otherwise qualified to vote) the opportunity to vote on tax questions submitted to the public. While statehood signified a new age of freedom and home rule, it did not automatically end many of the traditional political grievances about oppressive taxes, unqualified officials, or the power of special interest groups.[26]

Wyoming's admission took a little more effort. The territory's political leaders, Cheyenne's best-known sheepherder and now governor, Francis Warren, and his ally, territorial delegate Joseph Carey, led the statehood movement. The collapse of the cattle industry delayed consideration at home and in Washington. When that situation stabilized, the proponents redoubled their efforts and moved ahead. The constitutional convention saw some splits between the eastern and the western counties, but fortunately they were without lasting implications. To facilitate and speed the process, the constitution was copied, in the most part, from the ones recently ratified by Montana and its neighbors. Colorado had done the same thing back in the midseventies. After approval of the constitution by the electorate (only 8,000 voted), delegate Carey launched the battle for statehood in Congress, enthusiastically claiming a population of over 110,000 for Wyoming. He somewhat lamely claimed that the low ratification vote showed that "everybody favors the constitution, and what is the use of voting"! Skepticism about the territory's population proved to be the only hurdle, and President Benjamin Harrison signed the bill on July 10, 1890. Bells, whistles, firecrackers, booms, and "incessant yelling" greeted the news in Wyoming.[27] Montana was the forty-first and Wyoming the forty-fourth state to enter the Union.

Wyoming's constitution showed little originality, except in two areas: water rights and woman's suffrage. Wyoming recognized the doctrine of prior appropriation and went a step farther by setting up a complete system for state control of water, including a board of control, a water engineer, and the division of Wyoming into four water districts. An attempt to refer the woman's suffrage issue back to the voters was rebuffed; the delegates held firm, and women retained the right to vote in the "Equality State."[28] As Laramie's *Daily Boomerang* of September 9, 1889, quaintly expressed it, "It would [have been] an easier matter to level the mountains of Wyoming than prevent" the women from having the vote.

Washington's role in the Rocky Mountains during these two decades was similar to what happened in the neighboring states. The frustrations and the joys were not unique to the Rocky Mountains. One trend did become abundantly clear, for even with the breaking of the territorial bonds, Wyoming, Montana, and Colorado were, for better or worse, married to Washington, its programs, and its funds.

5 : NEW BONANZAS!

The "Big News" about the Rockies was not statehood or resolution of the Indian question; it was boom—mining boom. At last, bonanzas had returned. It had been a decade since metals maddened the region. Now Leadville and Butte roared into prominence in 1877–78, opening an era when gold faded, silver reigned as king, and copper waited to be crowned.

Colorado had been founded on a sturdy gold foundation; now silver surged to the front. The problems of silver—smelting, lack of investors, and isolation—had retarded Georgetown for years. Then came the news of a silver strike in Boulder County at Caribou in 1870. Over-exuberance labeled it another Comstock, but it never reached such heights. Caribou enjoyed over a decade of varying success before the mines faltered. Yet it managed to bestow a glimmer of hope on a dreary Colorado mining scene.

In the 1870s, Georgetown finally came into its own as a "silver queen." Hill's smelter solved some of the reduction problems, and the railroad arrived at last, showing once again the interdependence of the three. The amount of silver being mined in the state steadily increased as the decade moved ahead, jumping from 600,000 dollars in 1870 to over 4.3 million dollars in 1877.[1]

Georgetown and Caribou did not accomplish this feat all alone. Silver Cliff, Breckenridge, and even old reliable Central City (still the foremost gold district, as well) contributed their share of silver to the pot. Great expectations came with the opening of the San Juans in the early 1870s, which also created the aforementioned Ute problems. Small camps, such as Silverton, Ouray, and Lake City, and their surrounding mines promised a sparkling future, only to be derailed by the lack of a railroad. William Jackson Palmer intended to take his railroad (Denver & Rio Grande) in that direction until something interfered, and that something was Leadville.[2]

Leadville! Colorado had seen nothing in its history to equal it. Since 1860, miners had been panning and poking around California Gulch, where the little hamlet of Oro City clung to a precarious existence. By the 1870s, hard-rock mining predominated in the isolated backwash of a district that attracted few investors and little interest. Fifty-niner miner Horace Tabor owned the principal store and dabbled in mining; he and others knew well that the district contained silver, but they lacked the resources and the experience for developing silver ores. At that point, though, no rich veins had been discovered.

Everything changed in 1877, when George Fryer uncovered a rich outcropping on what became known as Fryer Hill; others quickly followed. Soon a new camp grew at the foot of that hill. The veteran Tabor packed his supplies and moved down California Gulch and a little northward. Though short in distance, the move represented a lifetime of implications. He opened another store, "H. A. W. Tabor general provisions and outfitting," in the town soon to be named Leadville.

That relocation set the stage for making the genial businessman a legend in his own time. News of the discoveries spread throughout Colorado, and the rush was on. "All roads lead to Leadville," declared Mary Hallock Foote, and she was right. By 1879, nearly fifteen thousand people had crowded into Colorado's second largest community. The business district had, for example, 25 clothing stores, 51 groceries, 5 daily and weekly newspapers, and 120 saloons. "This wondrous town," wrote *Leslie's Illustrated* in its April 12, 1879, issue, was the "seventh wonder of the world" and was "best from Saturday afternoon to Monday." Ernest Ingersoll described the immense business being conducted, the all-absorbing interest in mines, and the fact that "everybody is on the jump every minute of his work." Comedian Eddie Foy called Leadville the "greatest pandemonium and hurly-burly that I had ever gotten into." A traveling minister saw another side: "But how shall I describe the homeless, restless men that throng the streets, surging to and fro as evening comes on? I have never seen anything like it." Some Maine newspapers, on the other hand, waged an "anti-Leadville" editorial campaign. They apparently feared that people, money, and headlines would flee to Colorado, leaving staunch New England to languish.[3]

The mines captured the headlines and attracted the most interest locally and abroad. Nobody controlled any richer ones than Leadville's mayor (soon to be the state's lieutenant governor), Horace Tabor. In 1878 the Little Pittsburg and Chrysolite mines poured silver into his pocket, to be joined later by the Matchless. He became Colorado's first mining millionaire and its most enduring nineteenth-century legend. Leadville's fame and its silver could do that for an individual. Thanks to its rich mines, Colorado became the number-one mining state in the United States in 1880. Total production topped $23 million that year, with gold at $20 an ounce and silver averaging $1.15. Leadville's share was two-thirds of that total.[4]

Investors suddenly were falling over themselves in their haste to reach Colorado to purchase silver mines. Prospectors raced into the mountains, across the Divide, looking for another Leadville. Railroads hurried to reach the "magic metropolis"; Leadville did not have to bow and scrape to get its connections. So great was the pull that Palmer and his Denver & Rio Grande went into the mountains and never came out, forsaking the plan to reach Mexico. Denver soon prospered immensely as Tabor and other Leadville mining men came there to invest and live. Tourists beat a path to Leadville to sample the attractions that the railroads had brought within easy reach of Denver. A new day had dawned for the Centennial State.

Butte had not created the same sensation. It was older, having been around since the placer days. Its rich silver veins had been discovered slightly ahead of Leadville's. By 1876, Butte was basking in the glow of a major mining boom—major for isolated Montana, at least. It had become the territory's most important mining site. The Black Hills discovery hurt it, but progress was sustained and Butte survived that "fever." Then Leadville stole national attention away from it again, and Butte would have to bide its time. It attracted some local investors, including the astute Deer Lodge banker William Andrews Clark. When he began investing in 1872, claims could be secured for a pittance, a fortunate circumstance for a man who understood what the future could bring. Clark was so enthusiastic that he spent the winter of 1872–73 at the Columbia School of Mines studying ore analysis and assaying. His efforts paid off. He would go on to promote the area, interest Nathaniel Hill in starting a smelter (continuing the growing Colorado–Montana connection), and become a millionaire.[5]

The fickle future of Butte lay with neither gold nor silver. Copper would be its savior, a fact that Raymond noted as early as 1871. Copper, however, presented a multitude of problems, not the least of which were smelting and marketing difficulties. Those would take time to resolve. Montana, like Colorado, needed investment and the railroad, facts which Clark stressed when he presented an address at the 1876 Centennial Exposition. Montana contained five hundred gold-bearing gulches, besides numerous placer bars. She stood second only to California, the irrepressible orator proclaimed. And the wonder was that all her riches were within the reach of individuals who "possess the patience and industry to delve for [them]." He envisioned a wondrous future: "May her vigorous sons be unceasing in their industry until these rich words are completely earned and their application justified."[6]

His words were not mere flights of oratory. Philipsburg and Marysville also prospered, and the older districts, such as Virginia City, Helena, and Bannack, kept on mining, though at a reduced rate. Hardrock and placer mining ebbed and flowed throughout the territory, awaiting its salvation, the railroad.

Transportation remained Montana's greatest stumbling block. The wagon–river connections were simply not fast, reliable, or economical enough. The railroad could solve all these problems, but a huge expanse of unsettled prairie stretched eastward, slowing the advance of the rails. When the Indian war of 1876 ended, prospects brightened considerably. The railroad would be coming, but not in this decade. A shorter route north from the Union Pacific lines was also being considered. Up to this time, remote Montana's attractions and population had never been great enough to entice easterners and their money. The panic of 1873, with its subsequent lingering depression, killed interest, as did local jealousies when struggling communities fought each other over which one would become the railroad center.[7] Colorado, which was experiencing a railroad boom, understood where Montana languished in the process of securing railroad connections, because it had been there. Impatient Montanans anguished over the delays and unfulfilled promises. Everything appeared to be moving so slowly, and their morale suffered from watching rival Colorado surge farther ahead because of its rail connections.

Wyoming could not match its rivals with immediately available reserves of precious metals, a fact graphically shown by the 1870 census, which found only two quartz mines and no operating placers. The territory's dependence on the fortunes of the Union Pacific Railroad enforced a colonial status then unmatched in either Montana or Colorado. The UP continued to be the dominant private economic force, absorbing approximately 13 percent of the work force. As long as all went well for the UP, Wyoming could justify moderate hopes. The railroad, however, ran into troubles in the 1870s. During that decade Wyoming was an impoverished territory in an underdeveloped West.[8]

Wyoming's coal did not attract much attention, aside from the Union Pacific. The territory held first-class coal reserves, but they served little promotional good. Just how sparse the interest was in them was shown by the fact that the only comment about Wyoming in the *Engineering and Mining Journal* for the last half of 1872 involved a brief mention of a coal fire in a mine at Evanston. Coal simply did not elicit much excitement; Colorado's coal mines did not arouse any more interest than her neighbor's.

Something else, though, did call attention to Wyoming—diamonds. The discovery of almost anything seemed to be possible in the Rocky Mountains and, indeed, rubies and other rare gems had been rumored earlier in Colorado. Rawlins or Rock Springs appeared about to become the diamond capital of the world for a brief time in 1872. Two prospectors advertised to the public their discovery of diamonds across the Colorado line, southeast of Rock Springs. They organized a company, sold stock, and moved toward opening the diamond field. Then came the skeptics and an investigation; the discovery was proven to be "salted," and the great diamond hoax was exposed.[9]

Neither Wyoming nor the Rocky Mountains needed that kind of publicity. Swindles and scams—the salting of claims, wild speculation on townsites and mines, insider "freeze outs," real estate schemes—were as much a part of the history of the Rocky Mountains as their more legitimate cousins. P. T. Barnum may have been right when he supposedly said, "There's a sucker born every minute." In the rush to acquire wealth, some folks were bound to take shortcuts and live up to that frontier adage, "It is good to be shifty in a new country."

Rossiter Raymond urged strongly that mining be put on a legitimate basis. It can only be carried on successfully, he warned, "by a close adherence to principles of economy and experience." In the hubbub of Leadville, and to a lesser degree in every other district, that lesson would be learned repeatedly and expensively. To practice economy when silver and gold were cascading out of the ground often exceeded the capabilities of mortal man.

Even fewer people paid attention to the environmental damage that mining was effecting. The *Engineering and Mining Journal*, in describing hydraulic mining in Montana, warned that tons of soil were being washed out daily. Ranches and farms miles below the mines were being damaged by sediment. As the spokesman for mining at that time, the editor came to the following conclusion about the procedure: "But the mines have to be worked," he proclaimed, "and even should a few acres of land be covered up on the banks of Gold Creek, the new soil formed will be as good if not better than the old."[10] It was a time bomb waiting to explode.

The plight of the Chinese miners concerned the ordinary miner about as much as did environmental issues. The mining frontier had attracted a wide variety of immigrants, including mostly midwesterners and border-state people in the 1860s. Now, in the 1870s and 1880s, new immigrants arrived.

Those skilled miners from Cornwall, England, the Cousin Jacks, predominated in Central City and other Colorado districts. Their mining knowledge and skills came to the rescue of a languishing hard-rock mining industry. English, Scottish, and German immigrants crowded into Wyoming and Colorado coal and hard-rock camps, along with the small vanguard of eastern Europeans.[11] They were all welcome, because they had skills and money to share and came from similar religious and cultural backgrounds. Not so the Chinese, who found racism and discrimination to be a part of their Rocky Mountain experience.

Westerners had displayed antipathy toward the Chinese since the days of the California gold rush. Among other things, the Chinese were believed to be inferior, loathsome, and addicted to opium. The legend that Chinese miners rang the death knell for a district was carried throughout the mining West; it was claimed that they could make a living where a white man could not. Menial jobs, which others shunned, were left to the Chinese. Nevertheless, Chinese mined in Colorado throughout the 1860s and 1870s. The reaction to them was frequently like that of the miners at Caribou, who, after protesting the hiring of Chinese, simply drove them off before they could ever reach the camp. Leadville later proved even more unfriendly; when a solitary "John" arrived, he was driven out. Because of all the animosity, the Chinese migrated to the city, where safety, even if tenuous, came with numbers. The largest concentrations of Chinese lived in Denver, where they established a Chinatown and maintained an uneasy truce with neighboring Denverites.[12]

More Chinese miners came to Montana, drifting eastward with the frontier from the placer districts of Idaho. In 1870, nearly 10 percent of Montana's population was Chinese. They worked their own claims, industriously taking ground that other miners disparaged for yielding too little ore to be worked profitably. The Chinese impressed Rossiter Raymond with their frugality, skill, and industry; he sharply condemned "evil-disposed whites," who frequently maltreated them. When Bannack miners drove them out of that district in 1871, Raymond would not be silent, saying that "besides being bad policy, this course toward the Chinese is rank dishonesty. . . . Bannack will certainly remain a dull camp as far as placer mining is concerned." When the Montana legislature passed a bill prohibiting aliens from acquiring or maintaining any land title, Raymond exploded:

> Whether this sort of law is constitutional or not, it is
> certainly destructive of the interests of the community, as
> may be shown in numerous instances where the Chinese
> have purchased, for cash, claims which white men could no
> longer afford to work, and have proceeded to make them
> productive at a smaller profit to themselves than to the
> Territory. . . .
> I must candidly say, however, that while the legislation of
> Montana is outrageous, and there is a great deal of silly and
> wicked talk of the same tone among certain classes of the
> population, I have heard of only two or three cases of
> actually perpetrated injustice.[13]

Raymond pointedly described the whole situation as "indeed a ludicrous illustration of human stupidity."

It certainly was that, and here, as earlier in California, the Chinese were finally allowed to own claims and work them. One problem that deterred their acceptance was that most chose not to become permanent residents. Their society in the American West was largely devoid of Chinese women and was thus deprived of the traditional family unit, a requirement for fulfilling social and cultural needs. The men, therefore, planned and saved only to return to China.[14] Americans, who could not imagine not wanting to live in the United States, were appalled. Ironically, many of them, who had once planned to make the West only a temporary home, did not want the Chinese for neighbors under any circumstances. Racism here, as with the Indian, prevented the dominant group from appreciating the attributes of the minorities.

People might not read stories about the environment or the Chinese, but they pored over accounts of the booming mining districts and their communities. None sparkled brighter than Leadville as the decade turned to the eighties.

The town and district soared to their peak of fame in 1880; to the investing public, Colorado mining meant Leadville and its silver mines. Then, unexpectedly, came the crash. Several of the major mines (Little Pittsburg, Chrysolite, Robert E. Lee) exhibited clear signs of being worked out, and their stock prices collapsed. Investors began to think twice and shied away from what had been the Colorado mining market's glamorous attraction. Then came a labor strike, the first major one in the Rocky Mountains, and the camaraderie and spirit of previous years vanished. When the turmoil ended, Leadville emerged, not as a booming mining town, but as an industrial city of day laborers high in the Rocky Mountains. Its era on mining's center stage was over in three short years, but not because the district was mined out—far from it. The spirit of adventure and the carefree naivete that characterized its early years was simply replaced by the day-to-day routine of an industrialized society.[15]

There had been scandals, as well as profits, in Leadville mining. The bonanza had attracted all kinds of people, and the downfall of some of the mines had been hastened by stock speculation and inside operations. In the Ten Mile District next door, the Robinson Mine became infamous because of manipulations of its property and stock. One eastern investor summarized it: "I cannot but feel the officers & manager are playing a double game and have made the thing far blacker than it is . . . but it is safer to be out of such a company no doubt." Even Coloradan Ed Wolcott admitted that "none of us understand" the fall of the Robinson; he placed the blame on the "Californians [who] are managing the property."[16] He hit the mark: a group of speculators from California, via the Comstock, had dabbled in Leadville, then landed heavily in the Ten Mile District. Not all the ideas, experience, and individuals imported from older districts proved beneficial.

Appearances notwithstanding, Colorado mining was not finished. After Leadville's opening, Colorado surged into the eighties, which became the state's silver decade. Silver and Colorado were nearly synonymous. Aspen soon challenged the silver queen; by 1889, its production of 5.6 million dollars nearly equaled Leadville's. Aspen needed the railroad as much as the railroads needed a new market. Once that union was accomplished, the district prospered. As one D&RG official observed, the "mineral trade is well known to be the best a railroad can have." The mining population required the railroad to "carry all the necessaries of life, and a great many of the luxuries," as well as vast quantities of machinery, fuel, and stores.

"The second Leadville" had already passed through its frontier days. Aspen's *Rocky Mountain Sun*, in March 1887, observed:

> The steady growth of Aspen, its wealth, society, the
> architectural beauty of many of its buildings and handsome
> residences, make this city in advance of many mountain
> towns. The frontier atmosphere has long since departed, and
> Aspen presents the cultivation and order of older settled
> communities.

Earlier, the call had gone out for the organization of a "Pioneer Association" for all those who had come to the camp before the autumn
of 1881. All these developments occurred before the railroad reached
the town, whose population topped five thousand in 1890.[17] By the
late eighties, it had an opera house, a fancy hotel, telephones, a water-
works, a daily newspaper, and "all modern conveniences." An enthusiastic local booster gushed, "No town of its size in the state can boast
of a finer class of inhabitants or better society."

Poised on bonanza's threshold, Aspen's great years would come in
the 1890s; the district reaffirmed that Colorado's mountains hid a mineral treasure box. The only thing that the prospectors and miners had
to do was to keep looking, keep probing. The lure of the mining West
lived on, as fresh as ever, despite the Leadville miners' strike, which
seemed to indicate that the day of independence might be departing
and that of industrial conflict arriving.

The rest of the state tried to keep pace with the mining giants, with
varying success. Unlike the Aspen and Leadville districts, both limited
in size, the San Juans merged a conglomeration of many districts,
loosely tied together by virtue of their location in the San Juan Mountains. The three major counties in this region—Ouray, San Juan, and
San Miguel—all surpassed 1 million dollars in annual production by
the end of the decade. They had, however, remained in the shadows
of the two better known and richer districts. Investors and publicity
had been drawn to the bonanza towns, not to Silverton, Ouray, and
Telluride. Still hampered by cloud-touching elevations and mountain-
backed isolation, even though the D&RG had come in, the San Juans
awaited a better day. The promise persisted, but the required investment and development had yet to come.

The neighboring Gunnison country had not even done that well.
Its precious metal deposits proved shallow, and the coming of the
railroad would not be the anticipated savior. Fortunately, local coal
deposits gave the D&RG the profits it sought, but the days of the
Gunnison country's hard-rock mining lasted only briefly. Its little camps,
such as Tin Cup, Pitkin, and Ohio City, flourished and withered; others,

ers, less promising, died almost without notice. Crested Butte survived because of its coal, which was among the region's best. Not only did the area yield bituminous, but it also opened nearby the Rocky Mountains' major anthracite mines.[18]

Gunnison's ghost towns did not stand alone; others could be found in older Gilpin and Clear Creek counties, currently completing their third decade of mining. That endurance spoke well for the mineral reserves of these two. Gilpin County held its position as the number-one gold district (in the million-dollar range yearly throughout the decade) and contributed a little silver as well. The boys of 1859, with their pans and rockers, were gone, but the heady forecasts of the year defied time. Now, though, that early individualism had been replaced everywhere by drills and powder and company control.

The same kind of evolution took place in the life of the durable camps and towns. Amid the relics of an earlier age, life settled down to a less hectic pace. Many old-timers had drifted on to newer districts, proving that mining could provide at least a minimum local safety valve. Since the early 1870s, ever-opening new districts had been draining surplus miners and the drifting crowd from less promising areas. That exodus helped to prevent general labor unrest into the 1890s. In Central City, Black Hawk, Nevada City, and Georgetown during this time, the rowdyism of the boom days disappeared. The gentility of Victorian America had come (as much as it ever would) with churches, schools, a stable business district, and "society." It all told a quiet story now, a tale of might-have-been's and used-to-be's, of ambitions reconciled to the routines of a workaday world, of frustrations and achievements.

Not all the old mining regions were so fortunate. Boulder County declined, with no district taking the torch from depressed Caribou; Silver Cliff languished in equally bad shape; Park County only looked back to yesterday; and once-notable Summit County bumped along on an erratic course, despite its nearness to Leadville and the coming of the railroad.

Corporation control and organization had appropriated all the major districts and mines, leaving the independent miner the slim pickings of what was left. The miner found himself a hired laborer rather than a man who, after working for a season, could strike out on his own. By the end of the 1880s, there simply were no new districts to lure the adventurous with the promise of owning their own mine. Mining had always been hard, dangerous work at low pay for the risks involved;

now the lure of fifty-nine had been stripped away, leaving only that brutal reality.

All was not rosy for the capitalists, who appeared to have gained the upper hand over their workers. The railroad had assuredly helped to boost production; however, the owners found themselves forced to bow to the wishes of the iron horse when it came to freight charges. Complaints were also proliferating about the smelters, which were charging higher rates and moving toward more consolidation and dominance by eastern investors. And the costs of hard-rock mining were rising, while the average yield per ton was going down. Finally, the silver price per ounce was steadily declining. Colorado mining, tightly tied to the East and the world beyond, no longer could boast of its independence.

To try to resolve some of these problems, Colorado mining was making progress in the application of science to the industry. No longer would the "school of hard knocks" be good enough; college-trained mining engineers were needed. The new study of geology was also making inroads, a great boon to Colorado, whose ores proved incredibly complex and varied. The Leadville bonanza paved the way for Samuel Emmons's monumental monograph *Geology and Mining Industry of Leadville*, which became known as the "miner's bible." Leadville was the real key to these advancements, because it had the fame, the money, and the mines to allow serious study and experimentation and to attract the qualified individuals to undertake it.

Over the objections of some miners, power drills, electricity, tramways, and giant powder (dynamite) were being introduced to modernize the hard-rock industry. Great strides had been made to improve the efficiency and saving abilities of mills and smelters, a long-demanded refinement. Engineering and science were merging. Another concession to the changing times was the organization, on a December evening in 1882 in Denver, of the Colorado Scientific Society. Early members included metallurgists, assayers, geologists, mining managers, chemists, and mining engineers. This group successfully brought men of science into contact with those who needed to apply scientific principles to their everyday work. Colorado had come a long way since the days of fifty-nine.[19]

Montana's 1880s experiences paralleled Colorado's, and the younger territory benefited from its ongoing connections to that state, especially when Hill and Clark organized the Boston & Montana Company and opened a concentrating and smelting complex south of Butte. The firm pioneered in the application of the invaluable lessons learned in Colorado to the smelting process in Butte. Marcus Daly helped, too, by bringing reduction technology from Nevada and California. Butte was the beneficiary of a generation of western experience.[20]

Butte generated the major mining news in Montana during the decade. As early as the summer of 1881, the *Engineering and Mining Journal* reported that "Butte will produce as much bullion as the Comstock ever did." It matched and surpassed that, though in copper rather than silver. Butte, straddling a copper mountain, needed only three things to bring it into bonanza: the railroad, improved smelting methods, and an increased national and international market for copper. The first was resolved very easily, but the second gave more trouble. The older method of heap roasting the copper produced the aforementioned pollution that clouded Butte's atmosphere. Nor did it prove to be the fastest and most efficient method. The smelters had been improved, but it took experimentation to work the Butte ores profitably. It all meant that more smoke was added to the haze that hung over town and mines.

The outgoing, likable Irishman and experienced mine manager Marcus Daly came up with one solution to the smoke problem: build a smelter town elsewhere that would utilize the most modern plant available. This he proceeded to do, and his "pride and joy," Anaconda, came into existence twenty-six miles west of Butte. Daly had come to Montana in 1876 to manage a mine for Utah investors, and he stayed to become one of Butte's mining millionaires. Already on the scene was the grim William Clark, with a personality almost the opposite of Daly, but so like him in his ruthless drive and intelligence. Both men lusted after dominance of Butte copper and believed they had the power to achieve it. Daly, joined by that lover of poker and good bourbon, the shrewd mining investor George Hearst, controlled the incredibly rich Anaconda Mine, which, by the spring of 1883, had revealed a vein fifty to one hundred feet wide. The Anaconda typified a modern, efficient mine, one that Daly found pride in as fully as his smelter. Clark had pioneered in developing silver and copper in Butte and had built the first smelter.[21] The two men steamed ahead on a collision course that would make the political and business rivalries of the Leadville millionaries seem like child's play and shake the very foundations of Montana.

While the digging and smelting of Butte copper continued apace, the third question of the market hung as morbidly over the industry as its own pollution blanketed the town. For many years, Michigan had been America's leading copper producer, until it was challenged in the early 1880s by Butte and, to a lesser degree, by the small Arizona districts and Colorado. Primarily as a by-product of precious metal mining, that Rocky Mountain state had produced over a million pounds of copper per year. No threat to Montana, that copper helped Coloradans pay mining expenses. America's production quadrupled by 1888; without a corresponding market expansion, prices fell (to ten cents a pound in 1886, half the 1880 price). Overproduction and depression struck the industry. Angry Michigan mine owners, reacting desperately to this threat, dumped their surplus copper in the hope that their western rivals would collapse. Arizona mines did just that, but Montana hung on gamely. After a dismal winter in 1886–87 in Butte, when several mines closed temporarily, Michigan threw in the towel. It could not compete with Anaconda's efficient, mass production (78 million pounds in 1887) and its gold and silver by-products. By year's end, Montana pushed ahead of Michigan into first place among the copper-producing states. Clark, Daly, and the others had won what looked to be a Pyrrhic victory. A depressed, glutted national market still confronted them.

Then came an international challenge, an attempt by French speculators to corner the world copper market. This action temporarily raised the prices until the inevitable crash came in March 1889. Out of all these maneuverings came an agreement to try to curtail production, but that too failed. Copper continued to be one of the world's most competitive, turbulent industries.[22] The amazing fact that Butte survived these manipulations as well as it did gave it great hope for the future.

Stretching down its hill of copper to the valley below, Butte, by mid-decade, had edged past Leadville as the premier mining center in the Rocky Mountains and could lay claim to that status for the whole United States. Butte rushed into boom, and Montana's governor Preston Leslie boldly proclaimed in 1888 that Butte was "already the largest and most populous city west of Denver, between the Mississippi River and Pacific Coast and is the largest mining camp in the world."[23]

Its debut on the copper mining scene came at a fortunate time. The need for copper mushroomed during the nineteenth-century industrial revolution. The telegraph, telephone, and electricity all demanded copper wiring and conductors. In homes, businesses, transportation, and factories, copper was being utilized as never before, and the expansion potential looked to be infinite. Montana was doubly blessed, with both copper and precious metals undergirding its economy.

The rest of mining Montana basked in Butte's glow. Governor Leslie called it "booming and prosperous." When discussing silver, the governor was right; like Colorado, the 1880s were Montana's silver decade. Ore poured out of mines in a triangle with its sides drawn from Butte to Philipsburg and Helena. The railroads came, investors came, smelting technology evolved, and Montana dethroned Colorado as America's number-one mining state. Professionalism dominated the industry, as it did in its rival, and like its neighbor, impersonalism took over mining. The miners reacted more quickly up north and soon unionized; the disgruntled owners moved less rapidly. They did not like this challenge to their power, nor the threat to the free-enterprise system, which, according to their definition, allowed workers to sell their services for the best price in the labor marketplace. The Philipsburg and Butte miners organized because of the "fearfully hazardous nature" of their vocation, which prematurely aged the miners and caused "many ills." The Miners' Association challenged its members to "Act Justly and Fear Not."[24] Both sides looked warily at the other; distrust and anger had been sown.

As the decade came to a close, copper and silver rode high; gold, except as a by-product, lagged. Placer mining had already become a relic of another era. Although not as often as in earlier years, rumors of new "bonanzas" erupted in the spring, along with the warmer days. So did those ever-present mining swindles and scandals, which the *Engineering and Mining Record* encouraged both Montana and Colorado to expose and discourage.

Montana mining communities were tamed and became respectable, except for Butte. The chronicler of the age, Herbert Howe Bancroft, quoted an old mining saying when he wrote that mining towns were composed largely of "ophir-holes, gopher-holes, and loafer-holes." Then he emphatically went on to say that that description no longer applied to Montana. Elegant and comfortable homes, good society, education, religion, and established merchants had made Montanans equal, in their own estimation, to their counterparts back east.[25] The times were changing throughout the Rocky Mountains.

They were changing less in Wyoming, where the UP dominated the coal business and hard-rock mining dwindled to nothing. The census takers found only twelve mines in the territory in 1880, one-twentieth of Colorado's. Its annual gold production of four to six thousand dollars would have been a good day's work for many Colorado and Montana mines. But that did not prevent Wyoming from looking for another Leadville; it had as much optimism as the rest. Even South Pass reportedly drew interest. The *Engineering and Mining Journal* of

October 19, 1889, noted that eastern investors planned to build a stamp mill and other improvements. The Laramie *Daily Boomerang* said it best in 1883: capital was all that Wyoming required, and "when we get it, we shall make as good a showing as any mining region in the country—not excepting, Colorado, Nevada, or California." Wyoming did not get it that spring or later. Undaunted, the Cheyenne *Tribune* in 1889 called attention to the lesser minerals—mica, gypsum, granite, limestone, marble—all of which were "plentiful."[26]

Coal was a different story. With it, Wyoming battled Colorado for the region's lead and finally forged ahead. Wyoming had fewer, albeit much larger, mines. Montana trailed badly, evidencing more potential than tonnage. The dominance of the railroad was clear in the coal mining industry. Railroads needed fuel and an item to export; coal furnished both and could only be shipped profitably by rail. Typical of the national trend, Colorado's railroads also controlled its coal mines, though no road dominated to the degree that the UP did in Wyoming. Typical also of the industrial pattern of coal mining, both fields suffered disasters. Wyoming's first major one came at Almy in 1881, killing thirty-eight miners, and Colorado's at Crested Butte in 1884, killing fifty-nine. Most of the accidents involved only two or three miners, making them none the less tragic for their families and friends. The high danger underground and the growing company control kept any hard-rock miner "worth his salt" out of the coal mines. The public, which had always paid little attention to coal mining, seemed indifferent to the growing accident and death rates, and the government made only feeble attempts to respond. The laissez-faire philosophy and lobbying by the operators kept regulation to a minimum. Even the lenient laws and penalties were ignored. Always in peril, the miners kept on digging in the dark, dangerous mines. When disaster hit Wyoming cattle ranching, coal mining came to the fore as the territory's major industry.[27] A few visionaries held out hope for oil, but isolated Wyoming, and Colorado, too, would have to wait for a more favorable time and the invention of the automobile before their oil wells would gush profits.

It had been a lively decade for mining. The Rocky Mountains had managed to capture national attention and gain a measure of fame. Leadville and Butte both surpassed the fading Comstock and such lesser rivals as Deadwood and Tombstone. The Rockies epitomized mining, just as their millionaires proved what they could do for the individual. Their prosperity masked somewhat the fact that mining was generally developing the old, not the new. The decline in this industry of finite resources would inevitably come—but not for a while, it was hoped.

In September 1881, a writer from then young and booming Red Cliff, Colorado, summarized the high-riding days of the eighties when a pot of gold at the end of the rainbow seemed to be within everyone's grasp:

> If you want to see a lively camp drop down here and take a look at us. The very sight of the camp will put a bug in your ear, and give you some food for profound thought you bet— . . .[28]

6 : RAILROADS AND URBAN RIVALS

"A time to weep, and a time to laugh"—Ecclesiastes 3:14

A s Rocky Mountain mining boomed, so did its handmaiden, urbanization. Mining camp, supply town, and farming hamlet were all tied to mining, whose prosperity was reflected on Main Street and well out onto the plains.

The Rocky Mountains were heavily urbanized during these decades, more so than a generation later. The 1870s census takers found over 70 percent of the people in each territory living either in a community or in an urban environment within a mile of a mining camp. That remarkable statistic needs to be tempered by the realization that these three territories ranked forty-first, forty-third, and forty-seventh in population out of the forty-seven states and territories.[1] The urban trend continued throughout the decade, and the 1880 census showed little change.

The new catalyst in this urbanization was the railroad. Wyoming had already experienced this development with the Union Pacific, and now it was Colorado's turn. The classic story was that of Colorado Springs.

Because the far-distant transcontinental railroad ran from East to West, Colorado Springs saw the light of day. Civil War veteran and railroader William Jackson Palmer had a plan to build a North–South feeder line to tap the hinterlands from Denver into Mexico. Thus was born the Denver & Rio Grande, Colorado's so-called baby railroad.

The slender, scholarly appearing Palmer had arrived in Colorado with the Kansas Pacific Railroad, which, despite his hopes, did not push into the southern part of the territory after it reached Denver in 1870. Palmer, by then, had abandoned his erstwhile employers and had struck out on his own, determined to build a railroad along the mountains to the south, land that he believed held great potential. Enthusiastic Coloradans did not have the financial resources required for construction, so Palmer turned to the East and England. There the funds were found, and the decision was made to build a narrow-gauge (three-foot) line. The narrow gauge could be constructed more easily in the mountains and at less cost, not to mention its popularity with the British, who used the gauge and from whom most of the funding would be forthcoming.

Plans were formulated, and on July 28, 1871, the first spike was driven. Three months and seventy-six miles later, the D&RG reached the town and colony that Palmer organized, Colorado Springs. In Palmer were combined the hard-headed railroader and businessman with the social planner and town builder, an unusual merger for this era. He envisioned that his organization would be "quite a little family," with schools, libraries, and lectures for the workers, who would also have the opportunity to invest in the company. He planned Colorado Springs as a utopian society—a prohibition-ruled, residential community for his workers, British investors, and others who would come to enjoy its beauty and healthful climate. The imaginative Palmer laid out his city with an eye toward the nearby majesty of Pike's Peak. He saw it as "the one spot in the West where nice people could gather together and live out their days in gentility and peace," far different from the impatience and tastelessness that distinguished typical Rocky Mountain urban development.[2]

The vision required some imagination when the first train arrived on a beautiful autumn day in October. The special passengers, including *Rocky Mountain News* editor William Byers, beheld a community barely three months old, with only a few log cabins. After a tasty meal, the excursion party, led by the personable Palmer, toured the site, then climbed aboard the train and returned to Denver. Palmer's railroad and his utopian community were launched.

Within a year, the D&RG continued on to Pueblo, with a branch line to Florence and its coal mines; then its funding ran out. The national crash and depression of 1873 followed, putting Palmer's construction on hold. Palmer's setback was not unique; the Rocky Mountain region was not strong enough economically to withstand such a downturn, which served to emphasize its dependence on the East. The railroad, imitating the UP, had tapped the coal fields, needing coal for fuel and freight. Just as their eastern counterparts did, western railroad men aimed their lines at these kinds of tempting markets. Palmer was already displaying his hard-driving business side. At Pueblo, rather than going into the town itself, he had built the depot on land owned by the D&RG and called South Pueblo. Angered by this duplicity, the people of the county declined to honor a bond issue, which had been voted to help lure the railroad. The D&RG sued, lost, and delivery was never made.[3]

The love affair between westerners and their railroads would be a rocky one. The towns desperately wanted the connections, but, once in place, they found themselves under the thumb of their would-be benefactors. Palmer, though a visionary, was also a realist. He wrote to his future wife, "One thing I feel certain of—that amidst all the hot competition of this American business life there is a great temptation to be a little unscrupulous."

That temptation could have served as an epitaph for the economic development of the entire Rocky Mountains for years to come. Palmer himself should be remembered more for his visionary side. Colorado Springs best reflected that vision. This outstanding success story had grown by 1880 to over forty-two hundred residents, settled along its boulevards and streets. Not the "fruit of mining excitement," with its fortune hunters, Colorado Springs offered a quiet, steady, unforced growth with "social, educational and religious advantages."

Perhaps the crowning achievement of Palmer's dream was the establishment of Colorado College. The Congregational Church decided to organize a Christian college in a central location in Colorado and selected Colorado Springs because of the natural advantages of climate and scenery, and because the students would be protected from "dram-shops." It opened in 1875 with a tuition of fifteen dollars for the fall term, warning that "any want of diligence in pupils, or any disorderly conduct, will lead, first, to a warning to the pupil, then a notice to parents or guardian, last to dismissal."[4] Coloradans placed great importance on education; within sixteen years of the Pike's Peak rush, they had created a school of mines, Colorado College, and, a few months later, placed a state university on the drawing boards. For Palmer, Colorado College represented a major step in the development of his town, a town that never went through a frontier experience. Urbanization and transportation instantly came together to give birth to a planned community.

Promotional materials extolled the beauty of the site—Pike's Peak, the Garden of the Gods, Ute Pass, and the nearby canyons— and the romantic walks along the valley and into the mountains. One of the "most salubrious and delightful climates of the world" was lauded for its dry and invigorating atmosphere that benefited invalids "of all classes." Mineral springs, the "Fountain of Youth" at nearby Manitou Springs, had been attracting partakers long before 1859 and now were included in Palmer's plans. At both places could be found the "best" people, the "most refined class to be found anywhere." The British, with whom Palmer had an inside track for investment and settlement, especially fit this category. As resident James Rayner wrote his mother, "Johnie Bull is well represented here by moneyed men and smart women: I believe I could tell an Englishwoman anywhere."[5]

Visitors were impressed, even if they had been somewhat oversold by publicity. Helen Hunt, who would one day make it her home, first saw Colorado Springs on a gray November day in 1873: "I shall never forget my sudden sense of hopeless disappointment at the moment when I first looked on the town." She overcame that feeling, eventually married businessman William Jackson, and became an enthusiastic booster of her new home, "well nigh the fairest spot on earth." Critical English traveler Isabella Bird, who saw little attractive in most Rocky Mountain communities she visited, continued true to form: "To me no place could be more unattractive than Colorado Springs, from its utter treelessness." Nor was she impressed by that tourist attraction, the Garden of the Gods, where, "were I a divinity, I certainly would not choose to dwell."[6]

Colorado Springs had too many natural and manmade attributes to warrant Bird's acerb description for long. Pike's Peak and mountain scenery towered over its streets and homes, and its climate proved to be nearly as good as its boosters claimed. It had Palmer and his railroad. No longer did travelers have to suffer through rollicking stage rides, which Rayner vividly described: "[we] sucked in the mountain air through our teeth, and spit the dust out when our mouths were full." Colorado Springs had adjacent economic empires growing on each side of it, west in the mountains and east on the plains. Unlike other contemporary Colorado towns, it had been planned with tourists, business, and health seekers in mind.

Tourism, of course, was not an automatic assurance of prosperity. Outside factors obviously influenced travel. William Bell, Palmer's able English lieutenant, believed that the 1876 national Centennial Exposition in Philadelphia hurt all watering places "throughout the country," because all "who could afford it went" there. He complained in 1877 that the "want of prosperity" in England and the late European war affected travel. Then, a bitter American railroad strike in 1877 exploded, and the season nearly collapsed. Colorado Springs also had to overcome the winter image of the Rockies. As one booster explained, they had to induce winter visitors to understand what that season meant in Manitou and Colorado Springs, "basking in sunshine."[7]

Thanks to Palmer and Colorado Springs, Colorado was well on the way to becoming a mecca for tourists. They came on the railroad, and they visited the places where the railroad went. For the more adventurous ones, travel beyond the rails and into the deep mountain recesses of Middle Park or Estes Park beckoned. Unexpectedly, Isabella Bird fell in love with the latter site and her romantic nature soared. She described it as just the spot she had been seeking, encompassing "grandeur, cheerfulness, health, enjoyment, novelty, freedom, etc.," a glorious region that was "surely one of the most entrancing spots on earth." Down in Colorado Springs, William Jackson understood what was coming when he wrote to Helen of "how much of the prosperity of sections of Colorado is dependent on the receipts from tourists & strangers."[8]

The swift advance of the railroads in the 1880s transformed the Rocky Mountain region. Except for isolated, unsettled, and undeveloped sections, no new frontiers lay over the next mountain by the decade's end.

The construction of lines in Wyoming reached into its far corners, opening them to agriculture and coal development and providing local jobs and contracts. The Oregon Short Line built northwestward into Idaho, and the Wyoming Central from Nebraska to Casper crossed the center of the territory. The Burlington reached Cheyenne, giving that community another avenue to Colorado and access to its markets along the far-flung Burlington route. The completion of the Northern Pacific through Montana to Portland in 1884 served to open up northern Wyoming, even if it did continue to maintain Montana's dominance of Yellowstone's traffic and trade.[9]

The Union Pacific now found its grip on the territory weakening. In the areas near its tracks and in the coal fields, the UP remained dominant and its legislative voice commanded respect in Cheyenne. Elsewhere, railroad competition and a cattle-dominated economy gave Wyoming more political freedom than it had ever experienced.

Montana at long last secured its railroad connections. The days of the slow, expensive, and seasonal staging, freighting, and steamboating were numbered by the time the eighties arrived. Montana was the last untapped Rocky Mountain railroad region and one of the last in the West. It held out attractive possibilities for the line that would tap its vast distances and economic potential.

The Northern Pacific had been struggling to reach the area since it began construction in 1870. As luck would have it, the crash of 1873 came at a time when construction funds were exhausted. Adding insult to injury, its financial representative, the famous Philadelphia firm of Jay Cooke and Company, was the one whose failure precipitated the financial panic. Depression-ridden years, bankruptcy, and one crisis after another delayed the railroad's recovery. Under new management and improved finances, construction resumed in 1879. The NP reached Montana's eastern boundary in 1881, a year later it extended its tracks into the Yellowstone Valley, and by 1887 it had spanned the continent between Lake Superior and Puget Sound. Heartened by the end of the Indian wars, farmers followed the NP tracks westward in sizable numbers. Miles City, Billings, and other communities sprouted, and settlement took root in eastern Montana.[10] With its substantial federal land subsidy (ten alternate sections on each side of the roadway), the railroad became a landholder of consequence.

The Northern Pacific missed Butte, which did not grieve for long. The Utah & Northern was heading toward that mining center. Promoted by Brigham Young's son John, and financed largely by New York capitalists, the company survived a failure to gain tax-exempt status from the legislature, and it overcame other obstacles to reach the community in 1881. It made connections with the Northern Pacific two years later. Until the road converted to standard gauge, the costly loading and unloading of goods raised tempers and expenses.

On the way to Butte, the Utah & Northern gave birth to a number of new towns. In September 1880, the railroad purchased the land and surveyed the townsite of Dillon. Eager merchants and settlers purchased lots at auction, and the future of the town was assured when the railroad arrived that winter. Free lots for churches and schools brought respectability and designation as the county seat (the local precinct approved it by over 375 votes), taking that honor from declining Bannack; political dominance was thereby assured.[11]

The impact of the railroads became evident immediately. New communities, energized promotion, a boom in the lumber business of western Montana, invigorated mining, growth in the eastern agricultural region, increased tourism to Yellowstone National Park, comfortable and speedy travel, and lower freight rates came in the wake of the iron horse. Here, as elsewhere, railroads meant survival to an underdeveloped territory. Sometimes they promised (or settlers expected) more than they could deliver, but increased prosperity and permanent growth were almost guaranteed. All Montanans, however, were not enthralled by the arrival of the rails. Mary Ronan, on the Flathead reservation, admitted that the Northern Pacific brought her family closer to civilization, friends, and medical aid, "but put an end to the old idyllic days."[12]

Most residents did not lament the passing of the "old idyllic days," certainly not Coloradans, who gloried in the state's railroad boom. Colorado experienced its greatest railroad building frenzy during the 1870s and 1880s, the likes of which the Rocky Mountains have not seen since. Once the tracks reached Denver, Coloradans from all walks of life became enamored of the idea and could not wait until the noisy, smoky engines reached their own town or mining district.

The Denver & Rio Grande was the most active of all the lines. Fending off rivals and money woes, Palmer's enterprise reached the Trinidad coal fields and had moved farther west to Alamosa in the San Luis Valley by the end of the decade; from Canon City, it hurried on to Leadville. Not satisfied, the visionary president looked longingly across the Continental Divide to the untapped Western Slope, which promised a bonanza to the railroad that reached it first and seized control of the region. In a three-pronged approach in 1880–81, the D&RG raced toward Gunnison and Crested Butte for coal and silver, to South Fork beyond Alamosa, and far to the west to Silverton in the heart of the San Juans.

In the same month, on the very same day that Dillon was being launched far to the north, the D&RG was surveying a town of its own, Durango. Here, it tapped coal fields, built a smelter, opened farming land, nurtured a community, and, after a brief winter's pause, pursued its goal of Silverton and its surrounding mines. That same year (1882), it moved beyond Gunnison to Montrose and Grand Junction, opening up the heartland of the Western Slope, where only months before the Utes had prevailed. The D&RG, in its own words, had adopted a "progressive policy as regards extension" in relation to the "exceptional conditions which exist." It promised to furnish promptly connections to every mining camp whose business affords "the railroad a branch." It eventually went on into Utah, tore along to tap the Aspen silver bonanza, and built to Lake City and Ouray in the San Juans. The visionary Palmer was long retired by then, forced out by his own overexpansiveness; his projects never fully met financial expectations. Cutthroat competition and less idealistic stockholders contributed to his downfall.[13]

Although Palmer was gone from the game, his legacy to it lived on. Colorado's baby railroad had opened, promoted, settled, and developed vast segments of the state's western half, as well as planned and nourished communities. Mining, agriculture, urbanization, and tourism had all benefited. Colorado's Western Slope frontier quickly receded before the rails, and the state looked ahead with optimism. Coloradans owed a deep debt of gratitude to the D&RG.

But it was not all peace and profit for the railroad company. William Jackson had been named president in 1886 during a period of expensive internecine warfare, reduced revenue, and general economic troubles, which had led to the railroad being reorganized and the "friendly" sale of it to stockholders. Throughout this time, Jackson pleaded with his board for permission to build to Aspen; it hesitated because of the reluctance of foreign investors to stand the expense. One of the members advised Jackson to abandon Aspen, where "we can not possibly compete with the Midland [railroad]," and to strive instead to acquire all its Leadville business. Jackson succeeded in getting the Aspen construction started, but wore himself out in the process and retired in less than a year. One of his friends, a vice president of the Chicago, Burlington & Quincy, wrote that he was sorry Jackson was leaving, yet he understood: "After all I believe you will live longer and be happier out of the Railroad business than in it. No one knows what it is to have charge of a railroad property until they have tried it."[14]

The D&RG obviously never had Colorado all to itself, and the competition was ruthless. The aforementioned Colorado Central tapped the Longmont and Fort Collins agricultural valleys and the mining riches of Clear Creek and Gilpin counties. It never crossed the Continental Divide because eleven-thousand-foot Loveland Pass frustrated all its plans. The Denver, South Park and Pacific, under John Evans's direction, had been slowed by the 1873 depression before it finally reached South Park. Revived by the Leadville silver mania, it sprinted for Leadville and later raced the D&RG to Gunnison. Meanwhile, both roads fell under control of the larger, eastern-owned Union Pacific, a pattern that was typical for Rocky Mountain mines and railroads. The standard-gauge Colorado Midland joined the fray and challenged the D&RG in a race to Aspen. It lost, arriving months late in 1888.[15]

The railroads had to climb the passes and descend into the gorges throughout the mountain ranges, which led to long and roundabout routes. The airline distance from Denver to Leadville, for instance, is 75 miles; the shortest railroad route covered 151 miles. Because of these meanderings and a decade of boom to grow in, these lines gave Colorado more trackage than any of her other Rocky Mountain rivals by the end of the 1880s. The San Juans, the Gunnison country, Aspen, and mining stops in between found themselves on main or feeder lines, which stimulated production and exploration. Consequently, Colorado continued to be one of the nation's leading mining states. The promise of the railroads had been fulfilled. They had climbed mountains that people said could not be climbed; they had tied the Rocky Mountains together. But the cost had been high and not completely comprehended. Westerners were unprepared for the ramifications that involved freight rates, railroad economic dominance, political lobbying, and hidden expenses that would have to be paid sometime in the future. Similar to the attitude toward the government, a love–hate relationship ensued, almost as soon as the marriage ceremony ended.

Railroads intensified the trend toward urbanization. Communities like Salida, Dillon, and Durango were being planned and developed by railroad companies. More common were those such as Lusk, Douglas, and Billings, which grew because of the railroad, and Helena, Butte, and Denver, which were aggrandized by their railroad connections.

Denver defied its challengers and emerged as the regional urban pacesetter. The 1880s proved to be a progressive decade for this city, which leaped from a population of 35,000 to 106,000, the greatest single percentage increase in its history. Denver had become the third largest city west of the Missouri River. Leadville silver played a major role in this growth. Fortunes flowed downhill from there to the capital where, for example, Horace Tabor established his home and built the Tabor Block and the Tabor Grand Opera House, the finest between St. Louis and San Francisco. Denver's railroad system, too, touched almost the entire region, like "steel spiderwork." It became the merchandising, banking, smelting, and transportation hub of the Rocky Mountains, as well as the state's political, social, and cultural heart. Nearby coal mines, farms, ranches, and a small, but growing, industrial section gave it a potentially strong economic base.

Tourists found Denver to be the convenient starting and stopping point for the trains that took them to Manitou Springs, Pike's Peak, the mining camps, through the Royal Gorge, and along the Circle Route to Durango, Ouray, Gunnison, and back to the "Queen City." The Windsor Hotel and its competitors, plus some excellent restaurants (like Charpiot's, the "Delmonico of the West"), encouraged visitors to linger in Denver, which proffered its own attractions, ranging from the Tabor Grand to the ladies on Market Street.

While survival had been the concern of the leaders of the sixties and early seventies, now growth and boom occupied their thoughts. Old-timers—David Moffat, Walter Cheesman, Charles Kountze, John Evans—had been actively involved for years in business, banking, railroading, and a variety of activities designed to promote Colorado and to enrich themselves. Others, like Henry Wolcott, James Grant, and Charles Boettcher, arrived in the 1870s or later. Tabor and John Routt came with the Leadville bonanza. Nathaniel Hill, with his smelter, almost singlehandedly made Denver the regional smelting center, when he came from Black Hawk in 1877, seeking more accessible transportation, ores, and coal. German immigrant Boettcher made a fortune in Leadville in banking, hardware, utilities, and mining before moving to Denver. Wolcott had come west to join Hill in the smelting business, but instead he became involved in insurance, investment, banking, and railroading; Cheesman focused on utilities, from gas to water. Grant, demonstrating the multidimensional careers of these men, involved himself in banking, smelting, mining, the water company, and politics. With the last, he parted company with most of his business contemporaries; he campaigned and voted Democratic.

All these men became part of the power elite that managed Denver's fortunes and, to a lesser degree, Colorado's in the years that followed. They built their mansions, joined their clubs, worked with and against each other at various times in business transactions, and speculated in real estate and stocks. Denver's movers and shakers demonstrated remarkable skills and versatility. An almost "naive optimism" in their young city's possibilities undergirded them. They attracted outside capital for a diversity of investments within the city and state. Business, whether real estate, minerals, cattle, railroading, banking, or agriculture, was their "main business," as it was their community's. Their initiative and manipulative sagacity were crucial to Denver's growth. They also appreciated the natural advantages of their adopted city and used them as the basis for its emergence as the mountain metropolis. Without the energy and farsightedness of these entrepreneurs, Denver would never have become the "Queen City."[16]

What Denver had in abundance—conservative (yet speculative) and aggressive leadership—its chief rivals failed to produce. Cheyenne dropped by the wayside, unable, because of its lack of natural advantages, to attract the type of men who went to Denver; a cattle boom that busted doomed it even further.

Complementing, but also rivaling, Denver was the industrial city of Pueblo, a hundred miles to the south, the home of smelters and Colorado Fuel and Iron (the region's major steel and iron works).

Pueblo's population multiplied by eight times, to twenty-four thousand, during the decade of the eighties. The community had transportation but lacked the aggressive leadership, political power, and interior market of Denver. Southern Colorado was further handicapped by being outside the state's mainstream mining, Anglo, and Republican culture; its traditional Catholic and Spanish heritage and its coal and ranching economy caused it to be ignored by the majority to the north.

Denver had fended off Cheyenne and Pueblo's challenge to retain its claim as the "queen of the mountains and plains," but the crown rested uneasily. Now, Helena made a bid for the title. Though farther away, it had some of the same natural and manmade advantages as Denver, including agriculture, mining, and transportation. It was primarily Helena's future, not its present, that held the potential to mount a serious threat.

Helena's stock rose when the railroad finally reached the city, but it could never shake off Butte, which rode its copper into a boom. Helena's population grew from 3,600 to 13,800 by 1890, Butte's from 3,300 to 10,700. Despite the former's head start and early prominence, the gold, silver, and now copper rival could not be thwarted and gained steadily on Helena in all areas. It followed the traditional formula, evolving from log cabins to permanent frame, brick, and stone construction, and from general stores to specialty stores in a thriving business district. The railroad and its copper wealth gave Butte all it needed to spurt to prominence. Victorian cultural ornaments, such as the theater, clubs, lodges, and sporting events, took up more and more space in the columns of local papers. When the eighties arrived, Butte had progressed from a rough mining camp to a quintessential mining town, striving to overcome its youth, yet refusing to let go of its mining heritage—wide-open, tough, and fun-loving. Within a decade, it surpassed Helena in population, economic significance, and national publicity.[17]

Leadville had marshaled a similar challenge to Denver, before its high elevation and rugged environment drove many of its mining and business leaders to the more mild and lower-in-altitude capital city. Denver had been shaken, but not toppled, and within five years Leadville's major challenge had ended, leaving Denver stronger than ever. Helena would not be so fortunate; Butte sat on a mountain of copper.[18] Both Leadville and Butte, even with the latest in Victorian architecture and middle-class respectability, could never completely overcome their desolation and ugliness as industrial towns. Pollution, working-class "suburbs," and the drabness of surrounding mines left no doubt as to what moved the communities.

Bustling, wide-open Butte had become the region's foremost mining town. Its future looked prosperous, but it was paying a price for its industrial success. As one visitor noted, "This is a big town, but between the smoke from the smelters and the burning timber it is not easily seen." The burning timber came from the heap roasting, or open air roasting, of the copper ore, which became an environmental horror. "Yellowish, sulphuric smoke" rolled over the town, smoke which Eddie Foy called "almost stifling," when he played there. The noted opera star Emma Abbott nearly refused to give a concert in the town because of the conditions. Butte residents tried to make the best of their situation by claiming that the smoke was a disinfectant, which destroyed the "microbes that constitute the germs of disease." Mining man William Andrews Clark waxed positively eloquent about the "blessings" of smoke:

> I must say that the ladies are very fond of this smoky city
> . . . because there is just enough arsenic there to give them a
> beautiful complexion, and that is the reason the ladies of
> Butte are renowned wherever they go for their beautiful
> complexions.[19]

All such rhetoric aside, Butte was the first major Rocky Mountain community to confront a serious, health-threatening pollution problem. Actually ahead of it had been the mountain-locked smelter town of Black Hawk in Colorado. One tourist pamphlet warned its readers that its appearance was "highly suggestive of the infernal regions." When Nathaniel Hill moved his smelter to Denver, a smoke cloud hung over parts of the more spacious and open "Queen City." Resident Charles Harvey described it thusly: "The smoke from their furnaces darkens the sky in that direction [Hill's smelter on the city's north side] at all times . . ."[20]

Denver, then, was virtually unchallenged for supremacy during the eighties, giving the Denver power elite time to grow and multiply, time even to make and correct miscalculations. They would use their windfall well.

Other towns hoped eventually to achieve power similar to that of the regional giants but without their problems. Most strove more realistically to make ends meet and dominate their own small economic spheres. Dillon survived because it had the railroad, the county seat, a good location, and was not situated close to any serious rival. Although mining had brought initial development to the surrounding countryside, and still excited locals (mica was the great hope in 1889), ranching and farming now constituted the economic backbone for this community.[21]

Somewhere in the Rocky Mountains during the 1880s, every stage of urban development was taking place—birth, growth, boom, decline, and death. All the potential settler or investor had to do was to judge correctly what phase the community was in or about to enter at any given time, which was not an easy task. Then he or she had to make a choice and work for the best results.

Atlantic City, Miner's Delight, and South Pass, though continually optimistic, had all seen better days by 1880, when their combined population sank to fewer than 170 people. Rawlins, too, had hopes: "our town's development in the near future, if recent past and present are a fair criterion, is beyond calculation." Its railroad connections, commercial importance, and location assured it a future that its three northern mining neighbors would never have. Mining camps presented the most stark contrasts: Elkhorn and Philipsburg in Montana prospered, while old Virginia City and Bannack declined sharply. Some looked to be in better shape than they actually were. Anne Ellis and her family came to Bonanza, Colorado, in the fall of 1882, a camp that boasted thirty-six saloons and seven dance halls. "In speaking of the population, you don't count people, anyway, you counted saloons and dance-halls," Anne decided. She misjudged Bonanza, which never amounted to much. Philadelphian Owen Wister visited Medicine Bow on the UP line in 1885: "A fearful place: A *town*—consisting of the station and a dozen wooden horrors for various purposes." He would make it famous later, but, like Bonanza, it would not meet its founders' expectations.[22]

During this time, those two exceptions to the general urban pattern, Colorado Springs and Manitou Springs, hummed along as refuges for the leisure class. Manitou unabashedly advertised itself as the "Saratoga of the West," hoping to attract some of the fame and glamour of that well-known eastern spa. William Jackson described a week of socializing in June 1880, which included gardening, an afternoon musical, playing whist twice, an evening at the club, and a "lively time" at the home of Dr. Reynolds. However, he was afraid that the charm of it might end when the railroad came. "I don't think it will improve Manitou much. It seems to make it like other places of resort brot [sic] into close relation with the outside world by rail." Jackson, though himself involved in railroading, saw a limit to its appeal when it made an impact on Manitou and his own life.

Manitou survived and Colorado Springs prospered. According to its own promotion, Colorado Springs was a commercial point of no small importance and a "pivotal center of all natural enjoyments."[23] These two communities proved they could cope by appealing to specific classes of people; the West could be snobbish as well as democratic. It should be remembered that they also attracted tourists and invalids, who came to try the waters and breathe the invigorating air.

Such elitism was shocking to lovers of the western democratic myth. More significant to long-range development was the fact that the worldly urbanite forged well ahead of his country cousin as the regional mover and shaker. The comparison between urban and rural life was not flattering. Laramie's *Weekly Boomerang* of December 13, 1883, observed that while the season's inclement weather drove people indoors, that deficiency was more than compensated for by the social season, when the "evenings are long and friends meet to spend a few hours pleasantly." On the other hand, the reporter went on to observe how "dreary and desolate the winter months may be to those who live in the isolation in the country . . ." Urbanites had cornered the modern improvements, such as electricity and the telephone, as well as having better access to the best entertainment and medical, business, banking, and educational facilities. Politically, they represented the major voice in Colorado and Montana. The West appeared rural to the casual eastern visitor, but that was not the environment in which the "modern" westerner, seeking wealth, power, and the good life, wanted to live. It consoled the ruralite very little that the farmer was still considered the backbone of America and the cowboy the heart of western legend, when all the excitement took place elsewhere.

This urbanization gave Rocky Mountain settlement a special flavor, though one that sophisticated visitors sometimes scoffed at. The census-drawn population density in 1870 did not seem particularly high: Colorado .4 and Montana and Wyoming .1 per square mile. Certainly those figures were smaller than older Nebraska, 1.6, and New Mexico, .7, and compared favorably to North Dakota's, .1. Statistics can deceive, however. For instance, less than half of Colorado's land was open for settlement that year; the rest comprised the Ute reservation or the recently evacuated Cheyenne and Arapaho territory. Adjustment for the unavailable land ups the density to .9; the figure goes even higher when only the eight counties most heavily impacted by mining are included. For a territory only eleven years old, that was remarkable.

Twenty-nine percent of the population was found in the nine largest communities, a circumstance that further strengthened the impact of urbanization.

Denver, Helena, Central City, and Cheyenne evolved into the major urban centers. Three of the four worked hard to carve out their own economic niches, while Central continued first and foremost to depend upon mining. Colorado Springs represented a planned city, but most of the others developed in whatever space became available. For Denver and Cheyenne, that meant suburbs on flat, open prairie land; Helena grew out of its gulch. Westerners were proud of their "metropolises"; visitors sometimes scoffed at their pretensions.

Rossiter Raymond thought Helena's process of site selection committed the "same error so usual to mining towns." The combination of town and mines gave rise to vexatious litigation and traffic congestion. The Earl of Dunraven saw little positive in highly regarded Virginia City:

> Good Lord! What a name for a place! We had looked forward to it during the journey as a sort of haven of rest, a lap of luxury . . . There might have been laps, but there was no luxury. A street of straggling shanties, a bank, a blacksmith's shop, a few dry goods stores, and bar-rooms, constitute the main attractions of the "city."

Ernest Ingersoll wrote, "The less said concerning Rawlins the better." Isabella Bird dismissed Cheyenne as "utterly slovenly-looking and unornamental, abounds in slouching bar-room characters, and looks a place of low, mean lives." Colorado communities drew similar reactions from her. She described Boulder as a "hideous collection" of frame houses on a burning plain; it aspired to be a "city of virtue." She arrived in Golden at night, which by daylight "showed its meanness," every other house being a saloon.[24] Finally, at Georgetown, Bird found something praiseworthy: "It is the only town I have seen in America to which the epithet picturesque could be applied."

Helen Hunt Jackson, who was enchanted by Colorado Springs, did not think much of Nederland or Central City and warned her friend Mary Hallock Foote that she could not stay in Leadville, the "place was too unnatural. Grass would not grow there and cats could not live." These were not the kinds of opinions the locals wanted to hear. They much preferred those accounts that focused on the good schools, the thrifty business places, the mines in operation, the residents "full of ambition and enterprise," and the lawfulness. Each certainly seemed destined, in these writers' opinions, to be the "metropolis of the Rocky Mountains."[25]

The camps and cities became the centers of politics, business, education, and transportation, as would be expected in Victorian America. A materialistic world, but one with a spiritual heart, brought the church west on the trail of the miners. The Methodists and Catholics made up the vanguard, followed by the Episcopalians in areas of strong British immigration. Pioneers relished their memories of the first church service. More important to the long-range stability of the community, however, was the establishment of a congregation and the building of a church. The Lord's house rose or fell on the shoulders of the man who ministered to the flock; the world around him challenged the basic tenets of Christianity. In the words of Colorado's George Darley, he had to "tire and tire again"; his work was easier if he could meet the people on their own ground, in their homes and businesses. The men who willingly adapted to western conditions and were good preachers and caring individuals succeeded best. Even the nonchurchgoers welcomed the moment when "Jesus Christ arrived," for it proved that the community was gaining maturity and permanence, profitable developments for everyone.[26]

While Rocky Mountain women struggled to stretch the family budget and worried about how best to raise their children, they remained the backbone of religion. They still found time to continue their work in the church and to protest if the ministers failed to serve their congregations adequately. One irate Butte housewife wrote:

> Instead of sending the best men they have in the East into
> these newer countries where so much sin and vice has
> reigned so long, they send a substitute. The consequence is
> religion has done little or no good as yet in this Territory.

Bishop Ethelbert Talbot, of the Episcopal Church, could have explained the reasons to her, because he was having trouble finding good men. With the salaries so low and with the rugged conditions that were so hard on married men and their families, he felt compelled to hire only single men. The result, he bemoaned, was that either very young, inexperienced men fresh out of seminaries or nomadic clergymen answered the call.[27]

The church gave women an opportunity generally denied them elsewhere, the chance to lead and govern. Except for the minister, the mainstay of the congregation typically lay in its women. Women, too, had to adapt to western conditions. The successful ones stabilized the transient nature of their lives, acquired a new measure of tolerance for home life, and accepted friendship across social lines. Examples of these success stories abounded: Mary Ronan, who was "blissfully happy keeping house" and following her mining husband throughout Montana; the pleasant, friendly, "very intelligent" Mrs. Link, whom Isabella Bird encountered on the headwaters of the Platte River in isolated South Park, Colorado; "Grandma" at Garland City, who had two sons killed in the war and brought a consumptive son to Colorado (the son recovered and this "tall, thin woman" made a new home in the West). Not all were able to adapt. Perceptive William Jackson described "Queenie" Palmer to Helen: "She is not my kind of person at all . . . she appears to me to have no object in life except that of seeking a good time." "Queenie" never did fit into Colorado and her husband's world, despite all that her husband, William Jackson Palmer, tried to do for her.[28]

Women led the attempt to reproduce Victorian society in the Rocky Mountains. They organized reform drives, such as Sunday closings and temperance, and campaigned for schools and the establishment of law and order. Wyoming provided the advantage of the vote, and, at least in the 1870s, women served on juries before the practice fell into disuse. Without the vote, Colorado women were not so fortunate. The state legislature, following the mandate of the constitution, placed a woman-suffrage amendment before the voters in 1877. The national movement, encouraged by the prospect of a state vote on suffrage, sent in such famous leaders as Susan B. Anthony to persuade the men to give the women the right to vote.

The suffragists met stubborn opposition from the Catholic church and from some Protestant ministers. Worst of all was the latent male opposition, which a friend of William Jackson described. He admitted having some "sympathetic anxiety for women. But what little [time] there is left of [my] existence is now dedicated to a tender interest for the welfare and safety of men." Suffrage lost heavily, by more than two to one. The anti-suffrage Pueblo *Chieftain* crowed, "Goodbye to the female tramps of Boston." Colorado women had themselves to blame, at least partly. A few worked actively for the cause, others opposed it, and the rest were afflicted by apathy.[29] Over a decade would pass before another effort would be undertaken in Colorado; the state had forgone its best opportunity to advance the cause of woman suffrage. Rocky Mountain men, agreeable to granting women more status and additional rights, were still reluctant to offer political equality. Wyoming stood alone in the whole country.

Women dominated only the profession of teaching. Many occupations and professions remained closed to them, or, at best, barely open. They owned or operated restaurants, boarding houses, millinery and dress shops, and served as domestics, but Main Street stayed a man's domain. Tradition predominated, and the woman's place was still in the home in this male-dominated society.

A few families had come with the initial rushes, and their numbers gradually increased. Wives and mothers had to endure the isolation and loneliness that had confronted pioneering women for centuries. The burdens of managing the household and family fell to them, as they helped to bring permanent settlement to the Rocky Mountains. The mining camps provided opportunities for female companionship and a variety of social institutions—churches, literary societies, theaters, clubs—which had enriched women's lives in their previous homes. The pioneering farm wife lacked these amenities.

Urbanization also gave children the opportunity to attend school and to make friends, as well as subjecting them to the temptations of the world around them. They matured rapidly; childhood seemed fleeting. Isabella Bird realized this, saying that "one of the most painful things in the Western states and Territories is the extinction of childhood." She believed that the atmosphere of "greed, godlessness and frequently profanity" in which they were raised caused the problem. Even in such a refined town as Colorado Springs, mothers encountered difficulties. James Rayner wrote his sister, "You can form no idea of the amount of hard swearing done in this country . . ." Newspaper editors often corroborated those impressions, occasionally describing the profanity and the gambling and drinking habits of some of the younger members of the community. In a society short of women, girls matured especially rapidly, at least in the minds of unmarried men. In their early teens, as in the 1860s, they began to be escorted to dances by older men, and soon they were married.[30]

Mothers could not rest easily with their sons either. The attractions of the red-light district glittered, and, despite ordinances and curfew, it fascinated children. Their mothers led the fight to restrict or abolish the district, but the struggle was usually futile because the trade played such a vital role in the economic life of a community. A "real" camp's prosperity could be measured by the size of its vice district, because the "knights of the green cloth," the "erring sisters," and the other hangers-on followed the cry of gold and silver as surely as the prospector. They, too, dug for their gold where they found it.

The red-light district included a number of temptations—saloons, variety theaters, dance halls, gambling establishments, and cribs and parlor houses. Common in the mining camps and larger towns, a district could also be found in some farming communities and in a college town like Boulder. Wherever it was, it almost always attracted the attention of writers and visitors, especially the prostitutes who conducted their trade within its confines. Not all the women of the red-light district served as "brides of the multitude." The dance hall girls and the hurdy-gurdies could earn as much on their feet as the "light ladies" could in their customary professional positions. A few women dealt cards at the gambling tables, but they were more a novelty than anything else.

The "fair but frail" have become western legends, but their life on the line did not resemble the romance of that legend. The beautiful, heart-of-gold prostitute lost her luster with nicknames like Nellie the Pig, Madame Mustache, and the Galloping Cow. These women plied their trade in a sordid, exploitive world, which included drugs, alcohol, the threat of physical abuse, suicide, and very little hope of breaking out of the fate to which the job and the age inevitably doomed them. Some, like Helena's "Chicago Joe" (Josephine Hensley) and Denver's Jennie Rogers and Mattie Silks, became entrepreneurs themselves, hiring girls to work in their parlor houses and making investments in real estate. Most merely existed by making the mining camp circuit in the summer and settling in one of the larger towns in the winter.[31]

Westerners generally tolerated their vice districts, which sometimes proved to be more than just an attraction for bringing business to the larger community. An anti-gambling–prostitution ordinance could be a lucrative municipal fund raiser, when the vices were allowed to flourish while the monthly fines kept rolling into city coffers. These fines, along with occasional police-protection payoffs, cut into the profits of the girls and the madams, who also worried about pregnancy or contracting a "social disease." Despite the claims of a number of patent medicines, no known cure existed for syphilis or other venereal diseases.

Knowing the sordid life, why would a woman turn to being a "capitalist with rooms," a "soiled dove," or any of the other Victorian euphemisms for whores? The most common rationale involved the stilted story of seduction and betrayal; that did happen, and so did drifting into it unwillingly. More than a few women chose the occupation of their own volition because of the lack of other opportunities or in a desperate gamble for a better life. A poorly educated, unmarried woman from society's lower economic rung might find the profession attractive. No simple explanation serves for all individuals; a combination of reasons probably motivated each one. What they found was a line to work in, a Victorian society closed to them, and a steadily deteriorating image and role in the community.[32]

Victorian society was allying itself with middle-class standards—the women saw to that. Law and order came into favor, with vigilantism relegated to a fading past. The red-light district, too, was being limited by ordinance to a certain area or two within the community, a nineteenth-century form of zoning. The accouterments of society surfaced in the form of the "right" club, church, neighborhood, friends, and so forth, just as they had back home. Newspapers did not headline the wild side of life, featuring instead the church social, the literary society meeting, the banker's dinner party, the school news, and the fortunes of the town's baseball team. Denver's or Helena's society folks aimed to imitate the elite of the East in dress, fads, and styles. They did not care to associate for long with the miner or the cowboy. The old West at their doorstep seemed not quaint or romantic, but crude, ill-mannered, and the antithesis of their new West.

Minorities also flocked to the urban areas, a fact that many middle-class people felt was not a positive step. The Chinese, the largest ethnic minority, found the same attitudes that they faced in mining. In some ways it was even worse. Growing anti-Chinese sentiment was evident throughout the country as the decade opened. The hard times of the 1870s and the resulting unemployment solidified racist feelings. Those, in turn, had led to political pressure which, rather quickly, resulted in Congress passing in 1882 a Chinese Exclusion Act that suspended Chinese immigration for ten years and prohibited the naturalization of Chinese.

Rocky Mountain westerners had always exhibited ambivalent attitudes toward the Chinese; most of them bordered on, or crossed over into, racism. Newly established Durango, Colorado, settled almost entirely by midwesterners and Coloradans, contained only a small number of Chinese. Relations between the races proceeded smoothly until it was discovered that opium "dives" were to be found among the Chinese businesses. This discovery led to editorials questioning, "Shall Chinamen be allowed to live in Durango?" Racism, intentional or not, reared its head in references to the Chinese as "wearers of the pigtail." Fortunately, Durango came to its senses before it had done more than whip up latent racist attitudes.

Butte, with a much larger Chinese population, also had a large Irish contingent, which harbored strong antagonisms toward its neighbors.

The animosity led to an 1882 victory by a mayoralty candidate, who used the slogan "Cheap Chinese Labor Must Go." The Chinese, who had resided there since the placer days, refused to go. They had established a two-block Chinatown, with restaurants, doctors, rooming houses, tailor shops, and stores. Despite local friction, it became the Chinese trade and cultural center for the territory and adjoining states. As might be expected, Chinese workers cornered a large percentage of the lowest-paying, labor-intensive jobs, which other workers often shunned. These included porters, janitors, domestic servants, wood cutters, truck farm laborers, and odd job workers. They worked hard and represented one of the most "peaceful and diligent" groups in Montana.[33]

The Chinese had accomplished yeoman work as placer miners, railroad workers, and entrepreneurs, yet they could not escape prejudice and cultural stereotyping. An editorial in the *Helena Independent* of October 9, 1885, gave clear evidence of these attitudes. The Chinese were nothing but evil, the editor concluded, "and evil continually can come from a Chinese immigration which can never assimilate to our population and our civilization." Helena and Butte had Montana's largest "Chinatowns"; proximity and association did little to advance understanding.

The predictable ultimately came to pass—anti-Chinese riots. Denver, which also had a large Chinese population, wrote a sad chapter in Rocky Mountain history. Like most Coloradans, Denverites viewed the Asian immigrants as inferior-minded, subhuman beings. The *Rocky Mountain News*, for example, headlined an article, "John Chinaman—The Pest of the Pacific Coast—the Heathen Who Have Ruined California and Are Now Slowly Invading Colorado." On Sunday, October 31, 1880, a riot erupted, the immediate cause of which seemed to have been a poolroom fight. Before the violence had run its course, scores of Chinese were beaten, one was killed, and Chinatown was looted. Worse trouble was averted when the Chinese fled into hiding. Denver eventually reimbursed the Chinese for fifty-four thousand dollars in property damage, but anti-Chinese sentiment did not abate in the following years.

Even worse was what has been described as the "Rock Springs [Wyoming] Massacre" of September 2, 1885. Twenty-eight Chinese were killed, fifteen wounded, several hundred chased out of town, and 147,000 dollars' worth of property destroyed. The cause proved to be partly attributable to racial prejudice and partly to bitterness against the UP coal department, which had hired them as miners and ultimately used them as effective strike breakers. Resentment flared among the other coal miners. The Knights of Labor had protested Chinese employment earlier, to no avail.

Under army protection, the Chinese returned to Rock Springs, and the troops prevented another outbreak of violence. For the next thirteen years, the army was garrisoned in the town, a Wyoming tour of duty that proved much less desirable than Yellowstone. Their safety insured, the Chinese went back to work. Only after protests by the Chinese government did Congress finally pay compensation. Westerners flaunted their prejudice when a grand jury failed to bring in any indictments.[34] During a day and time when other Americans were inflicting similar injustices on black Americans and minority groups, it cannot be considered unusual that westerners found convenient ethnic scapegoats for economic and social ills and changes. Nor was it unusual to find a corresponding inability or unwillingness to appreciate and value the culture and contributions of the Chinese.

Blacks also faced discrimination. Western prejudice sought to keep them in their place. Not many blacks lived in the Rocky Mountains, but they encountered the familiar circumstances—the menial jobs, the last hiring, social isolation, and a wide disparity between the numbers of men and women.[35]

Hispanics made only minimal impact on early settlement in the Rocky Mountains. The largest groups of them inhabited southern Colorado and the nearby San Luis Valley, but they found themselves politically, socially, and culturally isolated. That unfortunate pattern would continue for the next generation. Discrimination in jobs and living conditions awaited those who migrated to the more prosperous cities to the north. The fear, it seemed, was that if the barrier was breached by one group, all would follow.

The lessons of racism had not been learned. Montanans, when discussing their proposed state constitution, debated not allowing the employment of Chinese on any state, county, municipal, or public works, except as punishment for crime. Wyoming became one of the states that limited occupations in mining to citizens of the United States.[36] Racism would not soon end in the Rocky Mountains.

Fortunately for their sanity, these late nineteenth-century Americans had many other things to worry about or to find pleasure in. Victorian America, with its culture, fads, styles, and ideals, swiftly overran the raw frontier. Women organized clubs and societies for purposes of reform, intellectual challenge, and sociability. When Laramie women sponsored the organization of a territorial WCTU, the ballot and political pressure to advance their cause, which included the fight against "demon rum" and narcotics. The old West was passing, too, when newspapers editorially expounded on kissing: "The kiss as a good, hearty, healthy luxury, is unequalled"; or told their readers to hang up the receiver after using the telephone, because if left dangling "you sever connection as completely as though you cut the wire." When Green River's *Sweetwater Gazette* told the boys "to put up your pistols" because carrying one violated the law, it became obvious that the women and their allies had almost completely tamed the "wild" West.

The theater, that herald of culture, flourished in the eighties. Denver hungered for what the West's other great cities, such as San Francisco, had; and rich layers of culture and sophistication and Horace Tabor gave them a wonderful boost in that direction. His magnificent Tabor Grand Opera House in Denver, the finest between St. Louis and San Francisco, ranked as the crown jewel of the Rocky Mountain theaters. Butte could have disputed that claim, when it opened its Grand Opera House in 1885, only to see it burn in 1888; Helena, Cheyenne, Central City, Leadville, and other communities also took pride in their own "opera houses." Opera itself was performed only infrequently, but other kinds of entertainment abounded, from plays to concerts to new "stereopticon" slide shows. Nonetheless, an opera house, or at least a theater, served as an important symbol of municipal pride. Before the coming of the railroad, repertory companies, such as the popular Jack Langrishe's, traveled circuits in the prosperous mining districts. They would present a full night of entertainment, including Shakespeare, melodramas, and the closing vaudeville numbers. When the railroad facilitated travel to the West, nationally known actresses and actors visited the Rocky Mountains; Tabor, to gild the attractions, established the "Silver Circuit," which gave them bookings from Denver to Salt Lake City. In their own eyes, westerners lost not a step to the culture of the East when it came to up-to-date theater.[37]

As the 1880s closed, it had indeed been "a time to weep and a time to laugh" for the Rocky Mountain communities and their residents. They tried gamely to re-create the life that had been left behind and their success measured the achievement of their generation in settling these mountains. The opportunities had been many, the pitfalls equally numerous; now they had an urban foundation to build upon.

7 : AGRICULTURAL HINTERLANDS: MAN VERSUS THE LAND

Not only the miner and urbanite came to the Rockies in the 1870s and 1880s; so did the farmer and the rancher, settling in the valleys and the plains along the foothills. Wyoming and Montana moved well ahead of Colorado, particularly in ranching. As aspiring rancher Gordon Tupper explained the attraction:

> One dollar in cattle here will make more than four dollars in business in the East. . . . Calves bought in the fall for $4–6 as steers are ready to sell at the railroad at $30. The expenses are light. Provisions are cheap and so are horses.[1]

He went on to explain to his sister that his lack of success stemmed from "Our bad luck . . . from bad management." Others were not so candid—it seemed so easy. The government provided free grass and water, and the rancher the bulls and cows, after which nature was allowed to take its course. On the plains of Wyoming and in the valleys of Montana, ranching took hold. When the final defeat of the Sioux opened the eastern portion of each territory, cattlemen trailed their herds to new ranges. Cheyenne finally latched onto its economic stronghold and became the cattle center of the Rockies. The British moved in to invest and play at being "cowboys," while hardheaded cattlemen ran their ranches for them.

Cattle was king and another legend was created, that of the free-spirited, fun-loving, and independent cowboy. He came up the Texas trails (a few stepped off the trains directly from the East) and settled permanently in the two territories, bringing with him his folklore and his rugged image. When the American writer discovered him, the western novel was born. There was money to be made in ranching, and the cattle business boomed.[2] Colorado's eastern plains also became the domain of cattle, and to a lesser degree, the cattleman ventured into the mountain valleys. This was not primarily a mountain business, however; it belonged on the plains. The cowboy rode far from sight of the Rockies in his meanderings.

Nevertheless, the rancher benefited mightily from the miner who toiled in those mountains. The market and the high prices in the mining districts continued to encourage the rancher, as they did the farmer.[3]

Yet of the three, the cowboy would become legendary, the miner semilegendary, and the farmer nearly forgotten. Easterners looked toward the Rocky Mountain region and came up with their own conceptions of it. Farmers they had back east, and miners looked like any other industrial laborers, but the cowboy had a mystique all his own. The old West lived on in the cowboy, even while it was evolving into the new West.

That old West, that land of opportunity, would not die. Since the days of Jamestown and Plymouth, the West had beckoned, a land in which a new start could be made, a fortune won. Though many chose to ignore the fact, it could also be the place where one could fail and the dream turn to ashes as many Rocky Mountain residents discovered when the cattle kingdom collapsed at their doorstep. There was a dark side to the western dream.

Building on the occurrences of the 1870s, a spectacular boom in the cattle business came about in the early eighties. From Colorado through Montana, cattlemen appeared to be realizing their ambitions, with generous help from a benevolent Uncle Sam. Whereas legendary mining barons dug into the mountains, their cattle-kingdom counterparts rode the range. Granville Stuart, who had seen it all happen in Montana, organized a large and successful cattle ranch and was joined by Bannack butcher Conrad Kohrs among the ranks of the cattle kings. Colorado contributed John Iliff, who operated the region's largest ranch for 150 miles along the South Platte, over which he ran a herd reported to contain fifty thousand cattle. "The squarest man that ever rode over these Plains," a contemporary called him.

Of the three distinct Rocky Mountain regions, Wyoming was the one most completely dominated by the cattlemen. Cattle raising became its economy. Pennsylvania-born Alexander Swan exemplified the apex of the cattleman's power. His Swan Land and Cattle Company, Ltd., ran cattle west from Ogallala, Nebraska, to Fort Steele, Wyoming, and its landholdings had a value of fifty million dollars. During the 1880s, Swan emerged as a major figure in Wyoming's political life, serving on the territorial council, among other positions. Political wheel-horse Joseph Carey ranched in several choice Wyoming locations, and John Iliff's cattle grazed on the southeastern plains. The list could go on; Wyoming was cattlemen's country. By 1885–86, an estimated million and a half cattle were pastured in the territory. The Wyoming range had reached its capacity in a decade.[4]

Emulating that typical frontier habit, Wyoming cattlemen organized into several county associations, which merged in 1879 to become the Wyoming Stock Growers Association. It grew to encompass associations from Montana, Nebraska, and Dakota Territory. The legislature recognized the power of the cattlemen by passing laws on "marks or brands," and one statute made railroad companies liable for killing or injuring stock. Even the all-powerful Union Pacific bowed to the wishes of the cattlemen. Other major concerns of the association were organization of roundups, freight rates, rustling, and control of disease. In response to range needs, it recorded brands of members, supervised roundups, hired detectives to apprehend cattle thieves, and lobbied in both the state and national legislatures. Colorado and Montana had their own associations, neither as influential nor as powerful as Wyoming's. Mining reigned in those two, with ranching dominating only the eastern plains.

Bill Nye of Laramie's *Boomerang* illustrated the ranchers' need to curb rustling. This Mark Twain–style humorist told a sly tale, which was given wide circulation:

> Three years ago a guileless tenderfoot came into Wyoming,
> leading a single Texas steer and carrying a branding iron;
> now he is the opulent possessor of six hundred head of fine
> cattle—ostensible progeny of that one steer.[5]

More than just a few accepted this classic story as true and saw it as an accurate indicator of Wyoming's cattle potential. The established cattlemen saw in it a grim truth amid the humor.

Intrigued investors saw only profit. With the range-cattle industry prospering, they turned their attention to it, just as they had turned to the gold strikes. Low expenses and the potential for quick wealth encouraged entrepreneurs from the East and from the British Isles to invest heavily in the cattle business. When an 1881 English parliamentary committee reported a 33 percent return to stock owners, the rush was on. In one year alone (1883), twenty corporations, aggregately capitalized at more than twelve million dollars, were organized under Wyoming laws. Rumors became reality when the Prairie Cattle Company declared a 42 percent dividend in 1882, on the heels of a 28 percent return the year before.

Aside from the profit possibilities, English traveler and writer William Baille-Grohman saw other "attractive inducements for the English character." The vocation would bring an infinite "amount of exercise on the bright breezy Plains" in a temperate zone with the most "delightfully bracing" climate in the world. He saw the life as a rough one, where the cowboy and his horse were one. But it was also a life well compensated by the "ever-present element" of manly sport, which would weed out the "effeminate and unmanly."[6] Wyoming, Colorado, and Montana cattlemen clearly did not appreciate the fringe benefits they were providing for their cowhands, aside from their pay and bacon and beans!

Of more immediate interest, fortunes could be made quickly—and lost just as quickly. And like mining, the cattle business attracted its share of fast-buck artists and manipulators. Plungers in Glasgow, New York, and London invested in herds they never saw, on land they never visited. The land existed, the cattle might not. No accurate system of tallying cattle had been achieved. When a rancher sold his herd, the number of steers was usually estimated. The same held true for the calves born each spring; it was a chancy business at best.[7]

In spite of that, Alexander Swan and his competitors rode the crest of prosperity. He, and Iliff before him, followed more ethical, conservative business practices, unlike many of the others, who went into debt to buy ranches, overestimated herds, illegally claimed federal land, overgrazed the range, ruthlessly fought opposition, lobbied for special interests, and singlemindedly drove to make money. They were not alone in their avaricious activities, for the business ethics of Victorian America, both East and West, encompassed many questionable practices.

Ethics aside, in the very success of the cattle kingdom were sown the seeds of destruction. Ranchers had feared the coming of barbed wire, which gave the farmer an easy way to fence the range; cattle did not tangle with those barbs more than once. The ranchers, who expected the "devil's hatband" to ruin them, soon began to use it to their own advantage. They could easily fence in the public domain and call it their own, while fencing out competitors at the same time. They could also easily replace the Texas longhorn with a better breed. Worried about interbreeding and the increasing incidents of cattle diseases stalking the plains, each rancher could use barbed wire to keep his cattle segregated. Fencing the range and placing better grade stock on it required investors to increase their contributions appreciably. Once more, it was costing money to make money. To make matters worse, these imported cattle, although purebred stock and better beef producers, were "pilgrims" when it came to western weather and open-range grazing. The gamble for higher profits could turn out to be unwise, but time would tell.

Washington had already instituted proceedings against fraudulent land entries (a not uncommon practice), and now it added proceedings against unlawful fences. Ranchers who had purchased Union Pacific land often incorporated the alternate sections of government land into their fenced Wyoming ranges.[8] Cheyenne's *Northwestern Live Stock Journal*, the cattlemen's mouthpiece, vigorously protested the unfavorable publicity in an April 1885 editorial: "Every Jim Crow paper from New York to San Francisco is branding us bulldozers and thieves."

Investigations and public revelations tainted the cattlemen's image. While they went on, the overstocked and overgrazed western range deteriorated alarmingly. Estimates vary, but probably close to two million cattle were grazing on Rocky Mountain rangeland by the early eighties. No large amounts of new land remained to be settled, and even marginal rangelands were overcrowded. Then came an 1885 presidential order that forced stockmen who had leased lands in Indian Territory to get out. Some 200,000 beeves were driven onto the crowded ranges that fall.

The cattle themselves faced competition for that very land. Sheep interloped onto some areas, as old-time cattleman Bryant Brooks observed, "uninvited, unwelcomed by the cattlemen." He did not like the appearance, taste, or smell of this "strange, unromantic animal." He and others contended that cattle would not graze where sheep had been. Sheep made an impact of their own on western Montana, Wyoming, and southern Colorado, where they had been raised for years. The conflicts between the two groups of herders for control of the open range grew into western legend. Some of the roots of the trouble were racial and cultural, not economic, in areas where Spanish–Mexican sheepherders worked. Belying the claims of incompatibility, a number of large operators in Montana, for example, ran both sheep and cattle, and the animals shared the same watering spots and range.[9]

Meanwhile, farmers were moving onto the plains, homesteading the range that the ranchers had been claiming illegally. Barbed wire helped them as much as it did the cattlemen, and both covetously eyed the water. Wyoming Governor Francis Warren declared, "I am convinced from conversations with practical cattlemen and what I have seen that losses from a want of sufficiency of water are greater" than from a lack of food.

Experienced ranchers grew alarmed as overcrowding, disease, government legal action, and a cattle surplus forced the sale of large numbers of steers and cows and depressed the price of beef. Instead of the four to five dollars per one hundred pounds earned in earlier years, the average dropped to three to four dollars in 1885. Hundreds of ranchers across the open range felt the squeeze of mounting costs and falling prices. The cattle industry represented a disaster waiting to happen.

Nature relentlessly ended the cattle era. Its demise began during the cold, blustery winter of 1885–86, which took a frightful toll of cattle on the northern plains. The hot and dry summer that followed shriveled grass on the overgrazed range, leaving the cattle to enter the winter in poor condition. That became a winter to remember. Montanan Herbert Lord recorded in his diary the variations: "Nov. 21, snowed all day, 15 above zero, Nov. 22, 18 below; Dec. 27 snow 20 inches deep; Jan. 11, 1887, 42 below." More blizzards ensued. Rancher Granville Stuart surveyed his range and found the streams and coulees strewn with dead cattle. "A business that had been fascinating to me before, suddenly became distasteful. I wanted no more of it. I never wanted to own again an animal that I could not feed and shelter." Cowboy Charlie Russell made a mark for himself with his sketch of the "last of 5,000," a scrawny, barely-alive steer. Interim manager Finlay Dun, reporting on happenings at the Swan Land and Cattle Company, described the aftermath to depressed investors:

> Hundreds of weakly old cows and their calves have perished and the tally demonstrates heavy mortality of two year old heifers . . . Several outfits after traveling with the round-up and finding scarcely any cattle pulled out and went home; the northern winter losses are currently stated at 50% and exceptional cases are even higher.

The prosperous days of the open range came to a tragic end.[10]

Winter losses had always been a part of the open-range cattle business, but nothing like this had ever happened before. Losses in Wyoming counties went from 5 percent to 45 percent, and in Montana they were even higher. Cattlemen and cattle companies throughout the Rocky Mountains were ruined. Membership in the once-powerful Wyoming Stock Growers Association plummeted, and its political power reached a low ebb by the decade's end. Montana, with both its copper and its cattle in the doldrums in 1886–87, also faced a bleak season.

Picking up the pieces in the wake of the disaster took years. Liquidation sales and bankruptcy pulled the industry down in the months that followed, and investors fled from the disaster.[11] It would take a while for the debris to settle, and for a general acceptance of what John Iliff had been preaching back in the 1870s. This farsighted rancher had advocated fences for the range and shelter and feed for the blooded cattle, combined with sound, conservative business practices and avoidance of debt. Those practices promised the rancher a surer and steadier income. When irrigation, crop and field rotation, and the acceptance of veterinary medicine merged with Iliff's ideas, the modern era of scientific ranching dawned.

The ending of the open range had been a costly lesson. For the first time on a large scale, the Rocky Mountains had failed their would-be conquerors and profit makers or, more realistically, the latter had failed to match the mountains' challenge and adapt to the environment. The dream had become a nightmare for them, and a generation felt the grim aftershocks. The rugged individualism, so prized by the cattlemen and the mythmakers, had led to disaster. The absentee investors, and even their western partners, had not clearly understood that the opportunity to make bonanza profits also carried with it the risk of failure. What had appeared to be almost a right now seemed more of an illusion. Nature could prove a hard taskmaster at any time, but never so much as when she allied herself with human greed and excessive optimism. That union could teach a brutal lesson. But had that lesson been learned by everyone involved?

Despite the hard times that came with the crash of open-range days, the legend of the cowboy and the free-wheeling days persisted yet a little longer, resulting in tragedy in Wyoming a few years later. The infamous Johnson County War pitted the big ranchers against the other settlers. It looked like a fight between the small man and corporations, and it smacked of trying to revive an individualistic West that lived more in the imagination than in fact.

Range conflicts had been coming for years, as the big cattle operations watched small ranchers and farmers crowding onto the land they had once so freely roamed. The hard-pressed cattle kings who survived the mideighties disaster saw nothing but trouble coming from these range rivals. The climax came over rustling in Johnson County.

Although there were arrests, the courts provided no comfort; juries of newcomers had no sympathy for their arrogant neighbors. Frustrated and angered over failing to get convictions, the cattlemen decided to take matters into their own hands. In the words of one participant, it was an "irrepressible conflict."

While large ranchers planned violent action, there occurred in 1891 the lynching and dry-gulching of several "suspected rustlers," who also happened to be small ranchers. Following that incident, a special six-car train left Cheyenne in April 1892, carrying twenty-five Texas gunmen, horses, wagons, and supplies, along with Wyoming ranchers and their friends. Detrained at Casper, the group headed for Buffalo. Others who were obviously privy to the plan included state officials, newspaper editors, and most members of the Wyoming Stock Growers Association. Known by various names—Invaders, Regulators, and White Caps—they rode in with secrecy that April, and secrecy and controversy rode out with them.

After losing much time for one reason or another, they besieged the KC Ranch, believed to be a rustler hangout. It required one long day for all these gunmen to kill two of the men they sought. News of the attack had reached Buffalo, and opposition to the Invaders was instantly galvanized. Unaware that the news was out, the gunmen hurried on toward Buffalo, fifty miles north. They never arrived. Warned that a superior force, armed and ready, would greet them, they turned back to a friendly ranch thirteen miles south. There, on April 11, the assault on them was almost as inept as the one they had undertaken earlier. Two grim days later, they were rescued by a detachment of cavalry, in response to the pleas of the two U.S. senators and the acting governor. Safe but embarrassed, the chastised gunmen were escorted by the troops to Fort Russell for trial. Later on, in Cheyenne, the Invaders pleaded not guilty to murder, but they never came to trial. After more than one thousand prospective jurymen had been examined without a jury being formed, the defendants were discharged.[12] Johnson County was bankrupt and unwilling to pay for the costly keep of the prisoners. With the need for gunfighters ended, the prisoners scattered.

The aftermath of the skirmish was hardly what the Invaders expected. Instead of earning acclaim for a worthy crusade, they found themselves pictured as "arrogant lawbreakers and cold-blooded murderers." Many people consumed a good deal of time that summer in covering their tracks and distancing themselves from the Invaders. Supporters of the gunmen in Johnson County had their property destroyed or carried off; a few were killed and more left altogether, never to return to Wyoming. Throughout the state, their backers used the summer to try to recoup the costs of the campaign. It is impossible to ascertain whether their efforts inhibited rustling, or whether some of the marked "rustlers" left Wyoming because of their campaign. The actions of the cattlemen evoked further distrust against wealth and power. The "little man" continued to settle the range, undeterred by threats of violence.

In his angry account of the invasion, *The Banditti of the Plains*, Wyoming editor Asa Mercer, concluded:

> Corporation rule dominated so long, and then the disgrace of
> the state's invasion came as a climax. Some of the invaders
> still hold up their heads and try to pose as men . . . From
> now on there will be a new Wyoming, purified by the
> people's rule.

For such heresy, Mercer paid dearly. Books were seized and burned, and he was jailed, charged with "sending obscene matter through the mails."[13] The dust slowly settled, but the hard feelings lasted for years. This episode, along with New Mexico's Lincoln County War, eventually entered western folklore as one of the great range wars.

This anachronistic vigilante effort did not enhance Wyoming's or the cattlemen's national reputation. The time had passed when such a low value could be placed on human life; vigilantism was scorned after courts and county and state governments had begun to function. The "war" can only be described as an indefensible and costly blunder—the cattlemen seemed to believe that they lived in a still unsettled, frontier era. Bryant Brooks, himself a cattleman and later governor, gave the episode the perfect epitaph, a "disgraceful, inexcusable affair."[14]

With much less attention and trauma, the farmer continued migrating to the Rocky Mountains, trusting in God or comforting himself with the belief that rainfall trailed the plow or was tickled out of the clouds by currents from telegraph wires or iron rails. The farmer of Colorado, Wyoming, and Montana labored from "sunup to sunset," struggling with scant rainfall; grasshoppers; heat; cold; short growing seasons; drought; the drudgery of planting, weeding, and harvesting; isolation; and the vicissitudes of a changing mining market. Except for the last, and the scarcity of water, many of the difficulties resembled those encountered in the Midwest. But in Wyoming, particularly, farmers faced nearly insurmountable problems, with shorter growing sea-

sons, fewer home markets, and less water than its neighbors. Montana's
Rocky Mountain Husbandman cheered them all on, declaring: "The heal-
thiest people on the face of the earth are those who follow the occupation of farmers. The farmer is the only true sovereign and monarch
among men . . . He feeds the world."[15] Health the farmer might have,
but wealth usually eluded him, just as it did the average miner and
the cowboy.

What had once been the "Great American Desert" was being converted to the "Garden of Eden" by railroads' wishes, promoters' pens,
and newspapers' print. Especially in eastern Colorado, where neither
ranchers nor Indians impeded their advance, the farmers settled in
large numbers. Railroad agents lured them to the rights-of-way of the
Burlington, Missouri Pacific, and Rock Island lines. The great hubbub
came in the eighties, when these tracks crossed the plains on their way
to Denver. The farmers moved in, purchased their land or home-
steaded, and established small farm communities, among them, Akron,
Eads, Flagler, and Springfield. The excitement was intense. In May
1886, Lamar was described this way:

> Only five short weeks ago there was not a sign of human
> habitation in sight save a single log building down by the
> cottonwood belt that fringes the stream. . . . Today there are
> five and twenty buildings completed or nearly so, many
> others are begun and active preparations are making to erect
> a large number more.[16]

The sodbusters had their own aspirations, like the miners and cattlemen before them. They gambled, also—that their dryland farms would
receive enough moisture to raise a crop on undeniably rich, virgin soil.
Only if the rains came could they succeed. Ainsworth E. Blount, head
of the agricultural experimental program at Colorado Agricultural College at Fort Collins, was one of those who arrived as a skeptic. In an
1886 interview, he told of being unimpressed seven years before, re-
garding the country "as a desert." Now, with new agricultural products, particularly wheat, he saw a future for farming. Less scholarly
farmers east of his campus agreed with him.

Farmers had not been so seriously affected by the dry summers and
harsh winters that killed the cattle kingdom. They had fortuitously
settled during the earlier wet cycle. This chance occurrence reinforced
the belief that rain really did follow settlement in some mysterious
way. But trouble was not long in coming. Dry years returned in 1889
and 1890, and worse times lay ahead in the new decade. The "rainbelt"

had not moved west at all; hopes and dreams shriveled in the dry, hot prairie winds. "The only crop was bankrupts," lamented one farmer. To paraphrase a popular saying. "In God we trusted, in Colorado we busted." The refrain soon grew old as the farmers made their exodus from the plains. The fledgling counties retrenched, and the once-promising farm towns stagnated. The same story, to a lesser degree, was told in Wyoming.[17] The first assault on the high plains had failed to sustain itself.

One earlier settlement did survive the tribulations of the eighties—the Union Colony, which founded Greeley. Completely forsaking the individualism that characterized the farm frontier, these settlers banded together. Settling along the South Platte, on some of Colorado's finest farmland, and with the Denver Pacific at their doorstep, the colonists utilized town and farm settlement to achieve a winning combination. Especially contributing to their success were adequate finances and resources to develop an irrigation system. The Union colonists enjoyed spectacular success in the 1870s (the colony ended its corporate status in 1880) and laid the foundation for one of Colorado's greatest agricultural achievements. Their success encouraged a flock of imitators on the plains and in the mountains, none of which realized the same prosperity.[18]

They did something else that would be equally significant to the history of the Rocky Mountains: they helped to develop territorial water law. Farmers in the South Platte Valley, as well as the Arkansas, needed water, as did the miners in the mountains to the west. Demands on the streams and rivers became overbearing; riparian rights, the outgrowth of British common-law doctrine that was brought from England via the East, failed to meet western needs. In the humid East, the doctrine had worked well, but the West required something more than the limited use of river water by adjacent landowners. Users in the East had most typically borrowed the water, using it, for instance, to operate a grist mill, then returning it to the stream in almost the same condition in which it had been taken out. Rocky Mountain miners and farmers wanted to take the water out and transport it for use where it was needed. When, and if, it was returned, after being used for irrigation, sluicing, or milling, the water often carried industrial pollution or ground salts. To complicate matters even more, stream flow could be changed radically by the demands of upstream users. The men who invested capital and labor to secure downstream agricultural diversions needed protection in law that would ensure them the continued right to draw the water necessary for their projects.

The Union colonists had committed their fortunes to transforming their land into the garden. They and their neighbors were not about to have that ruined by upstream users monopolizing water, and the debate over water rights exploded and quickly landed in the courts. Who would have what rights?

Colorado Supreme Court Chief Justice Moses Hallett expressed the concept well in 1872, stating that "in a dry and thirsty land it is necessary to divert the waters of the streams from the natural channels . . . and this necessity is so universal and imperious that it claims recognition of the law." From this necessity, there arose the Doctrine of Prior Appropriation (first in time, first in right), which permitted diversion of water without regard to ownership of land along the banks. First users were endowed with a permanent right to water so long as they needed it and continued to use it beneficially. Priority of diversion established priority of usage rights, regardless of the geographical location on the stream where the diversion was made. Used sparingly in California earlier, the doctrine was written into the state's basic document by Colorado's constitution makers. It would be challenged in state and federal courts, but the "Colorado system" would be adopted by Montana and Wyoming and other arid western states.[19]

As early as the 1870s, the water question had brought several western states together in Denver to discuss a joint appeal for federal aid in reclaiming western lands. Although Congress did not respond, the issue had already moved beyond the concern of just one or two states. Water that flowed out of the mountains in Colorado, Wyoming, and Montana flowed into other states. What rights might they have?

Corporation fights, hard times, water issues, rural problems—there was much of the twentieth-century Rocky Mountain West in all this. The nineteenth century, though, hung on grimly to this generation. It confronted the issues, but did not solve them. These unresolved issues were as much a part of their heritage to their grandchildren as were those legendary frontier days, which their descendants more joyfully accepted.

8 : TOURISTS FIND THE "STAR OF EMPIRE"

Already Washington and other outsiders were changing the Rocky Mountain region, but so were the pioneers themselves. They did it both intentionally and unintentionally, and in the process erased the frontier as surely as they paved the way for the new West. This evolution was no more clearly shown than by the creation of Yellowstone National Park, the country's first.

Considering the uncontrollable desire to exploit the natural resources of the Rocky Mountains, it seems almost incongruous that a preservation movement was started to save some of the natural wonders, such as geysers, falls, lakes, and hot springs. Occasional visitors and prospecting parties had entered the Yellowstone area, with the latter focusing their attention only on what minerals were to be found there. Fortunately, as Rossiter Raymond explained, it did not promise much "except sulphur, fire-clays and natural cements" to the wildly exploitive miners. A visitor, Nathaniel Langford, understood the significance of what he saw, and in an early 1871 lecture in Washington and New York he spoke for preservation: "This is probably the most remarkable region of natural attractions in the world." He called for setting Yellowstone aside as a national park.[1]

Later that same year, geologist Ferdinand Hayden led the first scientific party into the Yellowstone country, a trip he repeated in 1872. The resulting publicity, along with the photographs by William Henry Jackson and the watercolors of Thomas Moran, both of whom were members of the 1871 party, brought congressional attention to the region. All the while, Hayden and Langford pushed for a park bill, which William Clagett, Montana's delegate, introduced in December 1871. The bill's supporters were helped along by officials of the Northern Pacific Railroad, who saw a tourist attraction and tourist profits in the making. Although hundreds of miles of track from its terminus, the Northern Pacific and others saw a dollar-producing opportunity in Yellowstone and acted upon it by lobbying Congress.

Without much debate or newspaper notice, the bill sped through Congress, and President Grant signed it on March 1, 1872. He may not have realized it at the time, but it was his greatest contribution to the Rocky Mountain West. The act to create the park ran fewer than six hundred words. It defined boundaries and placed the park under control of the secretary of the interior, who could establish regulations, grant leases, and "take all such measures as shall be necessary or proper to fully carry out the objects and purposes of this act."[2] Almost without thinking, Congressmen had created a new federal obligation and then hurried off to shake voters' hands and get on with the presidential campaign.

This minor bill of the 1872 congressional session passed for three reasons: because the power structure wanted it passed, because it had hardly any opposition, and because the region was unsettled and located far away with a very small voice. For the Rocky Mountains, it signified the birth of a new era, one greatly distanced from the frontier that surrounded it. Although no direct mention had been made of the environment, of conservation, or the potential for tourism, a look between the lines of the three short paragraphs reveals that all of these factors were implicit. No consensus had been forged among westerners about the pros and cons of these issues as they related to development, but the Rocky Mountains would be changed forever by them.

A new theme emerged. At the moment, exploitation completely dominated; only a quiet voice spoke for something more than materialism. It had not been a particularly memorable year, either regionally or nationally; however, 1872 marked a milestone, uncomprehended then amid the business of settlement and development.

The easiest route into the park came not from Wyoming to the south nor from Idaho to the west. Montana won that prize. The first visitors entered from there; a few were exploiters, more proved to be protectors, and almost all were awed by what they found. Superintendent Nathaniel Langford, who had no salary, no staff, and no guidelines to follow, greeted them. He did recommend prohibition of timber cutting, fishing and hunting, and severe penalties for leaving campfires unattended. Tourists could be vandals even then, and Langford warned Washington as early as 1873 that several features "have been defaced by visitors."

The Earl of Dunraven came through the park in 1874. Like visitors before and since, he watched the geysers with wonder. He did get "mad" at the Mud Springs, which refused to demonstrate for him. Sitting in wait for several hours, he described the situation as "a ludicrous-looking group, three men and a dog, gazing earnestly at a lot of mud which slowly, slowly rose." He came to this conclusion: "I suppose, acting on the principle that a watched pot never boils, this geyser sternly refused to do its duty. It would not get angry." Dunraven and his friends tried their best to rile it, but they "threw sticks and stones into it to no use." After saying Yellowstone Falls were "quite impossible to describe," he rhapsodized:

> They have a savage beauty all their own, a wild loveliness
> peculiar to them . . . The scene is so solitary, so utterly
> desolate, the colouring is so startling and novel, the fantastic
> shapes of the rocks so strange and weird, that glamour of
> enchantment pervades the place.[3]

Although unimpressed with the Mammoth Hot Springs Hotel (where accommodations were in "inverse ratio to the gorgeous descriptions" contained in Helena and Virginia City newspapers), he enjoyed his visit. Westerners were prone to exaggerate in their eagerness to impress visitors with the contrast between yesterday's primitive frontier and today's modern developments. Tourists like Dunraven would not overlook those still rustic conditions and would grumble about accommodations in Yellowstone and elsewhere.

Robert Strahorn, in his promotional book on Wyoming, predicted only a bright future for this "great national pleasure ground." Colgate Hoyt, who visited the park in 1878, was simply mesmerized: "It contains in the same space probably a greater number of natural wonders & curiosities than any other region of the entire globe and this is rightly named *Wonderland*."[4] A wonderland it was, without doubt. And the most wonderful thing was that Americans were trying to preserve it. Perhaps they were doing it for all the wrong reasons—profit, tourism benefits, lack of developable resources—but their actions demonstrated that they could see a future for the Rocky Mountains beyond the almighty dollar, and that the Rockies could be more than just a pass-through on the road back home.

Strahorn touched upon the other bounteous Wyoming tourist enticements—the magnificent scenery, towering mountains, grand rivers, mineral springs of almost every nature, and the hunters' and anglers' paradise—and concluded that "she possesses more attractions for the tourist and health seeker than any other State or Territory."[5] Health seeker? Indeed, the Rocky Mountains had long been famous for their curative powers. From the dry, light air to the mineral springs, chronic sufferers could hope to find relief. The exuberant Strahorn claimed that those who suffered from respiratory diseases, consumption, general debility, nervous dyspepsia, and a host of chronic diseases would find Wyoming a "resort for invalids."

Wyoming's claim to that title would not go unchallenged. Colorado had made similar claims earlier, and only the difficulty of travel had kept people from quickly capitalizing on the hope that relief could be found in the rarefied air in the "bosom" of the Rockies. There being no known cure for tuberculosis, the consumptive deteriorated inexorably until death ended the suffering. No wonder these invalids grasped desperately for the elixir that a change in climate might provide. Colorado preceded both its neighbors in making good on its wonderworking claims. Thanks to local initiative, Colorado Springs was being planned and developed with one of its goals being to help the so-called one-lunged army of consumptives and those with other chronic illnesses.

The railroad, too, impacted tourism. The ease, comfort, and speed of travel allowed tourists, health seekers, and journalists to reach the Rocky Mountains in numbers greater than ever before. Their impressions of the plains and western Wyoming did not differ much from those of earlier travelers. Words such as "wearisome, endless, verdureless, monotonous," and even the old "Great American Desert," peppered their descriptions. Conversely, Helen Hunt Jackson was one who grew to appreciate the plains, "which have all the beauty of the sea added to the beauty of plains. Like the sea they are ever changing in color, and seem illimitable in distance." Some others, with a more practical bent, saw them as "magnificent grass for cattle."[6]

The Rockies continued to elicit admiration. Jackson spoke for many when she mused, "Whether the summits or the foot-hills are more beautiful one forever wonders and is never sure." Then, looking west from her Colorado Springs home, she asked, "Are there many spots on earth where the whole rounded horizon is thus full of beauty and grandeur . . . ?"

Miners spent little time contemplating the surrounding splendor while they dug into those mountains. Some writers romanticized miners and their industry; for example, Horace Tabor's legendary rise from rags to riches. But Jackson saw them more realistically, as in Central City, and classically described them: "Pallid, dusty, earth-stained, they looked like no joyous seekers after riches. Their begrimed and careworn faces, and ragged clothes, seemed a bitter satire on their words silver and gold." The miners cared not a whit about Helen's opinion of them; they had come to make money, not to pursue aesthetic pleasure or create a romantic appearance. Miner, rancher, and soldier Gordon Tupper spoke for his generation when he said, "I want to make money enough to come home," and concluded that the amount he needed would "take time you know."[7] For him, and others, it continued to be hard to settle in one spot, and few considered returning to the old place until they had their fortune in hand.

Even fewer people paid attention to mining's environmental damage. The *Engineering and Mining Journal*, in describing hydraulic mining in Montana, warned that tons of soil were being washed out daily. Ranches and farms miles below the mines were being damaged by sediment. As a spokesman for mining, the editor drew this conclusion about the procedure: "But the mines have to be worked, and even should a few acres of land be covered up on the banks of Gold Creek, the new soil formed will be as good if not better than the old. . . ."[8]

Despite the obvious improvement that had come to the West, and westerners' pride in them, some easterners still saw the Rocky Mountains as forbidding. Louisa Koppe said when her father left Tennessee in the 1870s for Colorado, "we all told him goodbye and he went up a hill . . . when he got to the top of the hill he stopped and waved to us." Then he was gone, and the family felt that he had disappeared from the earth. Others feared that by going west one "bid good-bye to school and churches" and entered the realm of the buffalo.

William Andrews Clark, in his 1876 Philadelphia address, tried hard to reverse that image, inviting the capitalist, laborer, miner, farmer, invalid, artist, and lover of nature to come to where they all would "obtain an abundant recompense for their toil" and have a reasonable hope of restoration of health. Colorado organized briefly a Board of Immigration to spread the word of its attractions with literature and promotional campaigns.

But, in the end, it was individuals writing and talking who perhaps did the best job of promotion. Gordon Tupper, trying to convince his unmarried sister to come out to Montana, spoke of the healthful climate, the abundance of marriageable-age gentlemen, and the better economic opportunities. The region was improving, and no longer could be considered a wild, untamed land, but Tupper concluded with an appeal that has resounded down the generations since: "You will have to live in a log house and wear calico dresses, but you can have a saddle horse of your own and go riding whenever you feel like it."[9] The marriage of the old West and the new West was well under way. These westerners would try to retain the best of both and capture the imagined charm of the earlier era—the Rocky Mountain frontier. Amazingly, in these fast-changing times, the pioneers of that frontier had been there, at best, only twenty years.

Part of that vanishing frontier was Yellowstone National Park, entering its second decade in the 1880s. With no park service or experience to guide it, the federal government found itself faced with perplexing problems. When the railroad eased transportation to Montana, tourism increased, at least in nineteenth-century terms. When President Chester Arthur and his party spent three weeks in the park in August 1883, Yellowstone attracted the widest publicity yet; the American public had never before read so much about this wonderland.

Most of the visitors came away enthralled. Margaret Cruikshank, a Minneapolis teacher, journeyed there with a party in 1883. She wrote, "It was dear Old Faithful—the never-disappointing, the beautiful, the grand, the typical geyser." Nor was she disappointed with the falls of the Yellowstone, which proved equally spellbinding: "We all agreed that earth could not furnish another such beautiful sight. I shall never forget it." Her guidebook, though, did disappoint Cruikshank because it claimed for the pools around Old Faithful "pink and yellow margins and being constantly wet the colors are 'beautiful beyond description.'" Not so, thought Margaret, "then all I can say is that I must be color blind. I could see a faint ashes-of-rose tint, a pearly gray, and the tawny yellow of iron rust, but 'brilliant beyond description' makes one imagine vivid greens, intense yellows, clear blues."[10] It was obviously possible to overpromote such a wonder as Yellowstone National Park. Westerners had always been adept at exaggeration, and they grew better at it as the years went by. The Rocky Mountains would never be undersold or underappreciated by their boosters and biased authors.

Some of the visitors ill-used the natural wonders. Owen Wister came west in 1887 and had harsh words for tourists who engraved their names on the sides and bottoms of hot springs and geysers: "I hope they'll have to write their names in Hell with a red-hot pen-holder." Philetus Norris, one of the best and most energetic superintendents of the park, suggested that a gamekeeper be employed to cut down on the killing of wildlife and to draw up rules and regulations for visitors.

The Department of the Interior did not concern itself with over-promotion; its primary responsibility was park administration. The administrations of a series of superintendents (including three in slightly over four years) had averaged out to a few successes and more failures. Faced with policing and concession problems, lack of finances, park vandalism, and staffing woes, these men had not always provided the leadership and protection necessary. To be fair, all the blame should not be laid to them; the federal government administered Yellowstone in a haphazard fashion. The economic depression of the 1870s forced a cutback of operating funds, and the park was remote, far removed from other, more pressing departmental demands. All considered, it was remarkable that the park was able to advance so steadily to become a Rocky Mountain attraction. Finally, in 1886, frustration led to a turn-over of park control to the army. With the Indian wars now history, new assignments became necessary and some military officers had always coveted a Yellowstone appointment.[11]

For the next generation, the United States Army policed Yellow-stone National Park. Visitors came to accept troops guarding and guid-ing in the park. When George Tutherly's father accompanied the first troops stationed in the park, a young boy's dream was fulfilled. He did not regret either the lack of a school or playmates, spending much time "in the saddle" during the summer and on "snowshoes" (skis) in the winter. Life at the post at Mammoth Hot Springs was full of fun for a young boy. Even with the publicity of President Arthur's earlier visit and promotion by the railroad, not a great many tourists arrived; to afford the train and stage fares and the hotel costs "required a fat pocket-book." Like many others, Tutherly concluded that the fall sea-son presented Yellowstone at its best, particularly for him, since almost no one remained there besides the troops.[12]

These westerners were a little bemused now when "cultured people from the eastern states and Europe," who had boldly journeyed to the Rockies by railroad in the 1880s, discovered a "newer, grander, and more beautiful world than has ever been found." The lure and charm of the mountains still worked its magic on inexperienced newcomers.

For tourists who wanted to experience something a little different during their visit, what became known as the dude ranch slowly evolved in the 1880s. Some emerged from working ranches, others from hunt-ing guides who broadened their appeal. In Middle Park, Colorado, and near Yellowstone National Park, travelers could relax at ranches that offered "good food," riding, fishing, guided trips, and other "western" experiences.

The easterners who came looking for the West of cowboys, outlaws, Indians, and adventure, so popularly portrayed in the dime novels and in Buffalo Bill's Wild West Show, were doomed to disappointment. Nor could they always trust their guidebooks, as in the case of Yellowstone. Denver might accurately be called a "beautiful city, beautifully situated," but nearby Littleton remained a long way from being the "location of the suburban residences of many of Denver's best citizens." As one easterner wrote, "You can never judge anything in these western places by their names, for the people seem to have a peculiar habit of giving high sounding names to the most insignificant places." That practice seemed only natural to the westerner, who was convinced that his or her community would grow up to be a city or, as one Butte resident humbly noted, the "Center of the country's interest and importance."[13] Inflated expectations died hard—William Gilpin and a generation of earlier boomers would have understood.

On this note the 1880s ended, and the 1890s were greeted by a proud people. The entire region was now part of the Union and vigorously intended to guide its own destiny. That "star of empire," so beloved by an earlier generation, firmly settled itself over the Rockies. Although the cattlemen might disagree, the last two decades had generally been good for the Rocky Mountain states.

It had been an interesting twenty years, full of the old and the new. Washington had played a major role and its services were required, but these westerners could never escape what they perceived to be entrapment in a colonial status.

Territorial political control had come from outside the region, but eventually that had passed away. Economic control was another matter. These Rocky Mountain miners and businessmen did not have enough investment capital of their own, and they were forced by necessity to look to the East and Europe. With those "foreign" funds came "foreign management" and the loss (or at least the curbing) of local control. Now it seemed they were in immediate danger of being an economic colony, not a bit more acceptable than being a political colony. What they planned to do about it awaited the new decade.

But as a result, in the Rocky Mountain states a general "we–they" opinion of outsiders permeated life and became ingrained in the region's consciousness; it would be passed from generation to generation. Be that as it may, these westerners continued to look to Washington, Wall Street, London, and elsewhere for the things they needed, complaining all the while about the loss of innocence and freedom that came as undesired baggage along with outside help. It seemed that only the land retained the flavor of bygone years and now they were marketing it.

Through it all, though, with typical enthusiasm, they looked forward to even better days in the nineties. With almost naive optimism, they surveyed their "empire's" wealth of resources and so much wide-open country and assumed it would last forever.

TOP: *Turn-of-the-century Butte proved that industrialization had triumphed. The Anaconda Mine sits in the distance. (Courtesy: Special Collections, Colorado College Library)*

BOTTOM: *In Butte, copper mining dominated; the mine owners ruled like feudal barons. Ore team, 1898. (Courtesy: Special Collections, Colorado College Library)*

TOP: *After environmental problems from smelting operations threatened Butte, the nearby town of Anaconda became the smelting center. (Courtesy: Special Collections, Colorado College Library)*

BOTTOM: *The railroad tied the Rocky Mountains together well into the twentieth century. Monida, Montana. (Courtesy: Montana Historical Society)*

TOP: *The serenity of this scene belies some vicious labor disputes that marred the prosperity of coal mining. Hanna, Wyoming. (Courtesy: Wyoming State Archives)*

BOTTOM: *The ethnic makeup of coal mining communities was evident in the Slovenian Club, Rock Springs. (Courtesy: Sweetwater County Museum, Green River, Wyoming)*

TOP: *"It was darn hard work, for darn little pay,"* remembered one cowboy. *There was little romance in Rocky Mountain ranching. (Courtesy: Patty McCall)*

BOTTOM: *Butte's Chinese community was the largest in the Rocky Mountains. Dr. Huie Pock's office. (Courtesy: Montana Historical Society)*

TOP: *President Theodore Roosevelt loved the Rockies, but some of his actions provoked the residents. (Courtesy: American Heritage Center, University of Wyoming)*

BOTTOM: *Baseball caught on quickly in the urbanized Rockies, and some towns, such as Trinidad, Colorado, built fine ball parks for their teams. (Courtesy: Jack Smith)*

TOP: *Yellowstone was still the region's most popular national park, but by 1915 there were three others to visit. Boiling Springs near Norris. (Courtesy: American Heritage Center, University of Wyoming)*
BOTTOM: *Rising Wolf Camp at Glacier National Park. (Courtesy: Montana Historical Society)*

Mesa Verde's ruins appeared like this to early visitors. Long House. (Courtesy: Mesa Verde National Park)

TOP: *Rocky Mountain National Park was the region's youngest, but soon became a very popular attraction. (Courtesy: Denver Public Library, Western History Department)*

BOTTOM: *Each state had an impressive university to woo students. This is the University of Montana's Main Hall. (Courtesy: Montana Historical Society)*

TOP: *The 1908 University of Colorado football team; "big time" sports were just around the corner. (Courtesy: Western Historical Collection, University of Colorado)*

BOTTOM: *When the automobile could reach the high-country mines, an era had ended. This one almost chugged up to the Tomboy above Telluride at 11,500 feet, but it had to have help from horses. (Courtesy: Patty McCall)*

9 : SILVER CRISIS

"A time to mourn"—Ecclesiastes 3:4

These westerners, who were convinced that they could guide their own destiny, were thwarted by the tiger that stalked the land. They knew it as the "silver issue"; easterners less poetically called it the "monetary question." By whatever name, it rampaged as the most emotional issue of the 1890s. A turning point had been reached, and politically and emotionally these people would never be the same again. The region would never return to the "old days," and those who lived through it never forgot what happened to their lives.

The issue was not a new one, just the immediacy of it. Although few were paying attention at the time, its origins dated back to what had become known as the "crime of '73." Hardly a crime, the measure had simply discontinued coinage of the silver dollar. The federal government had taken this step for the practical reason that the price of silver on the market ranged slightly above that of the federally regulated coinage price. As a consequence, silver dollars were being removed from circulation. Americans hoarded them for their silver, not for their coinage value. The government also intended to establish gold as the only metal for a coinage standard, thereby stabilizing the somewhat inflationary greenbacks, or paper money. By backing the paper with gold reserves, greenbacks would be placed on a par with precious metal, which had an internationally established value of twenty dollars per ounce.

In previous decades, both silver and gold had been used for coinage. By a curious and long-sustained coincidence, the relative value of the two metals had stayed almost constant, roughly sixteen ounces of silver equal to one ounce of gold. Gold did not fluctuate on the world market, as silver did, making it a sounder monetary foundation from Washington's point of view.

By the late 1870s, when the government finally succeeded in stabilizing greenbacks with gold (assisted by the earlier discontinuance of silver-dollar coinage), the United States went on a de facto gold standard. From the conservative, business perspective, this step represented a progressive advancement. It promised to end the specter of inflationary currency, "soft money," which had haunted the business world. Most of the European nations had also discontinued the use of silver currency, so America marched right into line with the rest.

These tedious monetary theories and discussions did not interest westerners in the Rocky Mountains who were busily mining silver. They actually created the problem. In Leadville, Butte, and other districts, as well as in Nevada's Comstock and smaller districts, production skyrocketed and silver flooded the market. Overproduction came at the same time that countries were ending silver coinage and that industrial and commercial uses were limited. The price of the metal declined as a consequence. Miners who would not have considered selling to the mint at the previous lower price now turned with alacrity to Washington, only to find, to their horror, that Uncle Sam had quit buying. Their habit had been to turn to Washington in times of distress, but this time the government failed to respond. What had once seemed a routine bill then became a "crime," and, as silver orators charged, resulted from an "international conspiracy to demonetize silver."

As soon as pressure mounted, politicians started to cave in. One of the first to recant was President Grant, who admitted that he had not understood what he had signed. Considering all that had happened during his administration, such a confession should not be deemed remarkable. Meanwhile, western senators and congressmen lobbied for resumption of silver purchases and coinage at sixteen to one. This goal, once attained, would bring the price of silver back up to $1.25 and make silver mining more profitable. Joined by others who supported the inflationary idea of more money and cheaper currency (not necessarily for any benefit to mining), the silverites succeeded in getting the Bland–Allison Act passed in 1878, subsequently overriding President Rutherford Hayes's veto of it. The act ordered the secretary of the treasury to purchase from two to four million ounces of silver per month and coin the lot into silver dollars. Although the coins were legal tender, the results did not fulfill expectations. The treasury purchased the lowest possible amount and at the prevailing market price. The hoped-for guaranteed price of $1.25 per ounce never materialized. And as western mining kept gushing forth silver, the problem of surplus production, price, and market only worsened. The price of silver continued to go down, from an 1880 average of $1.15 to $0.94 in 1889. Thus was born the region-wide "silver issue."

Silver spokesmen leaped to the podium and took up the pen in mining-dominated Montana and Colorado. There was little need for conversion efforts, since these people already understood well that silver undergirded their economies. Silver advocates preached unequivocally the doctrine of "free and unlimited" silver coinage at the price of sixteen to one. The miner understood the reasons behind this position, but wisely, the appeal was broadened. The *Boulder News & Courier,* in December 1880, clearly showed the new focus when it insisted that silver represented the "best money" for the whole nation. The editor later argued that to deny silver its place would "reduce the wages of the working man" and, at the same time, "increase interest rates." Other spokesmen contended that since both gold and silver had been used as money from the earliest age, silver embodied the money "of the founding fathers." In continuing their historic affirmation, they concluded that history proved that not enough gold existed to serve the needs of mankind. Senator Henry Teller, who became one of the leading silverites, summarized the positive aspects: free silver would stimulate commerce, trade, and industry, provide good wages and steady employment, and open new "manufactories and more employment."[1] Similar statements emanated from Montana and other western silver-producing states. Their arguments, accurate to some degree, evidenced mostly self-interest, emotionalism, and breast-beating. But these were times when rhetoric seemed to overpower reality in the Rocky Mountains.

That silver could actually accomplish all these miracles seemed perfectly logical to its advocates, but infinitely less so to eastern political, banking, and business interests. In their opinion, these radical, unsupportable heresies threatened to undermine American business and government. The undaunted westerners continued to hammer away, gaining new converts with increasing success.

Nonetheless, the cause might have died had it not been for the hard times facing the farmers. Ensnared by a western boom that went bust, they saw their hopes die. They had the ill luck of arriving too late for the party; the good days had been the ones just before they got there, a common western complaint. Harassed by the old problems of overproduction (as the plains states opened) and falling prices, and too often in debt (easy credit had rushed west with the boom), farmers searched for a cure. They were caught uncomfortably in the middle. The farmer envisioned himself as a small businessman, clinging to the dignity of working for himself rather than wages, but he was actually part of the system that he was fighting against.[2]

Miners and farmers had several complaints in common. They worked too hard for too little reward. Both were angry at the East, one for its gold stand, the other because it demanded repayment of those loans. Westerners had been begging for money for years, even though it came with eastern economic dictatorship, which they abhorred. Both farming and mining had seen the good times go and willingly placed the blame on outsiders rather than on themselves. Finally, each group had vague, uneasy premonitions about European bankers' attempts to regulate western development. Desperation bred rumors of plots and a willingness to grasp straws for solutions.

The characteristic individualism of farming retrenched, as farmers resolutely turned to organization to try to acquire some political clout. First came the Grange, which had failed them in the 1870s as a political and economic weapon but lived on as a social and educational outlet. Next came the Farmers' Alliances of the 1880s, with their meetings, publications, and candidates. By 1890, with the pressure of hard times growing ever more acute, most western alliance men were convinced that the only salvation for the farmers lay in turning their organization into a full-fledged political party. This they proceeded to do, eventually calling it the People's party or, as it was more popularly known, the Populist party.[3] In the election of 1890, the Populists made strides in the farming areas, even electing three governors and two senators. As the popular orator Mary Elizabeth Lease proclaimed, "What farmers need to do is to raise less corn and more Hell."

The only thing that remained to be accomplished was the unification of the farmers and miners in a common cause under a common banner. Realizing that state and regional gains were not enough, the party issued a call for a national nominating convention in Omaha in July 1892. Here, finally, everything came together; the issue had found its movement.

Not so much a convention as a revival, it was characterized by almost unprecedented enthusiasm. Reform simmered in the July heat of Omaha. Along with other reforms, the platform and supplementary resolutions, adopted on July 4 amid a roaring demonstration, called for a graduated income tax, shorter hours for labor, direct election of

U.S. senators, and a single term for the president and vice president. Most important for the Rocky Mountains, the Populists adopted a plank that called for the "free and unlimited coinage of silver at the ratio of sixteen to one."

The party performed amazingly well, achieving the best new-party showing since the Republicans of 1856, but it went down to defeat nationally. Colorado gave its electoral college vote to the Populist presidential candidate, James Weaver. Weaver almost captured Wyoming with 47 percent of the vote; maverick Montana marched to its own drum, with only 16 percent for Weaver, but the new party made a respectable showing in local and state contests. The same proved true for all three states. Excited by their overall western success, the Populists looked eagerly ahead to the 1896 presidential election.[4]

During this time, the silver interests had obtained a little more help from Washington by way of the Sherman Silver Purchase Act. Passed in 1890 as a political tradeoff with silver Republicans, whose votes were needed for a crucial tariff vote, the measure required the treasury to purchase 4,500,000 ounces of silver per month. This amount, the estimated output of all the silver mines in the United States, would be bought, not with a guaranteed price, but at the world-market price. With this incentive, silver rallied temporarily to more than a dollar per ounce before slumping again. By election time in 1892, it had sunk to a new low, averaging eighty-seven cents. Silver needed help, and the silver interests looked to the Populist party as their savior.

Silver had become a convenient symbol for the revolt against the "money power" of Wall Street. For Colorado, and to a lesser degree Montana, silver held the key to economic success for the mining industry. Free coinage would not only aid the producers, but it would also stimulate the entire economy, from Main Street to farm lane. Tired of being a colony for outside interests, and keenly aware of this economic dependence, Coloradans rallied to populism. They agreed with Professor Coin (William Harvey), when he lectured in his fictional financial school:

> The gold standard, now fitted to a shivering world, is squeezing the life out of it.

> The bankers of the great money centers must be given to understand that they must take their hands off the throat of government. That they cannot dictate to the government what is money.

> Gold is breaking down the fabric of our institutions, driving
> hope from the heart and happiness from the minds of our
> people.

> Silver is the money of the people. Its integrity and identity
> was respected by our forefathers.[5]

Populism had become a crusade, a crusade of debtors versus creditors, westerners versus easterners, of the common people versus monied interests. As the *Silver Standard* (Silver Plume, Colorado) expressed, "he [silver miner] should furnish the 'sinews of war' with which to carry on the fight in the enemy's [goldbugs'] stronghold."

They all came—the common folk and the famous, the wealthy and the once wealthy—to raise the silver banner. Mortgaged to the hilt, Colorado's Horace Tabor ardently supported the cause and predicted in 1890: "Let silver drop to 75 cents per ounce and there would not be a silver mine worked in America, and all our western cities would be paralyzed; our railroads would cease to pay." Old railroader William Jackson Palmer lamented the insufficiency of currency and supported the silverites. Tabor, Palmer, and other silver men in Colorado and Montana mustered to save themselves and their era.[6] Politicians rallied to the cause, and silver wings seized control of, or strongly influenced, the Democratic and Republican parties.

When 1893 arrived, populism had won over Colorado and had made strong inroads into Montana, although it failed to gain much lasting support in Wyoming. Wyoming had virtually no silver production, few crop farmers, and was dominated by two primary private industries— coal mining and ranching. Both of the older parties managed to keep their identity; using a divide-and-conquer approach, they kept populism from making significant inroads by at least sympathizing with silver.[7] Wyoming notwithstanding, the Rocky Mountain region was ripe for political revolution.

Populist rhetoric and Populist action were both part of the Rocky Mountain experience. Free silver might capture center stage, but other reforms took hold. In the aftermath of Populist success in Colorado in 1892, women revitalized the somnolent suffrage campaign. With the older parties in disarray and the men in a reforming mood, it appeared to be an auspicious time. The Populist governor Davis Waite cooperated by signing a Populist-sponsored bill that gave the voters another chance to grant women the right to vote. The women organized themselves, and the national movement sent in the enthusiastic, energetic Carrie Catt to help. Over the objections of the saloon–liquor interests and

other scattered groups, the male voters approved the measure in the
fall of 1893, and Colorado became the first state to grant women voting
privileges. Catt later wrote that the campaign had been neither as
elaborate nor as thorough as later efforts, but she believed Wyoming's
positive experience was a "factor everywhere." She and others credited
Colorado women with rejuvenating the movement at exactly the right
time and with conducting a successful campaign that "proved virtually
impossible to repeat until much later."[8]

Then, like a bolt out of the blue, came a staggering blow—the crash
of 1893. Banks failed, businesses closed, men and women were thrown
out of work, and bankruptcies multiplied. The depression reached its
depths in July. Despite the rallying cry of the *Rocky Mountain News* on
July 20—"Shoulder to shoulder, men, while the war upon Colorado
continues"—Colorado fell into desperate straits. How bad was it? Within
days, twelve Denver banks closed, real estate values tumbled, and by
September 1 a survey of the state revealed 337 business failures, 435
mines closed, and 45,000 persons "thrown out of employment since
July 1." Comments from throughout Colorado reinforced the depth of
the crisis: "No money in the country. Prices greatly depressed (Las
Animas County); Hard times and money scarce (Saguache County);
The situation is very bad, all credit business is stopped and many are
in need of the common necessaries of life (Garfield County)." From
the silver-mining counties came even worse scenarios: business, completely stagnated, "will get worse before better"; the people "are almost
destitute." After twenty business failures, ninety mine closings, and
twenty-five hundred men forced out of work, Leadville was reported
to be "gloomy," which matched the moods of Aspen, Ouray, Breckenridge, Georgetown, Silverton, and Telluride. The heart of Colorado's
economy had collapsed; the state was, according to one correspondent,
"very blue." One depressed miner wrote, "I must have my money, for
I am hard up."[9]

Wyoming did not descend so far into the doldrums, but its economy
shuddered and slipped. The cattle industry had not completely rebounded from the 1880s. When the UP went into receivership, the
depression made its impact on the people of the plains and mountains.

Montana's economy reacted much like Colorado's; in some ways,
the before-and-after contrast had been even sharper. It had expected
a boom in 1893; the *Helena Weekly Independent* of May 18 claimed that
it sat "at the threshold of an era of advancement." That threshold would
never be crossed. The silver districts caved in, their towns abandoned.
On the morning of August 1, the whistle at the Granite Mine was tied

down, screaming until no more steam remained; the silver era had ended. A. L. Stone witnessed the leave-taking at Philipsburg:

> It was the most complete desertion I have ever seen . . . Down the roadway on Aug. 1 came the queerest, most incongruous procession ever seen. No one had stopped to pack. Everything was thrown helter skelter . . . a continual stream of almost panic-stricken people leaving, perhaps forever, their home in the mountains.

Butte's copper shield failed to prevent it from suffering a "general business depression." In the winter of its despair, Montana's mining heart closed many of its mines and businesses, as laid-off workers gave up trying to find jobs. Montana had twenty-thousand men out of work. Butte teemed with idle men, its non-copper-yielding mines having long since closed.[10] Silver, once the vital, driving force of the economy of western Montana, was dead; copper would now dominate totally.

Samuel Hauser, in Helena, wrote to a friend in August, "You have no idea how broken up we all are." With 130 business failures statewide and thousands of men out of work, stopgap relief measures quickly played out. The destruction of silver "seemed to destroy all hope." To make matters worse, the depression stubbornly hung on, here and elsewhere. Rollin Hartt wrote to his mother from Helena, in December 1896, that "the one need of Montana is money enough to get back East. Nobody likes the West . . . Of course, this feeling would be different if money was free and plentiful as it used to be."[11]

Hope truly seemed to be destroyed, and money gone. Once again, the Rocky Mountains learned in a brutal way just how closely tied they were to the rest of the country and to the world. The crash had caught silver mining in a vulnerable period, with a low metal price (averaging seventy-eight cents that year), lower-grade ore, a shortage of capital, and higher mining and smelting costs. The panic and crash, however, had come from the outside, not from within.

Domestic and international problems triggered the disaster. Over-expansion and debt, a continued decline in farm prices that produced a correspondingly depressed farm belt, and reduced wages and buying power for industrial workers at home contributed their share to the tragic circumstances. A volatile world money market and financial situation, and an unfavorable balance of trade, set the scene. The panic erupted, though, over lack of confidence in the economy's future, allied with the emotional issue of a 100,000,000-dollar gold reserve in the federal treasury. In late April 1893, that barrier was broken when the treasury's gold reserve sank as a result of collapsing revenues and mounting expenses. Panic set in when the traditional belief was shattered that the government would stay solvent as long as that magic amount continued to be held in reserve. All the other factors reacted to that one, and the panic became a depression. Within a year, fifteen thousand business failures were recorded nationally, seventy-four railroads went into bankruptcy, and four hundred banks closed their doors, mostly in the West and South. Colorado and the Rocky Mountains saw themselves as the primary victims, but the whole country suffered equally.

A heavy burden had been placed on the treasury from a variety of sources, which led to the diminishment of the 100,000,000-dollar reserve. A higher tariff that reduced annual revenue, lavish expenditures of the Harrison administration, especially Civil War pensions, and the Sherman Silver Purchase Act had precipitated the fatal gold drain.[12]

The new president, conservative Democrat Grover Cleveland, promptly called Congress into special session to repeal what business leaders and others saw as the culprit, the obnoxious Sherman Silver Purchase Act. They assumed that this expedient would halt the decline and restore public faith. In the judgment of easterners, that would be the easiest choice to make, both politically and economically. Shocked western silver-mining interests mobilized to defeat what seemed to be the final blow to an already badly depressed industry. Senators Henry Teller, Henry Wolcott, and others led the fight. Young Nebraska Representative William Jennings Bryan gave an impassioned, three-hour speech: "On one side stand the corporate interests of the United States, the moneyed interests, aggregated wealth and capital, imperious arrogant, compassionless . . . On the other side stand an unnumbered throng." Wolcott complained of the pressure placed on him by eastern interests, but held firm, declaring that "any other course than the one followed would have been unfair to Colorado interests." For three months the fight dragged on, to no avail; the act was repealed. Within a year, the price of silver collapsed into the sixty-cents-an-ounce range.

The immediate result was renewed support for the Populists and free silver. The *Engineering and Mining Journal* consoled that no western state would go out of business, whatever the price of silver fell to, and chided Colorado for its complaining. But for Coloradans, it seemed that the end of their world had surely come. Admonishing that the depression "is teaching thrift, not only in the household, but also at the mine and in the mill," provided little comfort. Nor did Wolcott's hope for an international effort on behalf of free silver.[13] Coloradans and, to a lesser degree, Montanans clamored for action while the depression went on and on, refusing to release its iron grip.

Montana senator Thomas Carter caught the vision of what a silver victory would mean:

> Smoke will issue from the factories again; the laborer will joyously emerge from enforced idleness . . . confidence will mark the step of the plowman; the miner will strike the drill with renewed energy; the merchant will stock his gaping shelves anew; hope and determination will cheer and strengthen every citizen.[14]

The promised land once more loomed in view, just as it had in 1859 and 1862. It awaited only a political savior to bring it to hand.

Westerners achieved their goal in 1896. Over the protests of Teller and other silverites, the Republicans nominated William McKinley on a gold platform. The gauntlet had been thrown down. Teller and the others bolted and watched, as the Democrats, moved by Bryan's famous "Cross of Gold" speech, nominated the youthful orator, politician, and newspaperman and adopted free silver and much of the Populist reform idealism. The stunned Populists also nominated Bryan, stubbornly selecting a different running mate.

East versus West, goldbug versus silverite, debtor versus creditor, ruralite versus urbanite, old America versus new America—the battle of causes and standards was joined. Free silver now became the rallying cry for a multitude of groups, as Bryan took his campaign to the people. From Silverton, Colorado, to Butte, Bryan supporters organized, rallied, and concurred with the *Silverton Standard* that "Bryan is our man, first, last and always." Butte's James Daly was reportedly Bryan's greatest single campaign contributor. The *Helena Weekly Independent*, the *Rocky Mountain News,* and scores of Rocky Mountain newspapers headlined their editorial columns, "Bryan & Sewall." Even gold-dominated Cripple Creek came out for Bryan: "Bryan is one of the people—one of our people. Give him your support." Well-known mining engineer James Hague, on his way to examine the Tomboy Mine, wrote to his wife, "In Colorado Bryan is regarded as a Moses, a divinely appointed leader of the people, or, at least, a Lincoln, raised up to save and redeem his people."[15]

"The Boy Orator of the Platte" swept all three Rocky Mountain states; the Colorado results were astounding—nearly 85 percent of the vote. In La Plata County, Bryan won 2,796 to 88; in Pitkin County, 3,020 to 16; and in farming Mesa County, the vote was nearly as one-sided, 2,369 to 469. The dream was dashed, however, when Bryan and free silver failed to carry the nation. The East and Midwest had not heeded the message. For the Populists there would be no future—they had been swallowed by the Democrats. Free silver, too, was dead; although, in an unexpected way, it had lost the battle while winning the war. For a decade thereafter, Coloradans would be involved with the silver issue; politicians risked political suicide if they declined to support the cause. Montanans did not carry the banner that long; for them, 1896 was the high-water mark. Other issues and the strange developments in Butte took their minds off the stinging defeat, although they did not abandon their distrust of the East and large corporations. Wyoming, never so enthusiastic as the others, quickly returned to its traditional political individualism.[16] Bryan would be back, but not free silver; it died in the ballot box.

The 1896 election stood as the apex of political unity for the Rocky Mountain states. Two of the states had much in common, and the collapse of their silver mining, tied to the shock of the depression, solidified them as never before. Wyoming—also hit by the depression and incited by the decade's political emotionalism and the western appeal of populism—fell into step. The exigencies of the moment brought to the Rocky Mountains a unity and political momentum that would be rare in the twentieth century. What seemed like radicalism to easterners was really a defense of basic conservatism. To preserve their way of life, these westerners were willing to venture out onto a political limb—a reform movement whose sweeping implications they probably did not totally understand. They accepted the known and the unknown to preserve their unrealized hopes of achieving their promised land. In so doing, they made a significant impact on national politics. The attention of both political parties and the voters across the country had been attracted, either in support or in opposition to populism and free silver. The 1896 battle of the standards had been lost, and silver would not arise from the ashes of defeat. But the reform impulse lived on. Many of the reforms advocated by the Populists would reappear within a decade under new leadership.

10 : NEW WORLD OF MINING

Mining was down but not out in the Rocky Mountain states. Colorado would be spared further economic miseries because of a last great gold rush to Cripple Creek. Ironically, gold from this discovery, plus discoveries in other new districts in Alaska and Nevada, would do what many had hoped free silver would do—increase the world's monetary supply, allowing currency expansion. That development had not been in the mind of Bob Womack, a ne'er-do-well cowboy given to carousing, when he turned to prospecting while punching cattle on the west side of Pike's Peak.

Womack found some promising gold-bearing float in the 1880s, but he could neither find the source nor convince others to help him. Finally, in 1890, he opened a claim and at last attracted some attention from the other side of the mountain at Colorado Springs. For the next two years, interest mounted until promoter George Parsons was moved to say, "All Colorado Springs has gone into Cripple Creek, so enthusiastically that for the present, there is no use trying to get them into anything else." When the summer of 1891 arrived, claims had been staked on all the hills around Cripple Creek in the ten-thousand-acre bowl of volcanic rock. Showing little surface gold, these gold-bearing lodes ran so contrary to previous Colorado experience that the amateur was likely to do as well as the expert in the game to find the paying claim. Find them they did, and Cripple Creek concluded Colorado's mining epoch with the *real* Pike's Peak rush at last.

Its mines were producing over two million dollars in gold in 1893, and by decade's end, eight times that. Gilpin County and Central City were eclipsed in a twinkling by Colorado's new gold king. The *Engineering and Mining Journal* of August 26, 1893, had been absolutely right in declaring that gold, not silver, held the state's future. The editor predicted that men would look back sometime at "utterances of the present day [free silver] with simple wonder at the folly."[1] The chance that tomorrow might be golden consoled few, if any, silver Coloradans; however, the *Journal* had made one of the best predictions of the day.

Once more, a mining district had become legendary in its own day. Once more, the western vision of great fortune seemed about to be realized in the Rocky Mountains. Men could make millions at Cripple Creek, and Colorado would prosper once more.

Among the discoverers of bonanza mines was Winfield Scott Stratton, an itinerant carpenter and prospector, who had pursued his quest throughout Colorado without notable success. At Cripple Creek, his Independence Mine made him a millionaire several times over, before he sold it in 1899 to English investors for ten million dollars. Stratton headed a select company of at least twenty-seven, all of whom attained millionaire status, thanks to Cripple Creek gold. Shrewd and cautious, Stratton also owned the largest share of stock in the Portland Mine, which outproduced his Independence; in his own stubborn way, he became what Horace Tabor had been earlier.[2]

If all roads had once led to Leadville, they now led to Cripple Creek. That district, the town of Victor, and the satellite camps became national news; the curious and hopeful came to "see the elephant" one more time, just as they had thirty or so years before. Now, however, an urgency existed: they wanted to see it before it vanished for the last time. A thread of melancholy wove through the excitement, a feeling that the old West was passing and must be sampled now or be lost forever. Seeing the elephant had certainly become easier. There were no more long stage or wagon rides; the railroad had cut the time required for the trip and made it more comfortable, and it would soon reach the Pike's Peak area. What better jumping-off point than Colorado Springs?

James D. Hague, who, in the course of his long career, inspected many Colorado and western mines for investors, went to Cripple Creek in 1895. Much impressed, he correctly predicted that the district would maintain a "permanent mining industry for years to come," with its very favorable overall conditions, such as transportation, fuel costs, and ease of access. Hague had some concern about the validity of titles—the general surface seemed "to be deeply covered with a multitude of mining claims or locations." He feared an encounter with that curse of mining, the apex lawsuit, which provided lawyers and expert witnesses throughout the West with a comfortable living while it kept owners in a state of anxiety. With bitter-edged humor, some called the mine the "lawyers' pit." As mining matured and became more industrialized, it took on the complexities of modern American industrial life. The lawyer and the lawsuit were just two of the many aggravations with which Stratton and his generation had to contend, as mining evolved from the freewheeling days of yesteryear.

Hague had been sent to examine the Portland Mine. One of the potential investors in the mine warned the veteran mining engineer: "You will have to be very careful to avoid being fouled or salted, if I am to believe stories I hear about morality of Cripple Creek gentlemen!" He worried unnecessarily in this case. Hague spent nearly a month in the district and advised against the purchase, calling it "ill-advised and at the high price asked for is extremely hazardous." The asking price of 3½ million dollars was "too much for a prudent purchaser," and he feared that the property was subject to an apex suit. However, if Stratton included the Independence in the offer, "with its wonderful ore body," at "any reasonable price," then it would be a bargain worth pursuing.[3] The deal never materialized.

Danger lurked for the naive investor in the golden glitter of Cripple Creek. Mining engineer Ellsworth Daggett wrote to his friend Hague about a property he had examined. If the company's prospectus was correct, it

> indicates a very extraordinary, in fact an unprecedented state
> of affairs. For this amount of ore if assumed at the average
> thickness of all the ore that has been hitherto extracted
> would not only entirely fill the space between the two
> tunnels, but as it would go neither above, below or beyond
> the two tunnels would have to project as a slab of ore one
> foot thick and 181 feet high over 400 feet horizontally out
> into the air over and across Elkton gulch and probably into
> Squaw Mountain on the other side—why out in Elkton Gulch
> they would have to trestle up into the air three or four
> hundred feet to mine it.[4]

The buyer needed to beware. In the world of Rocky Mountain mining of the 1890s, a multitude of individuals, with varying degrees of trustworthiness, lay in wait to relieve the guileless of their extra cash.

George Parsons, a promoter and seller of mines, explained the problems from the other side: "The placing of mines is a delicate matter at the best, & the purchasers always hold the seller responsible if everything does not turn out as stated." He recommended that great care "must be taken not to misrepresent or overstate in the least." Even so, he berated one investor for trying in an "unmanly way" to get information, and to another he frankly wrote, "I cannot answer such abusive letters as you write."[5]

The rapid rise of Cripple Creek gave clear evidence of the changes that had materialized over the years. Railroads, telephones, electricity, and other modern improvements had come simultaneously with a stock exchange, college-trained mining engineers, the most improved mining equipment, incorporation, and dominance by large companies. Womack made little from his discovery and left the district for Colorado Springs to live with his sister. Stratton appreciated and remembered him with a five-thousand-dollar gift; few others honored him in more than name. The day of the hoary prospector and his mule disappeared along with the days of 1859. Modern industrial America replaced the poor-man's diggings and the independent miner who worked only to discover his big bonanza. Come to stay was the corporation, with its management, its investors, and a ruthless drive for profits. Stratton and some of his friends, like Jimmie Doyle and Jimmie Burns, were the lucky ones, the last of their Rocky Mountain breed. No more Cripple Creeks would be found over the next mountain.

Mining in the remainder of the Rocky Mountains, outside of Butte, Cripple Creek, and the coming-of-age San Juans, held out a mixed bag of possibilities in the 1890s and the early twentieth century. Dredging was doing well in Montana and gaining adherents in Colorado, bringing a new technology to long-declining placer districts. The boats and their ponds would soon churn up stream beds throughout the Rockies. Hard-rock mining in Wyoming suffered, much like old Atlantic City, which appeared to visitors as a "dilapidated looking row of buildings," and neighboring South Pass, a "sleepy place." Wyomingites still had hopes for precious metals, but they were forced to face the fact that unromantic coal dominated their present and would prevail as the state's mining future.[6]

In Butte, already self-proclaimed as the "world's greatest mining camp," the political shenanigans, the almost obscene crass materialism, the close ties between business and politics, and the clash of high-strung, egotistical individuals resembled what was happening elsewhere in the American business world. The eccentricities of the wealthy always seemed to catch the public's interest as a slice of contemporary

Americana. When placed in the romantic Rocky Mountains and mixed with the settlement of the West, they became particularly fascinating. For Montanans, caught in the "war of the copper kings" and forced to live with the results, the copper kings proved decidedly less enchanting.

Why they fought so bitterly in Butte was a puzzling question. Other mining districts had produced their millionaires, some of whom were every bit as driven, willful, and as jealous of each other as William Clark and Marcus Daly. The rapid industrialization and wealth that had come to this remote corner of the Rocky Mountains had produced an endlessly intriguing community and mining world. That combination helped to explain the background for trouble, but Cripple Creek also had a large measure of the same ingredients. The Butte stakes appeared to be higher, the personalities more sharply etched, than anywhere else in the Rockies or in the West of that day. Montana, large in size, small in population, could be manipulated, actually dominated, by a single industry and its kingmakers. With local and state control on the line and a copper empire to be gained, and with the tantalizing personal rewards that would surely come, the prize seemed worth the gamble. When strong-willed personalities and Butte's big money clashed, the shock waves rolled to Wall Street, Washington, and beyond. As a recent historian has noted, it was like "dinosaurs, mastodons, and sabertooth tigers squaring off for a fight."[7] Americans loved it.

Never before in the Rocky Mountains had two such strong, antagonistic personalities dueled, backed by more than enough money to achieve their ambitions. When Daly and Clark squared off, it would be a battle to the end. Both of these men had been fighting for fortunes since they arrived in Butte, and both had succeeded abundantly. In one corner waited frosty, tough, little penny-pinching William Clark, his lack of humor matched only by his ruthless ambition. In the other corner stood that stocky, gregarious, never-say-die Irishman Marcus Daly, the miners' miner. Not a few Montanans firmly believed that the two men had been born to hate each other. The origins of their feud were lost in the smoke of Butte, but it burst out into the open in 1888 when Democrat Clark decided to run for delegate to Congress.[8]

Much to his own astonishment, Clark was beaten, and he never forgot the injury to his pride or changed his self-righteous opinion that he had been the victim of political treachery. Clark had assumed the Irish would line up solidly behind his candidacy, but to his utter amazement, they voted Republican. Clark saw Daly behind his defeat; no doubt, a glass of beer here, a cigar there, and veiled threats about job security had done the trick. His ambition whetted, Clark ran for the senate in 1890, only to fall victim to disputed election returns; he could only stand by and watch as the U.S. Senate voted to seat the Republican candidate. Once launched, Clark let nothing stop him. He was determined to go to Washington. In 1893, Clark ran again, stubbornly opposed by Daly. Newspapers on both sides charged fraud and bribery, and the legislature could not reach a decision, adjourning in deadlock. For the next two years, Montana had only one senator.

These skirmishes served only as preliminaries to the main event, which pitted Clark against Daly over the emotional issue of the location of the state capital. As in Colorado, the Montana constitutional convention had dodged this thorny issue by providing for a popular referendum in 1892. Montanans turned out in record numbers to select Helena and Anaconda from among the contenders; a runoff election was scheduled in 1894. Clark and the "Queen City of the Rockies" (blatantly ignoring Denver's claim!) stood toe to toe against Daly's pet, a town he had created with his smelter. To some Montanans, the choice appeared to be severely limited: the town of entrenched political power and perceived snobbishness versus the company town, a tool of corporate power. The feud raged white hot until election day. Both sides organized clubs, campaigned, propagandized, and accused. Clark poured a reputed million dollars into the campaign, in exchange, apparently, for Helena's support in his next senatorial bid. Rallies, banners, slogans, and all manner of promotional hoopla inundated Montanans. Daly tried equally hard to stop Clark and secure a win for Anaconda. Finally, it all ended when voters decided to keep the capital at Last Chance Gulch.

November 6, 1894, became the single most important day in Helena's history. A thousand cheering inhabitants met Clark's special train and pulled him in a man-powered carriage through the streets. The celebration went on long into the morning hours, with liquor flowing freely.[9] This time Daly would neither forget nor forgive.

Clark's itch to go to the Senate apparently grew uncontrollable, and he launched another campaign in 1898. Daly's newspapers, influence, and money stood in bitter opposition. A rematch of earlier races unfolded, as the two sides tried to elect legislators sworn to their position. A Clark paper charged that "every irresponsible loafer and bum in the city [of Butte] was shouting for Marcus Daly and jingling in their pockets the price of their votes"; a Daly organ complained about "the lying and thieving tactics of the Clark forces." Daly gained the initial election victory, but Clark's money, reportedly 431,000 dollars, swung the needed legislative votes. Helena enjoyed another all-night binge, thanks to Clark.

Down but not out, Daly forces regrouped and accused Clark of buying his way to the Senate, producing evidence to support the charge. Clark found himself denounced in pulpit and press and attracted unexpected national publicity. Daly relentlessly carried his fight to Washington, where over ninety witnesses described the strange goings-on to a bemused committee and nation. Clark resigned, as the committee prepared to report and refuse him his seat. Completely impervious by now to shame or criticism, Clark then jockeyed to have himself appointed to the now-vacated senate seat. In the absence of Governor Robert Smith, a Daly supporter, the lieutenant governor named his friend Clark as senator! Clark made no attempt to take the post. The would-be senator returned to Montana, as he had promised, to vindicate himself; vindication would be made on his own terms, of course. At substantial cost and with a series of alliances, he won control of the state Democratic machinery and was elected to serve a full term in the Senate. By the time his triumphant rival was finally seated, Daly had died and the victory was a hollow one. The epitaph to the whole sordid mess reputedly came from Clark himself: "I never bought a man who wasn't for sale."[10]

The real crime had been the exploitation of Montana. The clash of these two egocentric personalities had brought unprecedented political turmoil and scandal. This classic confrontation of raw, unrestrained western capitalism had come to an end. Daly was dead, but he left a greater heritage than Clark—the organization that became the Anaconda Mining Company, one of America's great corporations. Subsequently controlled by the Rockefeller interests, this astutely managed, carefully integrated (Daly had brought together timber, coal mining, ranching, smelting, and transportation), and strongly independent company would continue the war of the copper kings for several years to come.[11] Clark, with his victory in his pocket, spent an undistinguished term in Washington, always tainted by the scandals that put him there.

Butte showed the naked power of mining millionaires irrationally fighting for personal satisfaction (rather like the legendary western gunfighter), and it was not over as the new century dawned. The cast had changed, however.

In a fuzzy series of developments, Daly had sold out (shrewdly taking stock with him) to Rockefeller interests (Standard Oil), which consolidated the holdings into the Amalgamated Copper Company.

The *New York Times* of April 18, 1899, observed that the consolidation "places Standard Oil capital and Standard Oil brains" in control of a very large portion of the world's copper production. Throughout American industry at the turn of the century, consolidation was emerging as a dominant trend. Central management promised more power and profits, and the Rockefeller group envisioned a copper empire that might eventually dominate the world market. Despite the fact that Daly served as president of the new company, the real power lay with the guiding genius behind the merger, Henry Rogers. To some, he was the embodiment of the perfect Victorian gentleman. A friend of Mark Twain and a generous benefactor, the intelligent Rogers became a brutal, ruthless, secretive, and driving individual when it came to business. Now a "foreign corporation with unlimited resources and vast power" controlled what Clark did not.[12] Montana had never seen its like before.

Winning that cherished Senate seat at last, Clark had gone off to Washington but continued to play a role in the final struggle. The Rockefeller group would not go unchallenged. Audacious, handsome, and amiable Frederick Augustus Heinze strode upon the scene and took on the company, with Clark's blessing. A Columbia School of Mines graduate with further study in Germany, "Fritz," who, as one historian noted, "was not heavily burdened by scruples," had arrived in 1889. After studying the "richest hill on earth," he set about to conquer it. His star rose spectacularly over Butte; he built a smelter, acquired control of several mines, and moved to play his game under his rules.

Unlike Clark and Daly, who had battled for legislative control, Heinze relied on the courts. His trump cards were the apex law and a "pet" county judge. He had once written his mother, "My dear Mother, I cannot fight a band of robbers by singing hymns and sprinkling holy water." Heinze used neither tactic when he claimed that two rich Amalgamated veins apexed on his property; therefore, he could follow them, "with dips angles and variations," downward to any depth beyond his sidelines. Amalgamated's attorneys fought back with legal actions, but Heinze's ever-loyal county judge, William Clancy, never swerved in his loyalty as he handed down decisions. Clark joined the fray, seeing it as a way to help him win that Senate seat and to humiliate Anaconda and, through it, Daly. Heinze needed Clark's money, and thereby an alliance was formed.

Through their newspapers, Heinze and Clark attacked "the trust" and, to top Daly's popularity, granted their miners an eight-hour day.

The dying Daly could only refer to Heinze as a "blackmailer, a thief and a most dangerous and harmful man to the business and property interests of Butte." Words alone would not stop him. Heinze made himself into a masterful orator, carrying his emotional arguments to the people. He pictured himself as a David opposing Goliath, a champion of the little man against the corporate evil. When Clark, his prize in hand, left the state, Heinze stood alone. Clark had no real quarrel with Anaconda, for he had secured what he sought. The Clark–Heinze alliance was dissolved. That action did not deter Heinze in the least; he went on baiting and attacking the "trust" with glee.

In Butte, lawsuit piled upon lawsuit, and litigation overburdened the court. At the height of this litigious period, thirty-seven lawyers labored on Heinze's behalf, coping with nearly one hundred lawsuits. Clancy and another pro-Heinze judge, Edward Harney, loyally supported their benefactor. Meanwhile, Heinze was mining ore out of Anaconda property, claiming the right by virtue of the apex law. Occasional underground warfare broke out: heads were bashed, powder was shot off, and smoke fumed through neighboring shafts. The miners suffered and several were killed.

Both sides broadened their base, attempting to control state, county, and judicial officials. Rogers and Anaconda managers confronted myriad tangled problems in a defensive, heavy-handed manner that often played into Heinze's hands. Money remained Anaconda's main weapon. Heinze's strongholds were in Silver Bow County and Butte, where he had become something of a folk hero by fighting the company.[13] Outside that area, he lacked the resources to compete on an equal basis with his rivals. To make matters worse, Anaconda bought out independent newspapers or forced them with threats to join a statewide network to wage the battle. Heinze had primarily only one on which to rely, the *Butte Reveille*.

By 1903, Rogers and his company had had enough of this upstart's aggressive attacks. They picked a good time to call Heinze's bluff, although they did not fully realize it at the time. Heinze was playing a bold hand, but his finances were nearly exhausted. His base, too, had eroded. Amalgamated exerted great influence in Butte; no matter how well the miners might love Heinze, Anaconda paid more of their wages. And the company's strength—its control of most of the newspapers—allowed it to paint whatever picture it wanted throughout the state. The cost was inconsequential, for the stakes were well worth the gamble. In late October, Amalgamated played its trump card by closing down mines, smelters, coal mines (it owned Wyoming and Montana coal mines), and lumber mills throughout its vast empire (which, incidentally, included the Butte Water Works)—everything, with the major exception of its statewide newspaper chain. Some twenty thousand men found themselves out of work. Charges and countercharges were bandied about. Heinze could claim that there was no reason to stop work, but Anaconda saw the matter differently.[14]

Regardless of the charges, this was no mere strike or shutout—it was the "bludgeoning of an entire state." Montanans everywhere were affected and read in the company-controlled newspapers that "crooked" F. Augustus Heinze was the cause of their troubles. Heinze hammered at the old theme of Standard Oil domination, less effective now that pocketbooks were hurting and desperation had set in. The Flathead *Herald Journal* correctly asserted that "a deep, dark, damnable game is being played." Both sides could have pleaded guilty to that charge. Anaconda refused to desist and made its next move, demanding that the legislature pass a "Fair Trials Bill," which would permit a change of venue if either party to a civil suit deemed the judge to be corrupt or prejudiced. Only then would Montana go back to work. Petitions and pressure, and approaching winter, worked; popular Democratic governor Joseph Toole called a special session.

Toole realized only too well that this kind of intimidation was an unprecedented coercion of state government. So did many of the legislators, who, in the face of bribery charges and other allegations, passed the "fair trial" law. Standard Oil won, Montanans went back to work, and "Fritz" Heinze went to the sidelines. With his control of the judges broken, he had no hope. In 1906, Heinze sold out to the company for 10.5 million dollars, and the "war of the Copper Kings" was over. In the process of tidying up the mess, all lawsuits were dismissed, the outspoken *Reveille* was closed, and Heinze packed himself off to New York to play the Wall Street market.[15] The progressive *Nation* summarized the outcome best in its February 22, 1906, issue: "Nobody comes out of the contest with clean hands, but at any rate there is now hope of ending it."

With a free hand, Amalgamated could consolidate its hold. It acquired Clark's mines and smelter and what few other properties remained on "the hill." They were all merged to become the Anaconda Copper Mining Company, which had severed its ties to Standard Oil. Colorado's time of troubles had been brief, but Montana's would stretch over the next generation. No other Rocky Mountain company would have so much control, so much dominance over an entire state's economy and politics. Blithely and relentlessly, Anaconda continued the tradition of Daly, Clark, and Heinze by compromising court and legislature and controlling information. Its methods might have been more subtle than the copper kings, but it achieved, on a grander scale, what they had started. Montana would be Anaconda's fiefdom.

Clark, Heinze, and Daly left behind this monument to unbridled capitalism in their adopted state. They epitomized the western capitalists, the ones "who truly built the West—at whatever cost!" They had expertly developed one of the world's great copper districts and, for two decades, used it and the state as their battleground, as personalities and egos clashed and scandal and corruption flourished. They had created jobs, supported a variety of auxiliary industries and communities, plundered and looted, and painted an image of western exploitation, extravagances, and eccentricities that fascinated Americans then and since.[16] They brought the western dream to its ultimate fruition.

Coal mining failed to capture such attention, even though Wyoming emerged as a major coal-producing state; production had increased from six million dollars in 1901 to eleven million dollars by decade's end. The coal-mining boom employed over eight thousand miners by 1910, with the majority coming from eastern Europe, particularly Italy. An inherently dangerous occupation, with its dust and gas, American coal mining trailed a record of disasters throughout its long history. Wyoming proved no exception, having experienced five major explosions that killed 448 men during this prosperous decade. The worst incident occurred on June 30, 1903, when 169 miners died at the Hanna No. 1 Mine. That same mine later killed 59 miners in two separate explosions on March 28, 1908. Edith Erickson remembered:

> There were several people at our house that day. Father, Andrew, Uncle Johnny, Uncle Andrew, myself and the baby, as we called her, and also two young fellows that were friends of Uncle Andrew.
>
> They all jumped up and put on their coats and left to see what had happened . . . The men asked me to leave the dominoes and drafts out so they could finish the game when they got back, so that's what I did. But they stayed so long I got the next meal ready for all of them, and waited and waited. At 10:15 that night it blew up again . . . killing all my family. The next morning was Sunday. I put the game away and the dishes of food I had cooked. You see, it was up to me to do these things. I didn't have a relative nearer than England, I was all alone if you understand what that is.[17]

The coal miners were all alone, too. They had never attracted the attention that hard-rock miners had. After the earlier explosion, the *Rock Springs Miner*, on July 2, 1903, simply described the dead as "100 Finlanders, 50 were colored, and the balance Americans."

In the rush for profits, coal miners paid the ultimate price with their lives. Not all the blame can be laid to the owners; some miners ignored the rules and their own safety in order to mine more tonnage per day. Economic self-interest created strange bedfellows. The story was the same in Colorado, where the horrifying total of 319 fatalities in 1910 stunned even the most jaded mine owners. Miners' lives were cheap (immigrants being particularly expendable); in fact cheaper, some argued, than the mules used to haul the coal to the surface. Living most often in drab, dirty, and isolated mining camps, far from the public eye, coal miners were largely ignored. Inexperienced in American customs and ways, they were exploited for their labor and, if necessary, for their votes. The companies ruled their lives from birth to death. As UP official D. O. Clark explained, "I would strongly recommend that we own the entire town site and control the entire business, building such buildings as necessary." Those were the circumstances in that industry, from the southern end to the northern tip of the Rockies. The mined coal was needed for the railroads, smelters, homes, businesses, and power-generating plants that underpinned the modern West, a West that almost totally ignored the ones who dug the coal, until it stopped coming.[18]

Protests about miners' working conditions were aired in the legislatures, but the legislators had shown only minimal interest after agreeing to some initial statutes. The safety regulations that were finally passed were undermined by a lack of, or only casual, state inspections and noncompliance by the companies. Wyoming provided for coal-mine inspectors, established ventilation requirements, and legislated other safety regulations: for example, as early as 1883, Colorado passed a Coal Mines Act, patterned after laws in Pennsylvania and eastern coal states. The legislation looked good only in the books.

Crass exploitation in the West was not limited to human beings; natural resources also came in for their share. To the amazement of some and the dismay of others, these resources appeared finite. Mother Nature's bounty had limits. The Rocky Mountains did not harbor an eternal mother lode that would extend from one generation to the next.

Wyoming's precious metal production, which had never amounted to much, collapsed to a total of forty-eight hundred dollars in 1909. Some copper excitement, especially at Encampment in the early 1900s, had kept hope alive briefly, but now even that flickered out. Governor Toole could exclaim in 1907 that "never in the history of the State has the magnitude of the mining industry been so impressive as during the past biennium," but he was referring more to Butte (the gold dredges and other corporation-controlled ventures), than to new rushes and poor-man's diggings. Taking out Cripple Creek and the San Juans, the same was true for Colorado; even those two districts were showing a slippage to lower-grade ore. Impressive amounts of gold and silver could still be mined in Colorado and Montana, however. In 1905, for instance, Colorado ranked number one nationally with thirty-one million dollars and Montana number three, with twelve million dollars.[19]

President Roosevelt, among others, had feared that the country was running out of resources, particularly coal and oil. Fortunately for the present generation, it turned out in both cases that the United States had plentiful supplies. New discoveries came to the rescue, postponing the crisis for another fifty years. The Rocky Mountains would experience its crisis much earlier—the era of precious metals was drawing to a close. It was time to look ahead to new resources.

Tumult and corporate control had dominated the major mining districts in the two decades that straddled the turn of the century. Like any other two-decade period, those years had their memorable moments and their regrettable ones, their good days and their bad. Many of the bad days had to do with labor relations, and nothing more clearly displayed the fact that Rocky Mountain development marched in step with the rest of America.

11 : ARISE, "ENFRANCHISED SERFS"

O nly a persistent Pollyanna among the miners could fail to see that mining had passed its high tide and the miners' profession was changing. Even the miners who flocked to Cripple Creek began to think of themselves as the last of their era. They found a new world awaiting them, one that many of them wished had never come. For a generation and until the 1890s, new districts had opened fairly regularly, allowing the dissatisfied and the hopeful to try their luck elsewhere. Now, the miners faced the brutal reality of being a hard-working daily laborer for someone else, who risked his money rather than his life.

Cripple Creek came at a most opportune time to relieve some of the pressure of the 1893 crash; miners gathered there from the demoralized silver districts. The last click of the safety valve only temporarily relieved the pressure. Cripple Creek at full steam could not absorb the labor surplus, nor could the maturing San Juans help much as their gold mines came to the forefront. The result was a surplus of miners, which presented an opportunity that did not go unnoticed by management, nor by the miners, who responded by joining a union. The potential for labor trouble sneaked into the district, just waiting for the chance to explode.

Unionism had been a factor in the mining West for years, with Nevada's Comstock being especially well organized. Its union maintained a four-dollar minimum wage and other benefits (including, at various times, medical and burial expenses) for its members, the underground workers, regardless of skill level. The union generously subscribed to the construction fund of St. Mary's Hospital and had "visiting committees" to contact ailing miners. Their union hall served as the center for meetings, social activities, a library, and theatrical entertainments; a complete set of prospecting gear was stored there to lend to members. Although they sometimes did strike, they usually tried to settle disputes more peacefully. With the Comstock peak a part of the past in the 1880s, the miners began moving to newer districts. As they spread throughout the West, they took with them their union concepts.[1]

No Rocky Mountain district ever completely complied with the pattern of Comstock unionism. Central City, Leadville, Butte, and other districts had their local unions, which lacked the unity and prestige of the earlier ones in the Comstock. The 1880 strike in Leadville had been the only major one, but still there were some very real questions about who motivated it and why. Management of certain mines had everything to gain and nothing to lose from a strike. Regardless of why it was undertaken, it was resolutely broken by the combined strength of the companies and the state, without granting any concessions to the workers. As long as new districts could lure workers with better prospects and higher wages, union advocates found themselves at a disadvantage.

This favorable situation, with new districts opening, eroded rapidly in Montana and Colorado during the 1880s. Industrialization, impersonalization, and loss of opportunity in the corporate-dominated world brought the hard, dirty work and low pay of the miner's life starkly into focus. Part of the price of precious metals was paid in advance by the men who worked in the mines—by the danger and death they faced every day. It did not take the miners long to realize that their labor conditions were changing. Their response was to form locals in such diverse points as Rico and Red Mountain, Colorado, and Granite, Montana. Unaffiliated with each other, the little locals gave the sense more than the reality of security.

In the early nineties, strikes were becoming more common, indicating the miners' growing sense of insecurity. Their insignificance in the industrial scheme of things made them extremely vulnerable to more powerful management, which was supported by conservative state administrations and courts. Out of this predicament came the call for a "grand federation of underground workers throughout the western states"; a bitter strike in 1892 in neighboring Idaho became the motivating *cause célèbre*. The Butte Miners' Union, one of the strongest, took the lead. Forty delegates convened in Butte on May 15, 1893, representing unions in Colorado, Idaho, Montana, Utah, and South Dakota. Out of their five days of deliberations emerged the Western Federation of Miners, the crucible for labor-management disputes for the next decade.

The WFM's purpose was stated simply: "men engaged in the hazardous and unhealthy occupation of mining should receive fair compensation for their labor and such protection from the law as will remove needless risk to life and health." It seemed a reasonable manifesto, considering the risks of hard-rock mining. The goals of the organization were easily understood, too. Among the ten were:

> To secure an earning fully compatible with the dangers of our employment.

> To procure the introduction and use of any and all suitable, efficient appliances for the preservation of life, health and limbs for all employees.

> To labor for the enactment of suitable mining laws, with a sufficient number of inspectors, who shall be practical miners, for the proper enforcement of such laws.

> To use all honorable means to maintain friendly relations between ourselves and our employers.

> To procure employment for our members in preference to non-union men.[2]

Miners applauded the achievement and joined the organization. Management, taken aback, watched warily; individual attitudes ranged from concern to outright hostility. In the beginning, the union made little impact, limping through the first year. Then a strike brought salvation.

Strikes had long ago given unions a bad name. As it moved west, unionism trailed a reputation for radicalism. The American public and conservative businessmen had not forgotten the violent coal miners and the railroad strikes of the 1870s. There appeared to be something suspiciously un-American about workers uniting and demanding certain conditions, made all the worse when foreign agitators could be found at the bottom of the trouble. For the workers, however, the union seemed to be their only hope against all-powerful management. Peaceful protests often failed; strikes furnished a viable alternative for the laborer.

Cripple Creek miners certainly agreed with the tactics. When the owners moved to reduce the standard $3.00 per day to $2.50 or, alternatively, to increase the work day from eight to ten hours at the same wages, the workers affiliated with the Western Federation. A miner with a family could barely make ends meet at the three-dollar wage. For the first time, Colorado miners had a strong union, dedicated leadership, and the potential support of fellow union members throughout the Rocky Mountains. The owners, however, were equally determined to show their strength and break the growing union dominance.

Unable to present a unified front on district-wide wages and hours, a group of determined owners took the offensive in January 1894. They also saw the opportunity to call the union's hand by forcing the issue. Unilaterally, they instituted a nine-hour day. Unimpressed by pious statements about hours in other Colorado mines and claims of how pleasant it was to labor in Cripple Creek's dry, well-ventilated works, the union struck. Its members stayed out in the face of threats and pressure. A few nonunion men, protected by armed guards, tried with scant success to keep some mines open. The strikers spewed venom, and tension mounted. Inevitably, the strike turned bitter.

From their headquarters on Bull Hill, near the extremely prounion town of Altman, the miners watched as the owners obtained a court injunction against strikers' interference, strengthened the pro-owners county sheriff and his deputies, and prepared to bring in nonunion miners. After winning the strike and breaking the union, they intended to prosecute union members for their "crimes." The pattern was all too familiar. Both sides armed themselves, organized small "armies," and waited for the war to begin. Observer Harry Newman predicted that "there will be considerable fighting and *blood* shed before the trouble is settled."

Trouble was not long in coming. A group of "bully-boy" deputies on their way toward Altman were routed, when the Strong Mine's surface workings blew up as their train approached, showering them with shrapnel. They hastened back down the hill. The next day, in a half-hour "skirmish," two men were killed and others wounded. The "armies" campaigned where a few weeks before miners had worked and mines had operated. Governor Davis Waite came to investigate personally and ultimately sent in the state militia. Under Waite's orders, the militia remained neutral while separating the two groups, but the issues were left unresolved. To avert further trouble, the owners' spokesmen and Waite, appointed by the union as its sole arbitrator, met at Colorado College in tranquil, antiunion Colorado Springs.

Waite was no typical conservative, business-oriented politician; he was a sixty-nine-year-old reformer, union member, and Aspen newspaper editor, who had been elected on the Populist ticket in 1892. Waite had earned a measure of national notoriety over his unsuccessful relief efforts, especially trying to coin silver dollars, and his statement, when discussing deteriorating 1893 conditions, that "it is better, infinitely better, that blood should flow to the horses' bridles, rather than our national liberties should be destroyed." If the owners expected help out of Denver, they were doomed to grave disappointment.

To the discomfort of the owners, Waite insisted on concessions by both sides and pleaded that "by-gones should be by-gones." The conference became turbulent, but with the governor stubbornly siding with the union, the outcome was decided: "I am at an age, by God, that I tell you, by God, you have got to concede something, that is all there is about it." When the two sides started wrangling about the statement that would be issued at the meeting's conclusion, Waite exploded again: "I want to make a sentence that means something. God damn those sentences that don't mean anything and take forty-five lawyers to say what they do mean."[3]

Waite's outburst proved too much for the disorganized owners, who had never been unified; Stratton had not cooperated with them or supported their goals. The National Guard disarmed the district, and the mines reopened. The Western Federation won a smashing victory over the owners, securing an eight-hour day at three dollars. The union rejoiced, the owners regrouped, and both waited for the next round. Interestingly, both sides lived up to the agreement in letter and spirit. The life of the state militia would never be the same; until now, it had been seen as a purely social organization by many of the recruits. There was nothing very social about dealing with irate owners and angry miners.

Never before had the Rocky Mountains experienced such fierce labor–management conflict. It was industrial and class warfare. Waite's idea of "good-fellowship" never materialized. No longer isolated from the rest of the United States nor, as was being abundantly shown, free from the economic and political problems that gripped all America, the new West of the Rocky Mountains looked remarkably like its contemporaries to the east. In silver's collapse, in the battle of the standards, and in the skirmishing at Cripple Creek, the old West was disappearing, while the new West was being painfully born. It was a strange time, when frontier attitudes and a generation of western experience collided with onrushing industrialized and urbanized America. The Rocky Mountain West emerged as only one relatively insignificant component in the national drama.

Like a snowslide roaring downhill and sweeping everything before it, the twentieth century exploded over labor relations in the Rocky Mountains. Where men had once fought nature to gain its rewards, now they fought each other. Travail and anger accompanied the new century as shapers of the new West. Those bitter days of the 1890s depression and the free-silver fight seemed tame by comparison.

The region had rebounded economically, which only made matters worse in the opinion of the leaders of the Western Federation of Miners. Its members were not enjoying the better times or reaping a fair share of the fruits of their labor. In their estimation, the "haves" were gaining at the expense of the "have nots."

From union headquarters in the "Gibraltar of unionism," Butte, union leaders saw WFM membership grow after the astounding victory at Cripple Creek. Under the aggressive leadership of presidents Edward Boyce and Charles Moyer and that militant labor unionist Secretary William Haywood, it became the dominant labor force in the ongoing industrial warfare that swept the region.

The victory at Cripple Creek was countered two years later by a defeat at Leadville. The depressed Leadville of 1896 would not appear to have been the best place to strike for three-dollars-a-day wages, but the overconfident union braved it. The owners, however, had learned some important lessons from Cripple Creek, and a conservative, pro-business governor sat in Denver; this time, management was unified and reacted swiftly, once the strikers marched out. Refusing to deal with the WFM, the owners fortified their properties and moved to bring in strikebreakers, or scabs. Both sides dug in. When hatred finally bred violence in September, the call went out for the National Guard. The troops quickly mobilized, sympathetic to management this time, and the strike dragged on for months before the union was broken. Loathing came to replace mere dislike, and violence superseded peacemaking efforts, while both sides waited for the next round.[4]

They did not have long to wait. Soon after the turn of the century, Colorado erupted again, this time in the prospering San Juans. When several brief strikes in the district in the 1890s revealed the undercurrent of discontent, ten WFM locals had shown some union strength. The energetic and successful Vincent St. John had made Telluride the strongest local in Colorado, much to the discomfort of the owners. It was only a matter of time before Telluride and the Smuggler-Union Mine became a battleground. It happened in the spring of 1901. The immediate catalyst was wages, but the underlying issue was control of the district. The result was tragedy. The familiar sequence of events ensued: a strike over management policies, which was responded to by the hiring of company guards and nonunion miners on terms denied to the union. Failing in attempts to induce the scabs to quit, strikers and their supporters attacked the night shift as it left work on July 3. Three men were killed, six wounded, and eighty-eight nonunion men were captured and brutally driven from the district—deplorable tactics for which union members would pay dearly before Telluride quieted. Each side blamed the other. Violence finally forced the two sides to sit down to discuss their positions, which was the only positive result. The isolated Smuggler-Union, unable to secure any state aid, angrily acceded to the union demands. Distrust and bitterness came out of the negotiations as the only winners.[5]

In the following months, the union attempted a boycott of the vehemently antilabor *Daily Journal*, a move countered by the formation of a businessmen's association to support the paper. A wildcat strike hit some of the district's smaller mines in January 1902, but the union gained nothing. Then came the unforgivable incident. Smuggler-Union manager Arthur Collins, a talented but stubborn Cornishman, was assassinated in November 1902, leaving a widow and two young sons. A "monstrous crime"—screamed the vengeful *Daily Journal*—committed by an "inhumane, cowardly perpetrator." That "dangerous agitator," St. John, and eight others were arrested. No proof of guilt was forthcoming, except for their union association, and the real murderer escaped. The unsolved murder infuriated the owners, who believed that nothing less than destruction of the union would bring a satisfactory solution. The conservative *Engineering and Mining Journal* (December 13, 1902) darkly hinted that socialism lurked among WFM goals. The specter of socialism terrified Americans more than any other threat.

There was a grain of truth in the rumor, for some of the WFM's leaders did lean in that direction; Haywood, for instance, later joined the movement. Regrettably, in light of the reputation the union later gained, those leaders marched far out in front of the other members. The frustrated rank and file read with interest the *American Labor Union Journal*, which argued that labor was entitled to all "that it creates" and must "emancipate itself from wage slavery." Socialism, the editor concluded, "is inevitable."[6]

While Telluride awaited trouble that was expected momentarily, the blow came from Cripple Creek. Both management and labor had been anticipating a rematch since 1894 in this strongly union district. Smart-

ing bitterly from their earlier defeat, the owners had organized themselves into a mine-owners' association. The mining union, with the
majority of the miners behind it, was determined to sustain itself and
the gains it had made in those heady days. Trouble started in the mills
at Colorado City in 1903, when the Western Federation attempted to
unionize the workers. Weakly organized there, it faced an uphill fight.
As a labor historian wrote, "precariously established unions always
have trouble avoiding industrial conflict." A strike erupted, and the
local would have been easily broken had not the powerful parent, the
WFM, come to the rescue. Many Cripple Creek miners stopped work
in sympathy, ultimately forcing concessions by management. In August, the mill workers went out again, this time attempting to win an
eight-hour day; the miners had joined them by the end of October.
For nearly a year afterward, Cripple Creek experienced scab labor,
company guards, and violence—a hauntingly familiar pattern in the
mining West.

The owners, whose association's avowed goal was elimination of
the WFM (and the elimination of highgrading), seized the opportunity
to call for the National Guard. They could not have asked for a governor
more sympathetic to their cause, the union-hating, arch-conservative,
Canon City businessman James Peabody. The owners had backed him
to the hilt and, for good measure, had worked to defeat an eight-hour-
day bill in the 1903 legislative session. They had strength never before
equaled to advance their cause.

The state would be forced to deal with the labor difficulties without
federal help. President Roosevelt, who had visited Cripple Creek during happier days in 1900 and again in 1901, had written a Colorado
friend, "I wish you could convey a hint to Governor Peabody that he
ought not, under any circumstances, to call upon me unless he is
powerless to restore order."[7] Peabody rose to the challenge; he was
not powerless and knew what to do. Colorado was plunged into a
costly, violent effort to break the Western Federation.

In came strikebreakers and professional gunmen, and out went the
blacklisted strikers. The Western Federation retaliated with violence of
its own, and the district was virtually divided into two armed camps.
The troops maintained an uneasy, and unneutral, peace. Terrorism
finally forced a declaration of martial law by the district's vainglorious
commander, Adjutant General Sherman Bell, who articulated his goal
this way: "I came to do up this damned anarchistic federation." Union
members were rounded up and deported, the local courts intimidated,
street meetings prohibited, and strikers' firearms confiscated. The pro-

union Victor *Record* was "captured" (union linotypist Emma Langdon crawled through a back window to publish one more issue). By February 1904, the situation seemed to have calmed enough to allow the National Guard to be withdrawn. Peace came, but at what cost to civil rights and personal liberties? The peace was dictated on the owners' terms, to a depleted union.

Desperation bred raw and brutal violence, which soon shattered the uneasy calm. Harry Orchard, a professional terrorist, dynamited the railroad depot at the Independence Mine early on the morning of June 6. He timed his deed to kill the nonunion night-shift workers crowded on the platform. Thirteen died, and many others were badly injured. The owners and the public promptly blamed the WFM. The whole truth has never been discovered, but Orchard was probably backed by the union. Swiftly, the owners moved toward final victory. Martial law and the National Guard returned, along with wholesale arrests, deportation (some were dumped out on the plains near Kansas and told not to come back), wrecking of the union hall, forced resignations of prounion county officials, and mob harassment of union members and sympathizers. By midsummer the strike was broken, although the shattered union stubbornly refused to terminate the strike officially.[8]

Back in Telluride, the union ("a band of terrorists, dynamiters, gunmen," according to eastern mining man Robert Livermore, who was working at the nearby Camp Bird Mine) was having an equally difficult time in maintaining itself. Flamboyant, controversial Bulkeley Wells, a charming, extravagant, and ruthless man, had replaced Collins as the leader of the owners. Inexorably, the nightmarish drama marched toward further tragedy.

In September 1903, while Cripple Creek seethed, the union struck Telluride in an attempt to secure an eight-hour day for the mill men. The owners stood firm, preferring to keep the plants closed rather than "submit to the dictates." Spokesman Wells confidently predicted, "The strike here and elsewhere . . . promises to be an absolute failure, and to cause the Federation a large loss of membership and standing."

The strikers hung on, determined. The WFM opened lodging houses and restaurants on a cooperative plan to sustain members; regardless of its efforts, many drifted away to seek other employment. Armed union pickets surfaced, while the mine owners weighed the use of "rapid-fire guns" to protect their properties. In the meantime, they brought in professional gunmen to serve as night guards. None was more feared than thirty-eight-year-old Robert Meldrum. The slightly deaf Meldrum, the rumored killer of a dozen men, made a dramatic debut. Coming off the evening train and into the Cosmopolitan Saloon, he announced, "I'm Bob Meldrum. You can always find me when you want me. Now, if any son of a bitch has anything to say, spit it out; otherwise, I'm going to take a drink—and alone." Later, when Meldrum was serving as daytime guard at the Tomboy Mine, genteel Harriet Backus recalled him as seemingly fearless, looking like the "typical intrepid westerner." The union imported its own gunfighter, but there would be no shootout at high noon.

Less dramatically, the plea went out for the National Guard, and it came in to patrol the district. Because Peabody's activities had severely strained Colorado's finances, the owners provided meals and quarters until permanent camps could be established. The crisis was now close at hand. The owners relentlessly brought in scabs, which allowed mining to resume. Union leaders were seized for threatening nonunion men, and striking miners, "mostly foreigners," were arrested. Charged with vagrancy, they were told to go to work, to jail, or to leave. Others were rounded up and shipped out of the district.

The WFM, which had shifted its headquarters to Denver, protested heatedly, to no avail; the conservative Colorado courts would pay little heed to its arguments. A bleak Christmas came and went for the strikers. The troops were being removed, when Peabody unexpectedly declared martial law. Basing his justification on information furnished by the owners, he ordered the troops to return. Press censorship, a curfew, searches for weapons, passes to walk the streets, restricted freedom of assembly, and more deportations followed, before the order was lifted on March 11. By then, most of the troops had been pulled out. Peabody, still nervous about the situation, saw a "state of insurrection and rebellion" and ordered the troops back in less than two weeks. By mid-June, the turmoil had ended. The mines and mills were operating, the owners were in complete control, and the union had been broken in spirit and in hope. To ensure union weakness, the mine owners, with Peabody's approval, imposed a card system for approved miners in both districts. That strategy blocked any resurgence of union prestige and power; Telluride's time of troubles was over.[9]

So, too, was Colorado's, but at a tragic price—trampled civil liberties; over 625,000 dollars in expenses (2 million dollars in the past ten years) to suppress the alleged "socialistic, anarchistic objects and methods" of the WFM; lost investments; and a reputation as a reactionary state. The owners sustained significant losses, too, in work stoppages, expenses, and the acquisition of an infamous reputation;

their stockholders were none too happy, either, with the decreased dividends. Colorado taxpayers were the losers, as well; they would carry for years the burden of paying for Peabody's campaigns and would suffer the consequences of their state's tarnished reputation. The Western Federation had suffered a fatal setback in the one-sided war over the destiny of the state's two major mining regions and would never regain the initiative. The miners suffered from lives shattered and lost, extinguished hopes, and finding themselves at the mercy of entrenched ownership. In the end, everyone lost. The promised land had turned violent.

The union could rant about "brutal barbarism," and Livermore could piously intone that Telluride had suffered too sorely to take chances on unionism. Peabody, in 1904, could declare, "I well knew the history and character of this organization. It is . . . a matter of common knowledge in Colorado that for ten years this Federation has stopped at nothing to accomplish its purpose." None of it made any difference.[10] Telluride would never be the same again, nor would Cripple Creek, or anywhere else that these two antagonists had fought it out in the past few years. Innocence had long ago fallen victim to violence. Trust, friendship, cohesiveness, and reputations were destroyed that year all along the Colorado Rockies and elsewhere. The old days, the old ways, disappeared in the debacle; mining would never regain its once familiar role and its relationship to the region. The new West would be a harder taskmaster than the old for the common worker. On the other hand, Haywood and other WFM leaders did not curtail their commitment to industrial unionism and militancy. There would be another day of reckoning.

Looking back over these unsettling events, Ray Stannard Baker, one of the best known of the day's muckraking journalists, lamented, "To this, then, have we come in these American towns at the beginning of the twentieth century! And why is this so? Why have the people borne these appalling usurpations?" The people had broken the law, he concluded, and they would have to assume the burdens of maintaining troops, of lawsuits, of lost business, and of rising taxes. "It is not cheap—lawlessness." President Theodore Roosevelt concurred and likewise blamed the federation. He remained unsure of just exactly what had occurred and wanted more information; or as he put it, "I should like to get the facts."[11] The facts told only part of the story; the rest would be recounted in lost ambitions and the death of an era.

Hard-rock unionism had been crushed in Colorado, but not in Butte, where the Western Federation remained strong. Butte would suffer no labor troubles now, but it chronicled an equally sordid story in the so-called battle of the copper kings. In this scenario, gigantic corporations and freewheeling individuals were pitted against each other, rather than against their sixteen thousand Butte employees. The tantalizing prize was dominance of Montana's copper industry, certainly a prize worth seeking. In 1905, over thirty-seven million dollars in copper was mined in Montana, 80 percent or more coming from Butte. It reigned as America's premier metal-mining center.[12]

If unionism aroused emotions, so did socialism, which flourished where it took root. Most Rocky Mountain folk were not at all enamored with the regional growth of socialism. Nor were many other Americans, who considered this form of "radicalism" an abomination, or worse, a threat to the American political system. It did, however, come as a natural outgrowth of mounting frustration on the part of some Americans. The workers, for example, saw the legal and political system as closed to them by the apparently unshakable dominance of business–corporation control. Some miners and others came from a European socialist background and saw nothing wrong with this alternative to the American system. To them, it was neither an aberration nor a fearsome political choice.

The leaders of the Western Federation of Miners also became more radical, as previously noted, when their union lost round after round in the fight against the owners. The union officers may have seemed more radical than the rank-and-file members because of their public statements, but even the diehard miner saw socialism as one way to balance the uneven contest between himself and management.

The most radical members would later march out to form the Industrial Workers of the World, further weakening the WFM. At the conclusion of the 1903–04 Colorado struggle, the union retained only one Rocky Mountain stronghold, Butte. As an antidote to the anguish, bitterness, and dashed hopes, socialism seemed to offer an elixir. For the workers, at least, it stirred as refreshing a breeze as free silver had done for the whole region a decade before. On the local and state levels, socialists attracted more support than they ever had before— or ever would again.

Easterners should have expected the growth of socialism in the West; it had also made inroads in the East during the progressive era. Industrial states published socialist newspapers and voters elected party members as mayors, as delegates to state legislatures, and even a few as members of the House of Representatives. Perennial socialist presidential candidate Eugene V. Debs polled nearly 900,000 votes in 1912.

Socialism had become a third force to be reckoned with on the American political landscape.[13]

Perhaps because of the distance involved, the labor violence, or the western image of activism, Rocky Mountain socialism appeared to be more radical, more threatening, than its eastern counterpart. The strength of Wyoming's Socialist party lay in its proworker platform. It was most successful in the coal towns. In Rock Springs, for example, the Socialists fared well in local elections, held their 1908 statewide convention there, and offered lecture courses in the local Grand Opera House.

Montana's socialist movement proved even more shocking to those who upheld the virtues of individualism and a simpler America. Organized under the banner of the Socialist party of Montana, twenty-five local branches had been formed by 1902; they were especially strong in the industrial counties. Their platform encompassed the eight-hour day, the outlawing of antiunion blacklists, workmen's compensation laws, and a host of other Populist and Progressive reforms. When the Socialist party won an Anaconda city election in April 1903, it was the first victory of the party west of the Mississippi River. In a company town that achievement was extraordinary, but understandable. With the unions sympathetic to their aims and with many supportive immigrants working in the smelter, the Socialists carried the workers' wards with them to victory. The shocked company reacted viciously, firing every Socialist or alleged Socialist sympathizer in its employ. The retribution took its toll, as did mounting public opposition to socialism. In the 1904 election, the Anaconda Socialist party was crushed. Far from dead, socialism continued to thrive in Butte, where it was closely interwoven with the Butte Miners' Union. In 1911, the two combined to elect a Socialist mayor and city government. The next year, their candidate for governor polled over 12,500 votes in Montana.[14]

A similar course was followed in Colorado, for where the Western Federation took root so did socialism. Although the cause–effect relationship was not that simple, the grievances that both attacked were. The popular Eugene Debs always attracted voters, but the party unsuccessfully nominated statewide candidates. What success it did achieve came at the local level. At Telluride and nearby Ophir, for instance, the party fielded a ticket and elected a few local officials. Telluride, the heart of the 1903–04 strike, held onto its socialist leanings into the 1910s. As in Wyoming, there was also socialist activity in the coal camps.[15]

Socialism reached its zenith in the Rocky Mountains during these years. The troubled times and the rapid changes accounted for the voters' allegiance to its tenets more than any doctrinaire commitment. Socialism's major impact came from its influence on progressivism. Both doctrines championed some of the same reforms and accepted the concept of a more powerful national state, supported by new regulatory legislation. Workers could accept more willingly the middle-class progressivism, which thereby gained a much broader base for its program.[16] To the hard-pressed miners, socialism seemed like a panacea; to others, it appeared only slightly more radical than some of the progressive plans.

Never before had the Rocky Mountains endured years like the ones that ushered in the twentieth century. The cost in money, lives, civil rights, and reputation had astounded residents and outsiders alike. The end result had been that big business reigned supreme and the miner found himself generally on the outside looking in. Socialism had proved no panacea, and the future looked bleak for the "working stiff" in the mines.

The dreams of 1859, 1862, and 1867 had turned, if not into a nightmare, then certainly into something less than what had been expected by the pioneers and their descendants. The Rocky Mountains, which they had opened, had become the plaything of eastern and foreign investors and their corporations' managers.

12 : CAMELOT LOST,
CAMELOT FOUND

T he times were changing across the face of the Rocky Mountains. The region, though still highly urbanized, was showing a percentage of urban decline by 1900. Farm population was growing, and many of the small mining districts were barely keeping afloat; not a few camps and districts had lost their vibrancy and become more ghostlike. Even in the major districts, business had stabilized and growth had leveled, maintained more by the emigration of people from nearby declining districts than by any major outside immigration.[1] The glamour of these communities was also fading; Butte, Aspen, Silverton, and Leadville looked more like industrial communities than "romantic" mining towns. Newness did not guarantee immortality, for Cripple Creek and Victor aged rapidly after the strike and the labor–owner split. The loss of opportunity, replaced by the more traditional workaday world, showed in people's attitudes and outlook. Anne Ellis knew all about this industrial world, and she saw little romance in it.

For two towns, though, the coming of the new century promised even more opportunity. Both Helena and Denver had outgrown their mining heritage to become regional centers. At the same time, they had maintained their political power and developed an economic versatility and a dependent hinterland, all of which promised them a bright future.

They had not accomplished these things without creating some ill will. The fight over the designation of the capital of Montana illustrated this, just as it had in Colorado a decade earlier. Some opponents called

Helena "hogopolis" because of its greed in trying to grab the largest share of the political spoils. The Montana legislature resolved some of these concerns in the first years of statehood by parceling out the higher education institutions throughout the state.[2] Butte, however, posed more of an immediate problem for Helena's boosters. Denver had no rival to compare with Butte. Butte, at the turn of the century, was larger (30,470 to 10,770), wealthier, and more newsworthy; its fatal long-range weakness would be its dependence on the one-pillared economy of copper. Retaining its hold on the capital had been the key to Helena's future.

Helena could lay claim to being the "queen city," but Denver already wore that title proudly. With a population of over 133,000, it had no rivals in size, transportation network, community leadership, cultural and social institutions, or a dynamic economy, all profitably balanced with commerce, industry, mining, agriculture, tourism, and banking. To be sure, there was still envy of Denver's power and prestige within Colorado and throughout the region. Ignoring the animosity, Denver achieved the goal that its founding leaders had set for it. Along the way, state rivals, such as Leadville and now Cripple Creek, had fallen by the wayside; Cheyenne had dropped far behind, after a brief challenge thirty years ago. Helena posed no real threat, since the distance involved removed it from Denver's basic sphere of influence, and it did not have the economic strength to mount a challenge that far south.

In the nineties, only the booming Cripple Creek district mounted any state challenge to the "queen." For all its publicity and wealth, it mustered only about ten thousand residents in 1900, at its peak. But for a brief, shining moment it had allowed another mining rush, with its boom and bonanza, to pass in review before it disappeared, never to reappear in Colorado.

Cripple Creek comprised a mixture of the old and the new. Its newspapers complained that Denver maligned it with misleading articles, and they countered by praising local mines and communities. Mining investor Harry Newman was one of those who rushed there and found in 1895 that it was "almost impossible to get rooms, the town was so crowded." The editor of the *Cripple Creek Guide* (April 25, 1896) saw, among the throngs, "corduroy suits, flannel shirts, leather jackets and natty black cloth suits." He even found time to praise this "orderly and law-abiding camp," whose "general morale . . . is so far in advance of anything that has hitherto been known." The words sounded familiar to those who had read about South Pass, Telluride,

Leadville, Butte, or any other mining town with a pretense toward improving its image.

The depression hardly touched this booming community and district, and Newman saw only bright tomorrows, declaring, "This is the only country to live in and make money." Even when the town suffered two major fires in April 1896, and Newman lost everything ("I have no more home than a rabbit"), he remained optimistic. People who had stampeded to scores of Rocky Mountain mining districts would have understood his attitude well. Amid the familiar, there were some new additions—the Victor Chamber of Commerce, the Board of Trade, the interurban between the various camps and mines, and all the modern conveniences gold could buy.[3]

Cripple Creek money went around the mountain to Colorado Springs or to the East; Denver did not reap the benefits of another Leadville. Because of this windfall, Colorado Springs was sheltered from the depression, as its growth (to twenty-one thousand people) and prosperity attested. There were 420 companies with offices there; bank deposits increased ninefold; and the number of millionaires residing along its expansive streets jumped from 3 to over 50. Neighboring Manitou Springs remained more of a tourist resort, one that did not tolerate "disorder & vice" and where "crime is practically unknown."[4] Tourists came to see the wonders of Pike's Peak and skirt its flanks to sample Cripple Creek at its roaring best.

From Main Street to mining camp, the scene was changing. Westerners were accumulating the accouterments of modern living in every aspect of life. They went to the motion-picture theaters and stared in fascination at the flickering black-and-white images on an improvised screen; in a really high-class theater they listened to a piano player set the mood. They were confounded by the flight of the heavier-than-air aeroplane and had watched agog as the noisy automobile chugged down their streets, frightening dogs and horses. If any one thing conjured the future, it was that vehicle, especially Henry Ford's Model T, which brought it within reach of the ordinary American. To inform themselves about the latest ideas and to sample a taste of culture, many towns sponsored a Chautauqua season, which included a variety of programs; Boulder, Colorado, achieved a permanent Chautauqua, to complement the university. Boulder had visions of itself as the Athens of the West.

Many businesses and homes already had electricity, and electrical appliances were helping to ease the daily burdens of the housewife. Box cameras preserved family memories, phonographs could be found in many parlors, and people were at ease with the telephone and "central." The latest styles and fads hit the region in season, not a year later. Newspapers published the very latest state, national, and international news. Their isolation overcome, westerners were now joined intimately with the rest of the nation. Newspapers were updated with photographs, better print, improved advertising, eye-catching headlines, and, in the bigger cities, special Sunday sections that included comics. Sports fans could keep track of the American and National League baseball teams or the week's boxing match, horse race, or football game.

The national pastime had taken solid root in the Rocky Mountains. Here, as elsewhere, it grew from urban roots. As early as the Civil War years, baseball had been played in Denver and, in the years following, throughout the mining camps and farm communities. Local pride, a chance for Sunday afternoon relaxation, and side bets heightened interest, when Helena took on Butte or when the Cripple Creek nine challenged its archrival, Victor. These were supposedly hometown teams, but players were soon being imported to bolster the nine for an important series. The 1881 Leadville Blues used the gimmick to the extreme when they enlisted four former or future major leaguers to play on a team that often won by twenty runs or more. Professional athletics were only a step behind, and Denver had a short-lived team in the Western League in the eighties. In the mid-1890s, the Colorado State League operated for a couple of seasons and, for a very brief time, had a Gillette, Wyoming, entry. Denver rejoined the Western League in 1900 and won the pennant; professional sports had returned to the "Queen City."[5] Denver was as current as most eastern cities of its size when it came to sports and sports coverage.

Though baseball garnered the most interest, college football was making inroads with college-age sports fans. Throughout the Rockies, state universities and colleges fielded teams; Wyoming and Colorado elevens frequently played each other. Later on, more distant Montana teams were scheduled. Athletic programs were not without their share of turmoil. In 1904 the University of Colorado withdrew from the Colorado Intercollegiate Athletic Association after being accused of "adopting every method that has ever been tried to put men on her team who had absolutely no standing as amateurs." The coach was denounced for importing "men merely to play football," who did not have "qualifications to pass examinations for the freshman class in high schools." Colorado University refused to "indulge in petty squabbles," pulled out, and scheduled games against larger "universities from other states."[6]

The next year, even with a victorious season that included a 69–0 thrashing of Wyoming, the University of Colorado contemplated giving up football. A rash of injuries and some deaths throughout the country motivated some Americans to call for the abolishment of the sport. University president James Baker finally concluded, as did others, that what the sport needed was reform, not termination. There existed, he affirmed, a "healthy public demand for strenuous athletics," which cannot be denied. He supported a one-year residency rule and "good academic standing" for athletes before they played, with no more than four years being spent on the squad.[7] All these rules were necessary and inevitable; they would come none too soon for some cases, in which players were on teams for five or six seasons.

The dilemma about intercollegiate athletics confronted the University of Montana a decade later. Following a successful tour of Utah by the debate team, the *Daily Missoulian* (February 17, 1914) raised the issue: "It may be old-fashioned, but there are some of us who feel that there is more glory in a debate victory for a university than there is in an athletic contest." The editor's supporters constituted a minority; the twentieth-century westerner reveled in athletics, not debate teams. University football and basketball teams already had become a symbol of state pride.

Football, automobiles, telephones—the twentieth century had come to the Rocky Mountains. High society promenaded in its own elite circle and resided on "snob hill." Denver had its select thirty-six, which Leadville's Molly Brown, made rich by mining, spent a fortune and years trying to crash, creating a legend in her own time. Helena prided itself on being the wealthiest town per capita in the country, with an especially opulent residential district. Other communities, several of them in the Rockies, legitimately could have disputed Helena's claim. Colorado Springs had a *Society Blue Book*, which included, among other items, a "Director of Society," a Club Directory, and advertisements for an "automobile livery," architects, and the local hotel haven for society, the Broadmoor. Butte had a *Blue Book*, too, but elite pretensions did not sit so well there, and it was discontinued after a year.[8] In between these extremes fell the rest of the Rockies' prospering towns. The newcomer quickly caught on to who were the right people to know and where were the right places to be seen. The previous generation's more egalitarian society was falling before increased wealth and assumed social position.

Urbanites could also snub their country cousins, who did not share access to their benefits and opportunities. The urban–rural rift widened as the cities moved far ahead in modern conveniences and quality of life. At the time, this elusive term, *quality of life,* was defined more by materialistic things than by aesthetic potential. The split became evident in a variety of ways—jokes about the "rural hick," disparate educational opportunities, and different voting patterns. In Colorado and Montana, for example, prohibition caught on in the farming counties, while Butte, Denver, and the working-class communities emphatically rejected the idea.

In this urban world, women were making gains. For example, married women's legal rights were also expanded. All three states had granted them the rights of property conveyance and inheritance. Additionally, they achieved the right to conduct business independently, without restrictions. The stereotyped image of the western woman—as a refined lady, a wife, or a fallen woman—does not hold up under scrutiny.[9]

Women were making strides on a variety of fronts. They had been active in the Populist party; one of their number, Ella Knowles, had been nominated for Montana attorney general. She worked hard, proved to be an outstanding speaker, faced some sexist "joshing," and lost. She later married the winner, causing one wag to comment that "politics make strange bedfellows." Women lawyers, mine managers, druggists, doctors, dentists, grocers, newspaper reporters, and town trustees (at least two city treasurers) all constituted pioneering ventures. With these occupations, and the more traditional hotel, boarding and rooming house operators, actresses, musicians (including the Ladies' Chicago Military Band), restaurant owners, laundresses, dressmakers, stenographers (even men agreed they operated those new typewriting machines faster), and the service occupations, women slowly invaded Main Street and the man's world of the professions.

For most women, like the now-married Anne Ellis, the tasks of mother and homemaker filled their days. Ellis wrote philosophically of the things that made her happy: "A woman may be very unhappy, not loved, and, she thinks, not understood, but a few paydays, a full cupboard, and some new clothes will grease the wheels of married life to a great smoothness." She needed all those and more, after her husband was killed in a Cripple Creek mine accident. A widow with children, she later remarried and her life went on.[10] When her second husband left the mines for clerking in a store, she was greatly relieved as she anticipated "losing the fear of accidents that ever hangs over a miner's wife."

Despite these advances, women, rural and urban, retained their classification as second-class citizens. Several eastern journalists traveled to Colorado in 1903 to observe how suffrage had worked in its first decade. One of them, Mary Slocum, described in *Outlook* how the difficulties of physical life and the obstacles to growth of the spiritual life "fall most heavily" on rural women. Conversely, she concluded that women had had a greater impact on rural politics by having more input and influence on local issues and political parties. Slocum, who believed that women had upgraded politics since they gained the vote, fell into a noisy argument with Elizabeth McCracken. McCracken wrote, "The possession of the ballot, and the employment of that possession, have hurt the women of Colorado as women can least afford to be hurt." The debasement had occurred because "her ideals have been lowered; the delicacy of her perception of right and wrong has been dulled."[11] The debate raged on, as it had since 1869 in Wyoming.

When the settlement of the Rocky Mountains began in 1859, one of the goals, as mentioned earlier, had been to re-create in the West the life that had been left behind. A generation later, certainly by the early 1900s, that goal had been achieved in an eminently successful, if unexpected, manner. Like the rest of the United States, the Rocky Mountain states confronted political scandals, discovered that a concentration of business power and corporations shaped much of their destiny, found their one major city (Denver) boss-controlled, and, finally, came to realize that their laborers had evolved into second-class citizens.

As in the rest of the country, these westerners searched optimistically for solutions to these and other problems, confident that they were inherently capable of resolving them. Americans launched a reform crusade, called progressivism, to effect change. Thus was born the progressive era, a child of populism and a product of the early twentieth century. Populists had planted the seeds and tilled the soil; the progressives would harvest the crop. The newer movement would be more moderate than its parent and more complex than populism had been; moreover, as the product of a more prosperous era, it was less rancorous. Its strength came not from angry farmers and miners, but from professional and middle-class Americans, who now manned the front lines.

At a time of political, economic, and social reform in the cities, the states, and the nation, the accession of that political virtuoso Theodore

Roosevelt to the White House in 1901 made a convenient national starting point for progressivism. Roosevelt himself was a progressive at heart, a vigorous, impatient man committed to the use of his office and the federal government to tackle the problems of the day. The government, he believed, should be "as well planned, economical, and efficient as the best machinery of the great business corporations." For the Rocky Mountains, this philosophy would translate primarily into conservation and reclamation programs. An activist and outdoorsman, Roosevelt came to view conservation as his most important domestic policy, because it gave him the opportunity for independent action that could not be duplicated elsewhere.

Progressivism differed most radically from populism in its roots, which grew primarily from an urban, middle-class response to abuses and evils generated by industrialization and metropolitan expansion over the past thirty years and to the ethnic tensions of the "new immigration." Progressives hoped to improve their quality of life in a fast-changing world that often left the middle class on the outside looking in. They took the "once-radical" populist ideas, clothed them in middle-class respectability, and made them acceptable to the average American. Progressives sprang up everywhere, visible and respectable.[12]

They possessed a great faith in the democratic system, the old populist concept of giving power back to the people. The Progressives were determined to use democratic means to galvanize local, state, and national action to promote general welfare and a larger measure of social justice. They did not simply talk and write about their intentions, for Progressives were both moralists and activists. They believed ardently in the inevitability of progress and the creative possibilities of social improvement, which, they reasoned, would be attainable by spirited individual and collective action.

In that bastion of populism, the Rocky Mountain region, Progressives found a host of allies and a natural home. For fifteen years, progressivism swept up and down the Rockies, touching village and town, the rural and urban alike.

These westerners needed their faith and optimism when they looked at Denver and Colorado. Throughout the country, there was great concern about the well-documented corruption and abuses of political machines that had become entangled with big-city government. Denver now proved that it was up to date in these deplorable developments. Denver had Mayor Robert Speer, who had organized a Democratic fiefdom, which rivaled the best that the East could offer. A complex individual, Speer had come to Colorado for his health, a member of the "one lunged army" who had recovered in the high, dry climate. Ambitious, friendly, and a natural politician, Speer eventually rose to leadership in the Denver Democratic party. He put together a powerful political machine, built on patronage jobs, city contracts, ties to the business establishment, contacts with the underworld, and some decidedly shady election practices. At the same time, he caught a vision of the "Denver beautiful" and was determined to transform the dusty town into an urban oasis. The civic center, mountain parks, Cherry Creek parkway, city park, and a tree-planting program resulted from his efforts.[13]

During the tumultuous years of 1903–5, it was not Speer's beautification plans that attracted public attention. No election in Colorado history was more corrupt than the one in 1904. Corporations controlled the Republican party (particularly Colorado Fuel and Iron, which was dominated by the Rockefeller interests, and the other coal companies). Speer wielded ultimate authority over the vital Denver Democratic machine. The result was chaos. Fraud, intimidation, and violence marred election day.

Republicans challenged Denver's voting returns, charging that Speer had used "repeaters." The Democratic machine had paid men and women to vote early and often, even holding a "school" before election day to give instructions. The scheme worked well. One precinct with 100 legal voters returned 717 Democratic ballots. Democrats pointed their fingers at "fraudulent" returns from Republican coal-mining counties. Immigrant coal miners were told which way to vote, risking their jobs for noncompliance. Votes were counted without opening the ballot boxes, and returns were sent in unaccompanied by the voted ballots. Democracy had descended to this state of affairs in the traditionally democratic West. Chicanery was not new to Colorado. In 1902, the situation had been almost as bad, and other elections gave evidence of similar, if less blatant, tendencies.

Reformer and renowned juvenile judge Ben Lindsey claimed that the people of Colorado were not free citizens, but only "enfranchised serfs." Though not an unbiased observer, having fought the Speer machine as well as corporations, he had put his finger on the truth. Much like what had happened in Montana (although not restricted to one company), corporations had involved themselves heavily in politics through the Republican party. They had bankrolled, guided, and generally controlled the party and the selection of its candidates for governor and senator. The results had proven highly effective in their decade-long fight against the Western Federation.[14]

This time, though, the tactics led to political travesty and miscarriage of justice. Democrat Alva Adams had won the election over incumbent James Peabody, who was running for another term on the heels of his fight with the union. No doubt both parties had committed fraud, but the Republicans perpetuated the most blatant one by appealing to and maneuvering the Republican-controlled Supreme Court and legislature. Democrats did not have enough votes to save Adams, and the Republicans were trapped with the highly unpopular Peabody. After two months of wrangling, Colorado endured the embarrassment of having three governors in one day, March 16–17, 1905. Under a negotiated compromise, Adams resigned, Peabody was appointed after agreeing to resign, and the lieutenant governor, Jesse McDonald, moved up to governor.

Outspoken Durango Democrat and newspaperman Dave Day would not sit still for all this maneuvering and blasted out, "Unseating Alva Adams was a steal, an outrage, and assault upon human liberty and the ballot." Said one Coloradan, "What is the use of voting? It isn't worth while to vote any more, I don't believe I shall ever vote again."[15] Fortunately for the future of the state, that kind of attitude did not survive for long.

The two political parties sneaked out of the limelight, but neither the entrenched Speer machine nor the corporations surrendered their influence and power. Ultimately, they would have to answer for the skullduggery, which reached its peak in 1904–05. The parallels between Colorado and Montana during those years were striking. The investing Rockefellers had used money and influence to achieve corporation profits and subsidize their interests in both states without regard for anyone else. In both states, the people's will was thrashed by special interests, and legislatures and courts were debased. The nation looked on, horrified and amused at the same time. The Rocky Mountain region had lost its appeal as the poor-man's paradise. It had come under the control and guidance of corporations, the vast majority of which represented eastern interests.

Fortunately for the Rocky Mountain region, neither Denver nor Colorado's political extremes proved to be typical. They did reflect, however, the type of problems that Progressives tackled with vigor on a wide front.

What did progressivism mean? In Durango, Colorado, it meant crusading against adulterated oleo and deceptive advertising. In Helena, it meant the civic club working for "better schools; better churches; better public buildings; better playgrounds; cleaner streets and alleys;

unsightly bill-boards abolished; better public service." Montana created a State Bureau of Child and Animal Protection. Wyoming adopted a direct primary law and limited expenses by, or on behalf of, any political candidate. Missoula, Montana, cleaned out its corrupt city government and adopted the commission form of government. Mayor Speer launched his city-beautification project and moved to acquire mountain lands for Denver's park system. At the same time, reformers were actively working to defeat his machine. In 1907, Montana established a Board of Railroad Commissioners and charged it with taking a hard look at rates and services, free passes, and railroad taxation. The "telephone octopus" attracted the attention of phone users in Meeker, Colorado. Kalispell, Montana, reformed its police department, and Denver's Judge Ben Lindsey took his crusade for social justice for young offenders throughout the region. His juvenile court became a model for national corrective institutions.[16]

It was truly a movement of people in action. Even the powerful Anaconda in Montana could not stop it. Governor Toole pointed out in 1907 that state progressivism had its limits: there was precious little that Montana could do to regulate so entrenched a corporation. Only the federal government, with its antitrust laws, could hope for success in tackling Anaconda or the Rockefellers of the day.

Perhaps, most of all, the movement was political, and it was from the political process that most of the reform emerged. Fed up with the old political traditions and with business leadership, and caught up in the new spirit of activism and progressivism, Rocky Mountain voters rebelled. They came to agree with President Roosevelt, who said, "I do not have to tell you that I believe in politics and in politicians . . . It is always a count in a man's favor if he is a politician—that is, if he is an honest one." In Wyoming, the new attitude reached its zenith with the election in 1910 of Democrat Joseph Carey, who had split with his old ally, Francis Warren, and quit the Republicans. His platform, typically Progressive, called for, among other things, a direct-primary law, initiative, referendum and recall, conservation of natural resources, and a law to eliminate the influence of lobbyists. Though not able to achieve all these goals, Carey nonetheless "proved to be one of the most outstanding governors in all Wyoming history."[17]

Montana produced a colorful quartet of Progressive leaders, all of whom would achieve impressive national as well as local distinction: Joseph M. Dixon, Jeannette Rankin, Burton K. Wheeler, and Thomas Walsh. While he was a congressman and later a senator, Dixon would become a great friend of Roosevelt. Rankin would work for woman's suffrage in the state, and Wheeler and Walsh would carry the reform banner into the New Deal era.[18] On the local level, Montana toed the Progressive line. Governor Joseph Toole brought the state a Progressive administration. That Montana did not achieve the sweeping reforms of the other Rocky Mountain states is understandable, for the others did not have Anaconda looking over their shoulders. Montanans did, however, in 1912—when progressivism reached its peak—initiate the direct primary, the presidential preference primary, and a corrupt-practices act.

While Montana and Wyoming jogged comfortably in the mainstream of progressivism, Colorado raced out in front. The reasons were obvious. The state was not dominated by one industry, as was Montana, nor was it as lightly affected by the era of disruption as Wyoming. Coloradans and their state had suffered greatly at the hands of the conservative, business-dominated leadership of the early twentieth century. They had anguished over the tragedy of the strikes and endured the national embarrassment over the disputed election of 1904. Their largest city manifested all the problems that the eastern Progressives railed against. Colorado had been a Populist stronghold, and its citizens had sincerely taken to heart the reform package that the party promoted. The majority of Coloradans stood strongly behind reform.

It came with the administration of Democratic Governor John Shafroth, nicknamed "Honest John,'" who had resigned his House seat in 1904, when he discovered that his victory had been tainted by Speer machine-voting frauds. This man of principle was elected governor in 1908 on a progressive platform, which he promptly and energetically set about to convert from words into laws. During his four-year tenure in the job (Colorado's governors served two-year terms), he used skillful political maneuvering and marshaled newspaper and public pressure to defeat the entrenched vested interests. Thanks to Shafroth, Coloradans secured initiative, referendum, and recall, all extremely popular because they gave the people the power to initiate laws, vote on legislative actions, and recall elected officials. Shafroth's influence did not end there. His administration and example led to the state gaining a campaign-expenses law, regulations of child and woman labor, the Australian or secret ballot, a state conservation commission, home rule for cities and towns, and a reorganized civil service commission. The voters actually approved judicial recall in 1912. Conservatives were astounded at how radical Colorado had become. Allowing the electorate to judge a state Supreme Court decision seemed to them to herald the resurrection of Danton and the Reign of Terror. At the peak of state and national reform in 1911–12, no state ranked ahead of Colorado in progressivism. Against the protests and delaying tactics of corporation and machine interests and the old guard of both parties, Shafroth successfully enacted the first progressive legislation in Colorado's history.[19]

Although the battle had not been entirely won in any of the Rocky Mountain states, a good start had been made in returning political power to the people in two out of the three. Democracy took on new meaning during the progressive era; there would be no turning back to the misnamed "good old days."

One important reason for the success of progressivism in the Rocky Mountain region was the prestige of Theodore Roosevelt, its perceived guiding light. The emotional fight over national forests did not diminish his popularity, probably because he traveled to the region more than any other president before him. He visited Wyoming in 1903 and relished a visit to one of Francis Warren's ranches. An advocate of the strenuous life, the president took a one-day, fifty-six-mile horseback ride from Laramie to Cheyenne, a vigorous outing that his host could not finish. He hunted on Colorado's Western Slope on several occasions, but his fame made it difficult to have a true vacation. He wrote his friend Philip Stewart in Colorado Springs that he hesitated to hunt because of the press attention it drew. He feared that Meeker would "literally be filled with correspondents," who would file all "kinds of wild reports." Roosevelt recommended that the hunt be conducted "in rather wild country, as it would discourage newspaper people from following us." Understanding fully that the press must be served, he arranged from "time to time" to put them in "touch with us."[20]

13 : UNCLE SAM'S NEW WEST

Theodore Roosevelt hunted, visited, and enjoyed the Rockies, and he fought to preserve western natural resources and environment. This was his greatest contribution, although not all locals appreciated his sentiments or actions.

Before President Roosevelt became active, Butte gave the region a taste of what was to come. It propounded the environmental themes that came to overshadow the Clarks and the Dalys of the district's heyday. By 1889, Butte's copper ores were being smelted by six of the "most modern and potent" smelters in the world, along with the old method of heap roasting in the open air. Butte's smoke problem could not be denied or explained away, except by the most ardent mining boosters, who still pontificated about the medical benefits of smoke, while the noxious sulfur, copper, and arsenic fumes were killing grass, flowers, and trees. Cats that licked grime off their whiskers risked arsenic poisoning. When Butte residents became agitated, the council responded by passing an ordinance against heap roasting, which was acknowledged more by being ignored than enforced.

Finally, in the last half of 1890, when over two hundred deaths could be directly or indirectly attributed to respiratory-related diseases over a period of six months, Butte residents arose in anger. Theirs was not an easy decision; born, bred, and prospered by mining, Butte knew no other heritage. The citizens took the desperate step of sending a letter to the *Engineering and Mining Journal* (on December 20), asking for help in finding a process to destroy the "gases and smoke emerging from the stacks." Now, the entire industry and the nation knew of Butte's problem. In the months that followed, a number of writers proffered some solutions for Butte.[1] But it would take action, not speculation, to remove Butte's crown of smoke.

Without that action, the "smoke nuisance" continued unabated. Mining's defenders relentlessly hammered away, claiming that the smelters had existed before most of the residents arrived; therefore, those who came afterward "knew what to expect." From an economic standpoint, they argued, it was simply not commercially profitable to remove the sulfur, unless the resultant sulfuric acid could be sold. There was no Rocky Mountain market for the amount that Butte could potentially manufacture, and shipment elsewhere was uneconomical.

When one smelter brazenly chose to ignore the ordinance, the city went to court to seek a permanent injunction. The company protested that the city had no authority to pass a smoke ordinance. Then, after heatedly denying that heap roasting or any other smelting operation rendered the "atmosphere of said city unfit for or dangerous to be breathed," the company lawyer warned that shutting down heap roasting would throw men out of work and damage the community's economy. The threats and denials failed; the judge supported Butte.

Challenged in one of its bastions, mining changed as little as possible while continuing its operations. Blatant heap roasting was gone, replaced more because of newer techniques than by anything Butte had accomplished. Twenty-six miles west, the establishment of the smelter town of Anaconda, with its modern mechanism, had also relieved Butte's smog. Western Federation organizer Bill Haywood traveled to the town in 1899 for a meeting; to him, the new Butte looked like the old. The "desolation" of the countryside amazed him. Of Butte, he later wrote, "The smoke, fumes and dust penetrated everywhere and settled on everything. Many of the miners were suffering from rankling copper sores, caused by the poisonous water."[2]

The ongoing fight would move from Butte to Anaconda. While the mining industry did, in fact, win the first round, the arrogant defense of its "rights" gained for it little sympathy. Its refusal to recognize the total industrial impact and to acknowledge its responsibilities exhibited a callousness and insensitivity that were all too typical of the era. Mining never came to grips with the basic issues, even when challenged and forced to retrench, if ever so slightly. Nothing had been fully resolved; here and elsewhere in the West, opposition to such flagrant disregard of the rights of others was slowly mounting. The terms *environment* and *environmental pollution* would evoke controversy several generations in the future, but at Butte the battle had already been joined.

Butte also became entangled in the first conservation fight in the Rockies, which involved the fate of the forested lands. Since the pioneering days, westerners had blithely cut timber and logged on federal lands. During the Cleveland and Harrison administrations, attempts were made to tighten federal regulations. Cleveland's secretary of the interior diligently exposed frauds by railroads, timber companies, cattle interests, and other groups. Daly and Montana lumber barons, who had illegally purchased large tracts of timberland through such activities as "bogus homesteaders," found themselves in court. They eventually received a slight slap and mild fines, but the actions did indicate that the government was taking a stand. Westerners, who believed it their "God given" right to utilize all nearby natural resources, were enraged.

As surprising as these actions had been, they paled in comparison to a more stunning development, the creation of federal forest reserves. In 1891–92, President Benjamin Harrison's administration created fifteen reserves in western states, including five in Colorado and one in Yellowstone, in Wyoming. This radical departure from the previous policy of individual exploitation caught westerners off guard. The initial reaction was subdued, although a few opposed this "damnable outrage" on economic grounds and as a violation of individual rights. Others were pleased to see the conservation of forests and water and the preservation of places in which to enjoy nature. For too long, the timber lands had been pillaged and despoiled by big companies and individual trespassers; now conservation would be given its chance. Enforcement would be the key to success, but in the Harrison years it was generally lacking and the federal forests suffered as they always had. The next president, Grover Cleveland, proved to be a much better "friend of forestry" during his 1893–97 term. His actions put conservationists and anticonservationists on a collision course and finally got westerners involved.[3]

Congressmen from all three states opposed the president's wishes and the new legislation, none more so than Senator Henry Teller. The champion of silver was also an outspoken proponent of maximum land use and staunchly argued against the forest reserves. He and the others managed to stem the conservation tide by refusing to appropriate money for protection and by defeating a Cleveland-backed initiative to save the reserves by selling marketable timber to the highest bidder. This policy, the opponents argued in true populist rhetoric, would enrich

corporations and harm the little man. They also accused ignorant easterners of trying to undermine one of the greatest pioneer heritages,
unrestricted use of natural resources. Without appropriations, Cleveland refused to set aside more preserves. Finally, in the last weeks of
his administration, the angry president, acting on the recommenda-
tions of the Forestry Commission and the pleas of conservationists,
set aside over twenty-one million acres in the West. Western opponents
were appalled. The *Rocky Mountain News* (May 30, 1897) summed up
the reaction of many people: the withdrawal had been at the behest
of "theorists, enthusiasts, and cranks." Conservationists, in the Rocky
Mountains and elsewhere, were just as adamant: "The preservation of
the forests is everybody's business."

While the debate raged, settlers took matters into their own hands.
Ignoring the law, they moved into the reserves and took out what they
wanted. Exhibiting a simplistic and long-ingrained attitude, they believed the forests existed only for immediate use and were important
only for how long and comfortably they could sustain their utilizers.
Miners, lumbermen, cattlemen, farmers, sheepmen, and townspeople
cared not a whit about presidential proclamations, congressional acts,
and federal rules and regulations. This damnable outrage exemplified
Washington's unnecessary interference in private matters. For them,
the forest reserves simply did not exist. Wyoming Governor William
Richards called the reserves a "farce," and Montana congressman Charles
Hartman decried armchair conservationists, who "sat down in the quiet
parlors of hotels in the various states and there from their inner consciousness . . . evolved the wonderful results." Conservationists protested in their turn. With neither side satisfied, each bided its time,
awaiting the right moment for the push toward final victory.[4]

The Butte smoke and the forest struggles, while hinting at the
future, also illustrated the freewheeling capitalism that characterized
the old West and much of America in the late nineteenth century.

The fight over the fate of Rocky Mountain forests followed the same
form in the new century, with much of the same type of notoriety. The
dispute between the pro- and anticonservationists took a new twist in
1901, when activist Theodore Roosevelt was inaugurated as president.
Roosevelt, who had personally experienced the West, understood its
problems better than any of his predecessors. With assistance from his
friend Gifford Pinchot, a trained forester and chief of what later became
the U.S. Forest Service, he made conservation popular in White House
and Washington circles. Furthermore, Roosevelt insisted on strict and
impartial enforcement of land, grazing, mining, and lumber laws and

diligently prosecuted those who plundered the public domain. West-erners had never faced a forceful team like this, but undeterred, they trotted out the old arguments and prepared to do battle. Roosevelt's first administration was marked by intense disputes.

Cattle ranchers jumped into the fray, protesting the grazing rules and regulations on forest-reserve ranges; for others, the old question of leasing of the public domain resurfaced. The cries were familiar. Outspoken Colorado state senator Edward Taylor, for example, argued that no federal policy should supersede the right of men to own their own land: "My own idea, is that what is everybody's is nobody's." Sounding the alarm, he warned his listeners, "We must strain every nerve to preserve the present condition of affairs."

That "present condition of affairs" was just what Pinchot and TR wanted to change, having defined it as that old freewheeling exploi-tation. Pinchot saw conservation as a social necessity, which would enhance man's environment, stabilize his life, and allow him to reach his full potential. With true populist conviction, Pinchot believed that conservation would protect the little man from the monopolists who had seized many of the West's resources. Pinchot realized, too, how intimately the destruction of forests was bound up with other prob-lems, such as soil erosion, clogging of river channels, and increasing potential for flooding. Roosevelt and others feared a "scarcity of natural resources," which would, they reasoned, undermine American soci-ety.[5]

Out in the Rocky Mountain West, that kind of abstract thinking and fear for the future did not endear either man to his constituents. There were, however, conservationists in the Rockies, even in the ranks of the cattlemen. Urbanites, from the larger cities especially, rallied to the cause, separating themselves from their rural brethren in yet another realm. The debate raged heatedly, from Denver and Helena to the halls of Congress. More than mere talk was involved in some instances; cattlemen openly ignored federal restrictions, and forest rangers were threatened, harassed, and occasionally arrested on trumped-up charges. On some reserves, rangers were "obliged to carry a six-shooter to emphasize [their] authority." When the Wyoming superintendent of the Yellowstone Reserve began to limit the use of forests, he was bitterly assailed in the press: "Mr. Anderson can by a single stroke of his diamond-bedecked hand put out of existence that noble animal [sheep] that clothes his unclean body."[6]

The conflict would not be settled in the West; it had to be resolved in Washington. Representatives there mobilized to defeat conservation.

In 1907, by using the groundswell of western opposition and adroit political maneuvering, the anticonservationists managed finally to pass an amendment to the Agricultural Appropriations Bill. It required congressional approval to create more forest reserves in five western states, including all three in the Rockies. Convinced that the president would not veto such an important bill, western anticonservationists celebrated their anticipated victory—prematurely, as it turned out. They greatly misjudged their opponents' determination. Roosevelt and Pinchot spent several days in withdrawing land from the public domain, some seventeen million acres of timberland in the states covered by the amendment. Little potential timberland remained when they finished. Then, and only then, on March 4, 1907, did the president sign the bill.[7]

Initially shocked into muteness, Roosevelt's antagonists quickly found their voices and screamed "presidential dictatorship" and "abuse of power," to no avail. The tide of opposition ebbed that summer, quelled by lack of unity, declining interest, and Roosevelt's national popularity. His calling attention to conservation opened a new era for the Rocky Mountains; conservation and other enviromental issues would dominate future years. The basic questions of development of natural resources, federal government regulation versus individual rights, and, to an extent, federal versus state jurisdiction would not die. The people had threatened revolt and would again; these westerners cherished their eroding independence.

The conservation movement had split ruralite and urbanite into two camps in the Rockies and, once more, had divided westerners and easterners. The national divisiveness was nothing new, for the East and West had disagreed on the method of resolving the Indian question, on free silver, and on a number of other, less explosive matters. Easterners sometimes had a romantic vision of what the West had once been, but they had some specific ideas about how they wanted to shape the West's destiny. The rural and the urban West, meanwhile, marched increasingly out of step, each to its own drum beat. What that meant for the future was not clear at this point.

Some Montana farmers and ranchers, joined by Uncle Sam, had a vision of what they wished the West to look like. It was not what they saw in their backyard, and so they took on Anaconda over the smoke-pollution question. The company's showcase smelter used the best and most modern copper metallurgy in 1902. A dust chamber and tall smokestacks were designed to reduce, if not eliminate, smoke problems. The chambers caught and settled harmful particles, and company engineers claimed that the stacks discharged sulfuric oxide smoke at so great a height that it never reached the ground in sufficient concentration to harm animal or vegetable life. Unconvinced, nearby residents brought a lawsuit to halt the spread of toxic substances over the Deer Lodge Valley. Remodeling of the plant did not quash the complaints, with the company insisting all the while that it had done everything that was economically feasible. Its remedial experiments were pioneering procedures in the copper-smelting industry, and it believed that it had produced an acceptable, if not a complete, solution.

The controversy evolved into a brutal fight, as Anaconda used all of its considerable power to defend itself on both high ground and low. The company paid claims whenever it became "reasonably satisfied that damage" had actually occurred; that concession failed to satisfy the protesters. Forced into court, Anaconda rehashed the classic arguments already heard in Butte: "We have a perfect right to carry on a legitimate business, and if incidentally we should pollute the atmosphere nobody has the right to complain until specific damage gives him a cause of action."[8]

Business, Anaconda piously intoned, had a right to pollute because it produced revenue through products, wages, and taxes. This assertion translated into total control of Anaconda's and Butte's economy, of the state's to a lesser extent, and even of the nation's to a degree. Only a dullard, or a newcomer, could fail to understand what had happened to Montana earlier, during the Heinze fight. The effects of a shutdown, the ultimate threat, would extend far beyond the state, creating a copper deficit in the world market and resulting in higher prices; Anaconda mined about 11 percent of the world's copper. This line of reasoning concluded with the logical assumption that the significance of the smelter far overshadowed effects on local farmers and ranchers. The *Engineering and Mining Journal* wholeheartedly concurred with that stand. A March 26, 1910, editorial stated frankly: "Even if it does [damage] it is better to suffer some damage than to check a mining industry upon which large cities, we might almost say the state of Montana, are dependent."

Aware of the benefits of improved public relations, Anaconda established its own experimental farms to raise crops and cattle within the shadow of the plant. It promoted agriculture in every way possible and praised the town of Anaconda for its pleasant, healthful atmosphere. The company also attempted to purchase land in the direction that the wind blew the smoke, in a further, unsuccessful effort to stop complaints.[9]

All these expedients having failed to stop the litigation, Anaconda marshaled its newspapers in an attempt to discredit the "smoke farmers." The company took a hard line and fired anyone who was found to have a relative involved in the farmers' association. Using another of its favorite tactics, it pressured and bribed Montana's politicians.

In the end, Anaconda won out. The court refused to grant an injunction and an appeal failed. There was no time to celebrate, however, because the company immediately found itself embroiled with the federal government over charges of smoke damage to trees in nearby forests. An agreement was reached that called for continued investigation and experimentation, to be overseen by a committee. Procrastination prevailed in this round. The study was carried into the 1920s, when a different governmental and business climate reduced pressure on Anaconda to respond further to the complaints.[10]

Nineteenth- and twentieth-century attitudes had clashed during this two-decades-long fight. Anaconda's power and wealth had proven too great for individuals to combat, even when they were organized. The corporation had won the battles, but the eventual outcome of the war remained uncertain. When their own economic fortunes were at stake, westerners took conservation and environmental issues to heart. Otherwise, and far too often, they cavalierly disregarded their impact on the Rockies.

Roosevelt's lasting legacy to the Rockies arose not from his visits, his obvious love of the region, his earlier ranching in the Dakota Badlands (which included an 1886 Montana hunting trip), or his multivolume *The Winning of the West*. It came from his heartfelt beliefs and his activism. The fight for preservation of forests exemplified only one segment of his many contributions. He enthusiastically signed in 1902 the epoch-making Newlands Reclamation Act, after pressuring Congress for its passage. The act authorized the secretary of the interior to construct federal reclamation reservoirs in the West, with such projects to be funded by a newly created reclamation fund derived from public-land sales in arid western states and territories. The Department of the Interior created the Bureau of Reclamation and reserved public lands in the reclamation projects exclusively for settlers, in tracts not to exceed 160 acres. Under Washington's direction, irrigation projects were to be surveyed, constructed, and maintained in conjunction with those reservoirs; local water laws would govern water distribution. The "Great American Desert" might yet blossom into the Garden of Eden; the West might still be the promised land for the small farmer, now that it had Uncle Sam's assistance and Roosevelt's blessing.

Colorado moved quickly into action with plans for a project in the

Uncompahgre Valley, using Gunnison River water. The project had been envisioned before, but not enough interest or money had ever been generated to dig a tunnel through the mesa that separated river and valley. The Bureau approved the project, and construction began in 1904. A promotional pamphlet predicted that the Uncompahgre Valley would become, in "a short time, one of the most beautiful and fruitful garden spots on the face of the earth." Not content with such hyperbole, the author went on to proclaim that the "Gunnison Tunnel and kindred projects are demanded by the time." They would serve as safety valves for eastern states "eagerly seeking some outlet for the overflow" of their population. Others concurred in that opinion. These projects, it was predicted, would evolve into a government-endorsed, back-to-the-land movement that would help to minimize the social violence, class warfare, and radicalism breeding in the cities.

At a cost of over ten million dollars and six lives, the tunnel and supporting canals were completed. President William Howard Taft, Secretary of the Interior Richard Ballinger, and Governor Shafroth drove across the sandy desert to the tunnel's western portal in September 1909. After the ceremonies, the president threw the switch to open the headgate of what was then the world's longest irrigation tunnel. The first water was delivered the following July, and the Uncompahgre Valley was on its way to blossoming like the garden.[11] The theory was a fine one, but the reality came with difficulty. Problems plagued valley residents for years to come; construction costs far exceeded estimates and the user fee for water had to be adjusted. Not all the "garden" proved to be fit for irrigation. Neither did it ever serve as a dependable safety valve for the discontented in the overpopulated East; located too far away and demanding agricultural skills most urbanites did not possess, the Gunnison project benefited only the surrounding region. For westerners, this project, and the many that followed in the Rocky Mountains, were godsends.

The Newlands Act worked well in this mountainous land. Water could be impounded easily behind government-built dams, without the silting that so hindered projects out on the flatlands. Irrigation became more commonplace. For every action, however, there is a re-action, and this one brought intensification of the thorny water questions. Reclamation projects demanded water; the crucial issue for the next generation would be who held claim to that water flowing out of the Rockies.

Kansas had already brought suit against Colorado and sixteen corporations over their diversion of water from the Arkansas River. Their actions left the western half of Kansas nearly high and dry by late summer. Colorado insisted that, by prior appropriation, customs, and Colorado law, it had the right to control and divert those waters. Furthermore, the moisture fell as either snow or rain within its boundaries. Kansas objected and filed suit (in 1901); her western lands would benefit by irrigation, but most of the Arkansas River water had been preempted.

The case proved to be a landmark in the history of water litigation. Colorado and Kansas and the United States, as intervenor, developed their cases fully. The Supreme Court handed down its decision in 1907, after hearing 8,559 typewritten pages' worth of evidence. Colorado won the case, with the court holding that the state had complete control of the waters within its boundaries. The judges, however, did give Kansas the right to reopen the case at a future time with new material evidence, especially if Colorado increased its diversions and upset the balance of benefits to both states. The first bullet of the interstate water war had been shot, and the fundamental issues would have to be resolved.[12]

The fact that the federal government had injected itself into western water matters did not sit well with Wyoming Governor Bryant Brooks. He fully understood that his state's water resources were of enormous value and wanted them to be developed for the benefit of Wyoming. At the 1908 governors' conference, he argued that the federal government had no control over the waters of Wyoming. Irrigation, drainage, and water-power privileges "are essentially local matters." Speaking for his generation, and laying a foundation of support for the future, Brooks emphasized that the people were "fully competent without any assistance from the federal government" to handle water issues.[13] The revolt of the Rocky Mountains against the federal government only intensified with the new century, but so did its fondness for federal funds and programs.

14 : RIDING INTO THE SUNSET

The major themes that would dominate the region for the remainder of the twentieth century had come into public view during the twenty years following 1890: relationships with Washington, corporation dominance, conservation and environmental issues, exploitation of natural resources (from land to water to minerals), urban versus rural controversies, and "colonialism." These issues had been there before 1890, but the focus became sharper, the stakes higher, and the emotions more intense as the years went by. Tourism also came to the forefront, with a vigor that only few had previously imagined possible.

In the same months that the Colorado suffragists campaigned, and during 1893, the first year of the nation's worst depression to date, America celebrated the World's Columbian Exposition in Chicago. The fair honored the man who, four hundred years before, had started the frontier rolling west, Christopher Columbus. Although it was a worldwide display of the progress that had been made since Columbus opened the New World, it particularly highlighted the achievements of the crown jewel, the United States.

Plans for it had been in the works for some time, and the Rocky Mountain states were determined to be well represented. And they were. Along with the fascinating midway attractions, such as "Little Egypt," the huge Ferris wheel, and that new taste treat, cotton candy, there could be found exhibits and some of the world's most advanced architecture. Buffalo Bill's fifty-acre international "Wild West" show, across the street from the fair, outdid itself in promoting a romantic vision of that never-never land. The Rocky Mountain states intended to convey the excitement of today and the promise of tomorrow. The hard times notwithstanding, all three states placed exhibits at the fair, with Colorado and Montana in special state buildings. Colorado's Spanish Renaissance–style edifice was found between California and Washington; Montana's more traditional Roman style sat next to neighboring Idaho and Utah, both on the northern part of the grounds. These two states were honored with a special day, while Wyoming seems to have been ignored. The organizers may have been offended that Wyoming had failed to construct its own building, or perhaps they thought that the home of the Johnson County War belonged more to Buffalo Bill's show.

Colorado and Montana earned high praise for their mineral exhibits. Aspen sent a ten-foot figure, "The Silver Queen," crowned with a "brilliant diadem of rich ores," and Montana displayed fifty tons of ore samples. Wyoming was proud of its "massive and creditable display," which featured a variety of minerals, including coal, iron ores, building stone, marble, and fifteen samples of petroleum. They all arrayed their grains, fruits, and other agricultural products, as well as photographs, to convince the visitors of the wonders of the region. Individual communities and counties sent displays that focused attention on their special attractions. Colorado benefited from one particular attraction, a cliff-dwellers exhibit that was housed inside a replica of "Battle Rock Mountain." The original stood far out in McElmo Canyon in the southwestern corner of the state. The mysterious former residents of Mesa Verde proved quite a hit with the fairgoers, who, if they wished, could discreetly avoid the room with the "mummies."[1] Tourism, agriculture, mining, industry, urbanization, and transportation were all represented, and the Rocky Mountains were well advertised. The new West could be experienced at the exposition, and the old West directly across Stony Island Avenue at the corner of Hope Avenue and Sixty-second Street.

Colorado had been involved in promoting itself since the 1860s, and the other two states fell into line as they matured. By the nineties they were all in full swing, assisted now by out-of-state private enterprise. The famous Baedeker Company published its first American guidebook edition in 1893. Colorado and Yellowstone National Park warranted the most coverage, with Wyoming given the least, although the editor did tell his readers that it was the "equity state," explaining that men and women had equal voting rights. With this book, the tourist found answers to most of his questions. Everything was covered—the primary attractions, the cost of Yellowstone guides (five dollars per day for the mounted tours), and advice: "*Warm Wraps* are very necessary in the Yellowstone, as however strong the sun is by day, the nights are apt to be very chilly." Finely situated Helena, pleasant Colorado Springs, and Denver (a "striking example of the marvelous growth of western cities") earned special mention. Less attention was paid to celebrated Leadville, "huge and bustling" Butte City, and smaller communities along the rail lines.[2]

Tourists were coming to the Rockies in unprecedented numbers, thanks to such promotions as the World's Columbian Exposition. They enjoyed the continued evolution of faster and more comfortable travel to the West. The last great railroad-building decade saw the giant of western railroading, James Hill, complete his Great Northern across Montana, along with smaller lines that rounded out Wyoming's and Colorado's rail systems. From isolated Mesa Verde to the fishing and hunting streams of Montana, visitors sampled the Rocky Mountains. Yellowstone National Park ranked at the top of many visitors' must-see lists. Some complained that the hotel at Mammoth Hot Springs was "a very aristocratic resort," or that the soldiers and rules made visitors uneasy; but most simply delighted in the vistas. Iowan Gardner Turrill and his party (including his wife, who was six-months pregnant) traveled by wagon from Kemmerer, Wyoming. They overlooked the "exasperating, audacious, Wyoming mosquito," isolation, "lonely mountain roads," and tourist vandalism to the park, and had a wonderful time. They looked for signs of the old West when traveling near a spot where they had been told a gunfight once occurred; failing in that endeavor, they found a substitute when they encountered an immigrant wagon bound for "some new gold diggings in eastern Idaho."[3]

The old West, which seemed as recent as yesterday, was passing from the scene. Both residents and visitors sensed it. The Colorado and Montana historical societies were working to preserve it, as the purchase of the first collection of Mesa Verde artifacts by Colorado indicated. "Old-timers" wrote their memoirs, telling newcomers how life had been back in the early days, and pioneer societies gave them a day to turn back the clock and tell a few tall tales.[4] Perceptive locals already realized that the old West had a market value and potential for profit. Tourists traveled to "see the elephant" at Creede and Cripple Creek before it was gone. Residents of Denver and Helena proudly pointed out some of their older buildings and sites, if for no other reason than to prove how far they had progressed and to contrast them with those wonderful new buildings framed by electric and telephone lines.

In the rush toward the new century, Rocky Mountain residents poised for a moment to honor the old. Then they plunged resolutely ahead to improve the roads, in which "future prosperity . . . is intimately bound up." They took the Spanish-American War in full stride, patriotically volunteering in unexpected numbers to "Remember the Maine, to Hell with Spain."[5] They, and most other Americans, only vaguely understood the full impact of the country's little "coming out" war. With the depression easing, the battle of the standards behind them, and labor turmoil on hold, the new century promised them it would be as exciting as the old.

Then came a boost from Washington, when Theodore Roosevelt became president. If reclamation and conservation held a large place in Roosevelt's heart, they shared that space with national parks. Among those that he created was Mesa Verde, the first cultural national park ever established. Since the "discovery" of the ruins in December 1888, the mesa had been attracting increasing attention from scholars, lay persons, and pot hunters, who ransacked the ruins for marketable artifacts. As a result of the depredations, a group of women headed by two redoubtable and remarkable individuals, Virginia McClurg and Lucy Peabody, led the fight to preserve the sites before vandalism and visitation left little to save or see.

The women overcame public inertia, lack of a strong political base, and the isolation of Mesa Verde by mounting a vigorous lobbying campaign that covered the state, the nation, and Washington, D.C. They petitioned, spoke, organized, marshaled support, raised money, signed leases with the Utes on whose land Mesa Verde stood, led expeditions into Mesa Verde, contracted for wells to be dug and roads to be built as well as surveys to be run, and wrote articles. Finally, in the winter of 1905–06, bills were reported favorably out of House and Senate committees. On June 29, 1906, Roosevelt signed the bill that gave the Rocky Mountains their second national park. It was extremely unfortunate that the women who had fought so long and determinedly to win that prize fell to fighting among themselves during the last months of the struggle. They split into two wings, which obstinately fought each other over the course of the next generation and managed to deprive all of them of their just credit. Mesa Verde did not become a popular attraction overnight. Located far down on the Rockies' southern fringe, it awaited better roads and the automobile to bring development and tourists.[6]

Roosevelt's support of the project had eased its way through Congress. Perhaps unwittingly, he was molding the Rocky Mountains' economic and tourist future, as well as making a significant impact on what a later generation would call the quality of life. Theodore Roosevelt was the first president to care about preserving and developing western natural resources. His popularity and charisma encouraged others to follow his lead. It would take yet a while, but eventually there would be a conversion from the strictly materialistic and developmental philosophy of the nineteenth century. The grow-or-die mentality would ultimately become outmoded.

Meanwhile, the tourist came not just to see natural wonders; the Rockies also held the fascinating possibility of sampling the old West before it was gone. After all, the census bureau, scholars, and others were already telling them it was too late.

What they found typically reminded them of their homes. Prohibition, Arbor Day celebrations, the Salvation Army, antigambling laws— where had the old West gone? Cowboy T. B. Long thought it had gone to western Canada, where he went in 1905, declaring that Montana was becoming too crowded. Montanans, meanwhile, were openly disobeying their antigambling law; and individual towns in Wyoming and Colorado were achieving no better success with enforcement. In 1907, Governor Joseph Toole was forced to recommend that either the citizens capture a "newborn zeal for enforcement" or recognize that the time for repeal was at hand.[7] The Salvation Army continued its appeals for funds, and schoolchildren planted trees without any controversy.

The old West could be found mostly in literature, paintings, the theater, and the newfangled motion picture. That West would live eternally in the imaginations, the myths, and dreams of its vicarious participants, safely downwind from its historical antecedents. Occasionally, it would be resurrected and the legends reinforced. The Chicago, Milwaukee and St. Paul Railroad construction camp of Taft, Montana, with its "human machine" work gangs, achieved great notoriety. The Chicago *Tribune* called it, in 1909, "the wickedest city in America," a "plague spot of vice." Taft's moment of fame was as brief as its life.

The myth assumed a life of its own. The mass-produced, adventuresome, larger-than-life dime novels had started the trend, which was abetted by stage plays (as early as the 1870s had come the first western, "The Scouts of the Prairie") and the highly popular Buffalo Bill Cody Wild West shows. Dime novels, many of them based partly on fact and real individuals, placed their characters in a fictionalized, simplistic, and stylized western setting. Kit Carson, Jesse James, Buffalo Bill, Wild Bill Hickock, and Calamity Jane would not have recognized themselves, but the average reader did not understand that the real West bore no resemblance to its fictional counterpart. Colorado Kate, Montana Nat, and Wyoming Zeke were no less real to their fans than authentic historical personalities. Even William Cody eventually found himself unable to distinguish between the facts and the fiction created about him. Buffalo Bill had become the first romantic, western mythic hero created "by a mass medium to pander to a mass taste."[8]

The dime novel flourished because the public loved it, and it shaped forever their view of the West and westerners. The critics deplored dime novels and declared they never would provide much of permanent literary value. The tradition they continued sprang from James Fenimore Cooper's "Leather-Stocking Tales." Cooper's five novels in this series were romantic and adventuresome and featured his hero, the noble, generous, resourceful, and brave Natty Bumppo. Nineteenth-century Americans were enthralled by the tales, and the western novel was born.[9]

The western novel was kept alive by authors such as Mary Hallock Foote, who lived in Colorado and elsewhere in the mining West with her engineer husband, Arthur. Less successful and popular than Cooper, she nevertheless captured the "local color" of Rocky Mountain history in the 1870s in her articles, illustrations, and novels. Hers was a genteel West, populated by respectable Victorians and a few rascals. From her sheltered Leadville home, that was the kind of world she had experienced, which may account for her lack of lasting popularity with the general public. She did combine the written with the visual, bridging the gap between the two mediums in presenting the West. Far less successful were such local writers as Emma Thayer, Mary MacLane, and Hattie Louthan.

The region was also beginning to attract writers to come and utilize the setting for novels. Gertrude Atherton used Butte for her *Perch of the Devil*. Her brief visit to the town was proudly noted by the *Butte Miner*, which commented that "the famous novelist is in Butte to gather material for a novel she is just now writing."

This literary genre could not hope to compete with the shorter, less expensive, and less intellectually demanding dime novel. All that changed when Owen Wister came along with his novel *The Virginian* (1902), often called the "quintessential Western." Pennsylvania-born and Harvard graduate Wister, a lifelong friend of Roosevelt, had first come to the West, to Wyoming in 1885, for his health. *The Virginian* became a sensation almost overnight, and its hero, the strong, silent, and brave cowboy, quickly became the ubiquitous literary hero of western fiction. That hero was someone who was not native to the West (usually an easterner, but in Wister's story he was a southerner), who then moved west and came to terms with a totally different life. He was transformed into a new man by a moral environment that clearly distinguished between black and white, good and evil. The simplistic nature of the story; the triumph of good; the virtue of the heroine Molly Stark; and the rugged and manly, yet gentlemanly Virginian confirmed in readers' minds an image of the West that had been circulating for several generations.[10] Because they wanted so much to believe the fantasy, they latched onto this one with alacrity. Wister had hit the bull's-eye, giving them the vision of the knightly hero, with a sense of honor, who had the capacity to exceed the villain in violence, if necessary, to bring peace to the land.

Wister's nostalgic look at a West that contrasted so sharply with the twentieth century, and had never actually existed except in the pages of literature and art, reinforced the image created by Fremont and Bierstadt. The larger-than-life Rocky Mountains and the people who conquered them, the transforming nature of the West, and the heroic saga of its settlement emerged firmly fixed in the American mind. The contemporaneous picture would have been considerably different if described by an 1860s settler who had crossed those mountains, lived in that elevated and isolated environment, and scratched out a living in the not-so-promised land. That same individual, a revered pioneer now, might have been just as captivated by the bewitching nostalgia, however. He or she had been a real live part of it and would always relish the remembrance of its exciting elements. So the pioneer fed the myth, giving it additional credibility, and the legend moved on, unhindered, into myth.

The myth also distorted visitors' accounts. *Century Magazine* published this description of the westerner: "Today in the recesses of the Rocky Mountains you come upon steady-eyed eagle-faced men . . . whose masterful, unswerving will and fierce impatience of restraint remind you of their spiritual kinsmen, the heroes of the Icelandic sagas." Katharine Ellis wrote several articles describing her visits to Montana—what she saw and what she felt. She praised the ease with which westerners overcame their difficulties, which would have loomed insurmountable in the East. One couple, starting with three hundred dollars and a pair of horses, had built up a ranch and a "good living income" in twelve years. "We must do it all ourselves," the western wife observed. Ellis wrote movingly of the components of their lives: the neighborliness and tolerance of these Montanans, the beauty of the scenery, a 1909 two-room log cabin with a dirt roof, and a July 4 picnic and its fireworks, which "gave evidence that it was no *common* picnic or dance, but was *the* event of the year." Her account, though accurate, reinforced the epic proportions of the people and their land.

Ellis's account was not restricted to the old West. She saw the changes and understood what they meant to young and old. Two widows with whom she talked on a train from Butte to Salt Lake City told her of the loneliness and hardships of the pioneering days; they were on their way to California to spend a warm, comfortable winter. Ellis saw nothing in the appearance of a young ranch wife and her children, whom she met at Dillon, "to indicate that they were from a Montana ranch high up in the Rocky Mountains." A friend described in a letter to her how much life had changed in the basin—the nine-month school, her neighbors and their problems, and "above every-thing else the telephone, connecting them with town and with each other," and thus providing "the greatest blessing."[11] Ellis observed the old and the new and left her readers to make their own judgments about the Rocky Mountain West. They wanted to believe that the ro-mantic adventurous West still existed, because the newer one sounded much more like their own daily lives.

Katharine Ellis was not the first nor the last to wrestle with that dichotomy. The legendary Montana painter, one-time cowboy Charlie Russell, struggled with it all his life and the old won out for him. He observed the world of the airplane and the automobile and worked hard to produce an exhaustive record of the old West. Painters and illustrators, as much as writers, had shaped the image of the Rocky Mountains and the western epic. Thomas Moran and Albert Bierstadt captured the essence of the mountains better than anyone else of their generation. Moran, as already mentioned, helped promote interest in establishing Yellowstone National Park. He also caught the region's majesty and beauty and made his little contribution to the legend, when he used artistic license to stroke American chauvinism into his "The Mountain of the Holy Cross." When one viewed Moran's painting of a cross naturally embedded in the Colorado Rockies, it did seem that God himself had blessed the westward course of empire and these beautiful mountains.

Photographer William Henry Jackson also visited the Mount of the Holy Cross, and even he could not resist embellishing his work. He touched up his photograph so that the cross would look more dramatic than it appeared in real life. Jackson and his camera photographed it all (both the old and new Wests) from the mid-1860s through the next fifty years and stimulated interest in preserving all four national parks that were created in the Rocky Mountain region prior to 1916. He gave the era and its people a visual immortality that was denied to earlier generations. The painter and the photographer complemented each other, but the former had more impact.

Bierstadt, one of the most popular American painters of the nineteenth century, worked to capture the "colossal drama" and the romantic, breathtaking landscape of the Rockies. His sweeping and powerful canvases seemed to give the viewer a window to a land that dwarfed anything to the east of it. He shaped the concept and matched it repeatedly in his paintings; visually, he was the master of the legend.[12]

What Moran and Bierstadt did for the land, the illustrator, painter, and sculptor Frederic Remington did for the inhabitants. He, too, came west, fell in love with the adventure and the era and spent the rest of his life glamorizing the trooper, the cowboy, and the pioneer. The myth of the West leaped from his work.

That was where Charlie Russell came in, as the myth and the reality merged. He also journeyed west and stayed there, unlike the others who went back east. This cowboy turned artist knew and loved Montana and the passing old West as few others did. He painted what he experienced, as well as what he imagined before he arrived. Charlie maintained a melancholy attachment for the best of the old. Without question, Russell painted with a genuine feeling for the nineteenth century and kept the pioneering spirit alive in the public's imagination. Russell and Remington brought the viewer up close to the people and revealed all that seemed necessary to know about their lives, their dreams, and their adventures. Their audience saw men and women struggling for survival in a rugged land, portrayed on a canvas filled with action and adventure.[13]

The West of the artists, the writers, and the photographers became the public's West. It needed only one more ingredient—a low-cost and mass-produced visual art form, which would add animation unfettered by the constraints of the stage or arena. That innovation came with the motion picture. The first western, "The Great Train Robbery," trailed on the heels of *The Virginian*. By 1913, even Buffalo Bill had joined the movie industry with his epic production "The Indian Wars Refought." With these silent films, the western galloped into everyone's lives; the old West could be seen, felt, and experienced without traveling far from one's home. It would never die now, for the western Camelot had become the American legend.

A fitting epitaph was written by an enthralled visitor to the Rocky Mountains in 1901:

> The wonders of the Rocky Mountains, revealed to many of
> us for the first time, remain a pleasing picture in our minds.
> The grand and picturesque scenery along the route through
> the mountains has been talked over many times.[14]

Everything that comprised the old West would be talked about for generations to come and would produce increasing tourist revenue. Meanwhile, the new West went about its business of replacing the old with the new, as it had done for fifty years.

15 : TOMORROW IS TODAY

As the twentieth century entered its second decade, the lure of a promised land danced temptingly once more. Again, the ever-optimistic farmer did not hesitate to tempt fate; this time he gambled and won and personally resolved the debate concerning the "Great American Desert" versus the "Garden of Eden." He now held a new golden key to unlocking the garden and conquering the desert—dryland farming.

The prairies that stretched east from the Rockies enjoyed another boom, the second and third time around for some of this land. Wrote one Montana editor, "The old-timer dies hard and loathes to see these fertile prairies adorned with claim shacks, but the tide of immigration that has set in this direction cannot be stopped." Assisted by new drought-resistant crops, new tillage methods, and special equipment, the dryland farmer conserved as much of that precious water as he could each season. He was aided by the region's agricultural colleges and by the Department of Agriculture, which conducted a variety of experiments to improve seeds and methods of cultivation, and published bulletins on the results. The federal government modified the Homestead Law to allow 320 acres to be claimed, a better size for dryland farming, and reduced the residency requirement for ownership from five years to three. The Rocky Mountain states added their own promotion, as did the railroads, which also conducted agricultural experiments. The railroads, of course, would sell the farmer as much land as he wanted, at their price, and would eagerly transport his crops and necessities. No longer did the homesteader have to do it all "by the seat of his pants," so to speak.[1] He had several partners in the struggle to reach and conquer his promised land.

The boom hit full stride, and Montana farm acreage jumped 2,325 percent in the new century's first twenty years. "In competition with the world, Montana wins," boasted the state Department of Agriculture. By 1915, Laramie County, Wyoming, had over 591,000 dryland farm acres on its tax rolls. The population of Cheyenne County, Colorado, jumped by a startling 635 percent between 1900 and 1910. As Wyoming's Governor Brooks enthusiastically predicted in 1909, "Experiments so far have been very encouraging. Unquestionably, a considerable portion of our remaining public land has some value for agricultural purposes."

Along with the farmers and their families came their supply towns. Built around the grain elevator, the depot, and the bank, they were "grimly utilitarian." A church, school, one street, and no trees or grass created a stark appearance that sometimes caught visitors by surprise. These communities looked vaguely like what they aspired to be—transplanted midwestern villages. Once the bloom began to fade, however, they did not offer enough to entice many visitors or new residents. There would be ghost towns on the plains as well as in the mountains.

Out on the farm, families lived in tarpaper shacks or, occasionally, in sod houses; they worked and dreamed, borrowed and dreamed, and awaited the new millennium. They gambled that good fortune would smile on them on the public domain. They would have argued vociferously with the historian who later described the homestead program as the "original relief fund for farmers." For them, the public domain was a birthright, not a grant to the poor.[2] Nature was kind: a wet cycle brought rain. As another historian observed, dryland farming succeeds best in wet years. Between 1910 and 1915 the price of wheat also went up, as did land values. The farmer borrowed more money bought more land, improved his equipment, and waited for even better times.

The ancestors of these farmers had trod this path before. With unbridled hope in their hearts, most did not pay heed to warnings, such as the one that appeared in the August 1913 issue of the *Wyoming Farm Bulletin*:

> the farmer who comes to Wyoming cannot expect to always
> tread a path of roses . . . Some land has been taken up
> which might better go back to cattle and sheep ranges until

224 Chapter Fifteen

such time as we are in greater need of land than we will be
for some time to come.[3]

Life for the homesteader and the rancher had not changed much
over the years. In a bittersweet, yet touchingly humorous series of
letters, Elinore Stewart related to a friend her experiences as a wife
and mother in western Wyoming. By train and stage, which acted "as
if it had the hiccoughs," she reached Burnt Fork. During haycutting
season, she worked in the field, milked seven cows every day, cooked
at night, and had time to put up thirty pints of jam. It was not all
work. Elinore delighted in planning for Christmas 1912: "I never had
so much fun in my life." For some of the neighborhood children, it
was the very first Christmas tree they had ever seen. "We all got so
much out of so little. I will never again allow even the smallest thing
to go to waste."

She became housekeeper, nurse, doctor, rancher, farmer, and general overseer, and proved to herself that women could homestead and
ranch. Any woman who could stand her own company, could see
beauty in a sunset, loved growing things, and was "willing to put in
much time at careful labor" would succeed, Stewart believed. With
confidence and pride, she boasted, "I have tried every kind of work
this ranch affords, and can do any of it."[4]

Water controlled the present and the future, for dryland farmer and
rancher alike. When the rains failed to come, they felt betrayed and
resorted to desperate measures. Rainmakers made extravagant promises as they brewed ill-smelling, secret concoctions and tickled the
clouds with electric current. They would work their magic, for a fee.
Occasionally, rain would ensue, but it was doubtful that they had
earned the credit for it. Rainmaking, nevertheless, became a part of
folklore, if not science; in some ways the rainmakers were simply ahead
of their time. Rocky Mountain clouds would be seeded and squeezed
in future generations.[5]

Government-sponsored reclamation projects promised a more permanent solution to the water problem. Irrigation could make the desert
bloom only if everyone had plenty of water. The early-day reclama-
tionists conjured grand visions of what lay ahead; unfortunately, those
visions turned out to be mostly mirages. In Montana, dams and irrigation systems brought the precious commodity to nearby farmers and
their land, but left most of the wide-open spaces unwatered. Wyoming's reclamation projects turned into a three-ring circus of federal,
state, and private enterprise. A mad scramble for water rights led to

a state report, which concluded that "every spring and rivulet is now as eagerly sought for as if it were in fact the last available supply of water in the state." Filings on reservoir sites and irrigable land multiplied, until by 1910 virtually all feasible projects appeared to have been taken. But demands for more did not abate, as farmers struggled to make their land bloom.[6]

Neighborhing Colorado, likewise, went through a boom, both in the mountain valleys and out on the plains. The state benevolently watched over these developments, doing what it could to help. The legislature passed a district irrigation law, which allowed landowners to organize irrigation districts capable of issuing bonds, or to levy taxes on land to purchase or construct canals and reservoirs. It created the position of state engineer to oversee equitable and regular water distribution.

Colorado, with streams aplenty and normally sufficient water flow, had been temporarily stymied by the *Kansas* v. *Colorado* case, but it had ultimately won. Or so it seemed; a warning flag went up when the Supreme Court announced that it would umpire quarrels in the future.

That future came quickly, involving not Kansas but neighboring Wyoming. The two states soon found themselves at odds over stream flow and appropriated water rights. Both Colorado and Wyoming irrigators used water from the Laramie River; when Colorado started to divert a larger amount for the Cache la Poudre Valley, Wyoming protested. Wyoming, which jealously guarded its available water supplies, heeded the pleas of its voters, who claimed that the additional diversion would interfere with their appropriations. The basic dispute did not involve the doctrine of prior appropriation, which both states recognized. Rather, the argument centered on the quantity of water used. When Colorado refused to respond to complaints, Wyoming filed suit before the Supreme Court in 1911. In 1913–14, evidence was taken and hopes ran high that a speedy opinion would be handed down. Those hopes would be dashed. Not until 1922 did the court reach a decision.

Wyoming got its way. The Supreme Court awarded to its irrigators the amount of water they had claimed to have appropriated and gave to the Colorado farmers the remainder of the unappropriated flow, or not more than 15,500 acre-feet a year. What was more significant in the long run, this landmark decision brought federal regulation and protection to interstate streams. The Supreme Court, not the states, would determine equity.[7] It became open season for water lawsuits; water lawyers and water experts had found *their* promised land.

All three states pointed with pride to their agricultural achievements. Pamphlets highlighted the average yields and profits and featured model farms and ranches. Colorado waxed enthusiastically about its sugar beets, and Wyoming and Montana to a lesser degree. Eastern and Western Slope farmers caught the "sugar vision." Cool weather, high altitude, and controlled irrigation combined to make Colorado the nation's leading producer of sugar beets. The progress that had been made in agriculture over the past decade was certainly worthy of the pride the farmers took in their accomplishments.

Farmers harvested heartbreak, as well; with the prospect of getting rich came also the possibility of going broke. Nowhere else in the Rockies did so many manage to fall victim to that latter possibility. The jury remained out on dryland farming, but irrigation held great potential, as earlier experiments in the Union Colony had proven. Irrigation required more capital and equipment and was already revealing some natural, but nonetheless disturbing, trends. The average farm size was growing larger and the number of family-owned farms began to decline, if ever so slightly.[8] Another barely perceptible trend was noticeable, at least in Wyoming: farmland was being returned to livestock raising.

To the farmer, the region still looked to be the promised land, for at least a little while longer. As long as the wet cycles continued and World War I provided unexpected access to foreign markets, the prospects would be good. Like the miner before him, the farmer could not function as master of his own destiny. That role fell to others outside the Rocky Mountains. A classic example came from the sugar-beet industry. Its continued prosperity would always rely on tariff makers in Washington and their willingness to protect the industry from foreign competition.

Denver's prognosis for prosperity proved even better than the farmer's. Unchallenged as "Queen of the Mountains and Plains," it thrived. With a population nearing 250,000, the city had far outstripped any regional rival. And it was growing ever more "respectable." Billy Sunday and Carrie Nation came into town, and the red-light district on Market Street closed down. The state, too, cooperated by changing its image. In 1914, the rural prohibitionists, assisted by their city brethren, passed a statewide prohibition law, which went into effect on January 1, 1916. The "drys" envisioned a quick end to poverty, crime, drunkenness, and other assorted vices, while at least some of the "wets" planned ways to circumvent the law. Montana and Wyoming joined the "noble experiment" somewhat later.[9]

Elsewhere, urbanization declined. Only Butte, among all the mining communities, more than held its own; the rest leveled off, retreated, or disappeared. In spite of the decline of urbanism, the focus of the twentieth century would be on the townspeople. They had achieved maturity and stability and gained polish and worldliness, and were now aggressively seeking new economic opportunities. They had lost the naivete that had characterized some of their ancestors' actions, particularly in despoiling the continent and dealing with the Indians. These twentieth-century westerners looked and acted very much like their cousins in Chicago or Boston.[10]

The urban influence in all three states did not prevent rural voters from exerting political power over their urban brothers. Through legislative apportionment and because of the rise in the agricultural economy and population, the rural electorate quietly succeeded in gaining the upper hand. Misunderstandings between the two groups created a future that was ripe for conflict.

For the time being, as the decade reached its halfway point, the political implications of this change in status were unrealized. To the urbanite, rural life and its troubles seemed far removed. The contrast between the two resembled the contrast between the two centuries. The "country bumpkin" and "the rural hick" were the butt of vaudeville jokes. Few urbanites had any wish to understand rural America; they simply wanted the meat, bread, and potatoes that it sent to the neighborhood grocery. Rural visitors, though bewildered by some aspects of city behavior, could not resist the modern life and the bright lights. Theodore Wiprud, who was stationed in Butte in 1914 during the union troubles, remarked that some of his fellow National Guardsmen sought out the red-light district, for, as he put it, "Most of them were like me, from small towns where proper behavior was taken for granted." Visitors enjoyed the glamorous side of urban life, but its workaday world drew little attention. Leslie Wilkinson remembered her mother at Cripple Creek: "Bake Day, Mending Day. A certain day for a certain thing. That's what I remember, those special days that my ma had. Ironing, cooking and washing every day."[11]

Montana women worked hard for the cause of suffrage. Led by energetic and friendly Jeannette Rankin, a whirlwind campaign was organized in 1913–14. A graduate of the University of Montana and one of the "new" women of her day, Rankin proved to be an efficient organizer, an intense speaker, and a tireless worker. With perfect timing, as progressivism reached its flood, the campaign brought victory on November 3, 1914. Not missing a beat, Montana's new voters organized a Good Government Association the following January and continued their quest for political power.[12] The quest, which had started back in Wyoming in 1869, achieved a complete victory for Rocky Mountain women.

Not all struggles for equality ended so successfully. The coal miners of Colorado could testify to that. Their grievances had ranged from wages through working conditions, to economic and political exploitation. Like their hard-rock contemporaries, they had looked to unionism for salvation. To help them, the United Mine Workers sent out organizers, who, despite strong company opposition, had made some headway early in the century. The predictable result was a series of strikes, which climaxed in 1903–04. Completely overshadowed by the troubles in the hard-rock districts, the coal miners lost.

Neither side was happy with the outcome; the union lost, but it had not been crushed completely. The miners still had grievances, and the owners hated the union and its continuing organizational efforts. A second series of strikes erupted in Boulder in the northern fields and ended in the southern fields (the Walsenburg-Trinidad area) in a vicious 1913–14 strike. Once more, the decades-old standard procedure was followed: In came company guards, and eventually the National Guard, and out went the miners and their families from the company towns into tent colonies. The miners demanded, among other things, a wage increase, union recognition, and the enforcement of Colorado mining laws, including safety regulations. The strike dragged on all winter before it exploded into violence at a railroad siding called Ludlow on April 20, 1914. Someone fired a shot, and frustrated miners and militia set upon each other; nineteen people died, including thirteen women and children. "Remember Ludlow," the strikers cried. "Down with the militia, To Hell with the Law," became the rallying cry, as the coal miners vengefully took over the district, driving out the company guards and state forces. Federal troops finally intervened and restored order. The "Ludlow Massacre" again focused unwanted, unfavorable national attention on Colorado.[13] Nobody won. An exhausted state saw twenty years of labor turmoil come to an end, at the cost of additional taxpayer expense and a further besmirched reputation.

An equally tired Western Federation of Miners hung on just as grimly in Butte. Confronted by the all-powerful and insensitive Anaconda, divided by ethnic tensions, challenged by the more radical Industrial Workers of the World, and infiltrated by company spies, the old union began to break under the strain. Conservatives opposed radicals, both electioneering for local offices and union power. Charges

of socialism, a "company slate," election frauds, and too-heavy as-
sessments heated the short-tempered spring of 1914. Confusion, insecurity, and anger prevailed.

The tension exploded on June 13, Butte's usually festive Miners'
Union Day. The reform, or radical, wing boycotted the parade, then
attacked it. Before the day ended, the union hall had been sacked. The
reformers promptly organized their own local, and a jurisdictional quarrel
broke out immediately. Ten days later, at a regular union meeting,
shooting erupted. Two men were killed and the evening ended with
the destruction of the union hall. Anaconda sat smugly on the sidelines
and watched its labor adversary tear itself apart.

For weeks afterward, the city quivered on the brink of anarchy;
local officials were unwilling or unable to restore order. Finally, because
of the threatened burning of Butte and the existing "lawlessness and
defiance of authority," the governor declared martial law and sent in
the National Guard. One editor declared that the situation resembled
the "great war in Europe" because each event had been so long expected
that fears were allayed that either would really happen. Nevertheless,
it had happened, and the WFM would suffer the consequences. Union
leaders were arrested, and Anaconda announced it would no longer
recognize the union, promptly instituting a policy of "open shop."
Following a grand jury investigation, the socialist mayor and sheriff
were removed from office. At the "Gibraltar of Unionism," the WFM
lay shattered and helpless; organized labor had been totally defeated.
Butte miners worked in the hated "open shop," much to the "great
satisfaction of everyone," concluded the conservative *Engineering and
Mining Journal*.[14]

In the two once-strong union states, the owners had emerged totally
triumphant. The hopes of the miners lay crushed in the smoking ruins
of Ludlow and in the dynamited union hall. The end result could have
been predicted, despite the appearance of strength and solidarity pro-
jected by the miners. The workers had never been completely unified,
and they lacked the financial reserves, solid resources, and political
power of the corporations. Increasing frustration led to increased radicalism in both Colorado and Montana and to mounting public reaction
against the unions. The tradition was all too universal, for it had happened in the eastern states earlier. The heritage of the old West clashed
with modern capitalism and industrialism, and the winner gained dominance in the new West. The result could also have been predicted by
noting the trends of the pioneering generation, which had been building toward this conclusion since its arrival.

Even though the miners lost, mining itself did not win. Except for Butte, and to a lesser degree Cripple Creek, the bonanza days were fleeting memories of a bygone era. Unable or unwilling to accept that reality, all three states optimistically awaited a revival. Hope sprang eternal in South Pass, for instance, where "the district will again become a steady and probably a relatively large producer." The truth was that only a "small quantity of placer gold" was produced in 1915. Studies were made and articles published about how to stimulate a mining comeback; the Denver Chamber of Commerce established a committee to boost Colorado mining and made efforts to attract outside capital. Those endeavors did not prevent ore grade values from continuing to sink, while expenses were climbing and no new districts were opening. Production totals remained fairly constant, except for the base metals, zinc, lead, and copper, which were needed in the expanding war-related industries.[15] Corporation-dominated mining tenaciously hung on to its fading claim as the number one industry in the Rocky Mountains. Daily laborers dug where independent miners had earlier waited for the next stampede. Dull, dirty industrial mining towns sat where a new camp over the next mountain had once created new hope.

Financially strapped Victor, Colorado, scratched up fifteen dollars in 1915 to buy flowers for Decoration Day, but it could not contribute to Denver's Children's Hospital. To the west, once promising St. Elmo, nestled between two fourteen-thousand-foot peaks, managed to collect $500 in taxes and licenses, which failed to cover the $671 spent to keep town government functioning. Mining and its camps collapsed together.[16] The dreams of fifty-nine had come to this ignoble end at last, and nothing emerged to take their place for those who still believed.

Maybe it did not matter anymore, except to the declining numbers of miners and their families. Montana boldly declared in 1914 that it was "no longer of the 'wild and wooly' West." To the first generation of twentieth-century westerners, relics of the old West were nice to visit and speculate about, but it was time to be getting on to new things. Tourism, for example, held out much more promise for them than mining.

Something old, something new. The twentieth century brought worries about "good roads" and how to achieve them. Associations were formed to lobby and work for them, as in the days of the pioneers. Roads were not intended, however, for bringing mining equipment or supply wagons; they were meant to ease the way for the tourists who would come.

"Americans Should See America First" became a popular theme of the 1910s; and a modification proclaimed, "Begin with Montana to see America." Tourists should pay particular attention to the "Playground of America," the Rocky Mountains, which offered more in scenic attractions, curative mineral springs, and climatic advantages—and in number and height of mountain peaks, more than the famous Swiss Alps. The Rockies "are not a harsh, bleak region"; thousands could roam them "in happiness & security." They were "a paradise of pleasure," a vacation land "arranged to suit any taste and any purse." The magic of the mountains had come full circle. Westerners had learned well the lesson of tourist promotion. Now they learned what the economic impact could be.

Travelers usually came by train. Rested and ready, they visited the easily accessible attractions. Each year, however, more and more "auto tourists" were braving poor roads, few maps, sand and mud, and flat tires to reach the "playground." Denver already had a "Motor Club," to which prospective visitors could write for information, and in 1915 it opened its first municipal auto camp. "In many cities automobiles are not allowed to camp inside the city limits." In Denver, they were "received with greatest hospitality," proudly emphasized the city park commissioner.[17]

Not so many people visited the hot springs, and they slipped out of vogue. A few visitors were intrigued by the remains of the mining frontier and the "ghost towns." More came for hunting and fishing (Wyoming limited fishermen to no more than twenty pounds of trout and no fish less than six inches), or for a relaxing time in a "sage & pine" filled atmosphere. Dude ranches slowly gained in popularity, with the Yellowstone region being particularly attractive. Montana got into the game and, in 1911, lured the Owen Wister family to its isolated JY Ranch, 104 miles by wagon from St. Anthony, Idaho. The infirm and the ill still came seeking relief in the sunshine and dry climate; numerous sanitoriums opened their doors to them. Most came, however, simply to visit the "panoramic" mountains, perhaps including an easy trip up Pike's Peak by cog railway or a tour through the national parks. One author advised that the large hotels were expensive, on a par with other "resorts the world over." One advantage offered by western resorts related to dress, which called for the "usual conventional wear, somewhat simplified." When camping out, one could wear old clothes and spend less than five dollars for a month's supply of food.[18]

Yellowstone held its position as the most popular attraction, topping fifty-one thousand visitors in 1915. They toured a park still policed by the army, but one in which marked improvements in roads, lunch stations, and hotels had been made over the past twenty years. The Old Faithful Inn, opened in 1903, had become a favorite stop on the leisurely, several-day stage tour. After rocking along the dusty Yellowstone roads, travelers found the inn a haven for the weary. The trip around the park seemed so tame that it bored some blasé tourists, after they had seen and snapped photos of several geysers and hot springs. Bear-feeding at the hotels was one of the more exciting activities. Not yet overwhelmed by sheer numbers, Yellowstone could still provide a sample of a wilderness experience; it was a golden time to visit Yellowstone.[19]

Mesa Verde did not enjoy the same fame or development. Although western author William MacLeod Raine called it "one of the most interesting features of Colorado," most vacationers overlooked it because, until 1913, roads had not been improved enough to drive a wagon or a buggy up the mesa and over to the cliff dwellings. Before then, the visitor could expect at least a three-day round-trip on horseback from Mancos. When autos arrived the next year, "old Dobbin" retained the right-of-way. Drivers were required to honk their horn at every bend of the road, and when a team approached they were forced to take the outer edge of the roadway and then stop. Speed was no factor—automobiles were limited to 8 mph (within the year, it was increased to 15 mph) on straight stretches, less elsewhere. The roads being what they were, that limit was understandable. The 1915 Mesa Verde pamphlet bluntly warned,

> The trip over the Government road should be taken only by
> parties experienced in handling and controlling of horses . . .
> The road is very narrow in places and makes sharp turns . . .
> All strangers traversing this route should be accompanied by
> an experienced guide.

The 663 brave visitors who came anyway found rather primitive accommodations at Spruce Tree camp; they saw a hint of the future when telephone lines were strung to the camp that year.[20]

Where visitors once had a choice of only two national parks, now they could select from four. If women deserve the credit for saving Mesa Verde, then two men deserve most of it for establishing Glacier and Rocky Mountain national parks: George Grinnell and Enos Mills. Establishment of the parks had to overcome suspicion and, at times, outright opposition from a variety of local, regional, and national economic interests. Interestingly, both the Forest Service and the Reclamation Service opposed the expansion of the park system as being contrary to the proper management of the public domain. Mining and timbering interests also objected, as did some nearby ranchers, homeowners, and the diehards who opposed more government involvement in the region.

George Bird Grinnell, author, historian, and outdoorsman, championed Glacier. As isolated in the northern Rockies as Mesa Verde was in the southern, Glacier had lured Grinnell for a visit in 1885, and he had returned almost every summer, beginning in 1887. He fell in love with its beauty and conceived the idea of preserving the most spectacular segment of the Continental Divide as a national park. "Here is a land of striking scenery," he wrote, "the Crown of the Continent." Trying hard to describe its wonders, Grinnell found himself at a loss: "No words can describe the grandeur and majesty of these mountains, and even photographs seem hopelessly to dwarf and belittle the most impressive peaks."[21] Like Virginia McClurg, he had found his cause.

The first obstacle was cleared when the Blackfeet agreed to sell the land to the government, which then opened it for settlement. Unfortunately for Grinnell's hopes, copper ("bigger than Old Butte") and gold and silver were reportedly discovered. Early in the century, the numerous prospect holes had fallen far short of Butte, and mining faded away. Grinnell, meanwhile, was enlisting the endorsement and support of Louis Hill and his Great Northern Railroad. Hill shared his father's instinct for profitable investment, and the Great Northern would enjoy a monopoly over passenger traffic, should a park be created. Grinnell slowly generated the backing he needed. Then it took Congress two years to deliberate about the possibility of a park. Not until it became obvious that little grazing land existed, that timberland was inaccessible, and that the area was too rugged for agriculture did Glacier finally achieve national park status in 1910. With nothing else to exploit, a park might just be "good business." Western opposition managed to water down the bill and somewhat limit the park prerogatives; summer homes, mining, and grazing rights already established could remain and leases would be given to those wanting summer homes. Water for irrigation purposes was reserved. The seeds of future trouble had been planted.

Unlike Mesa Verde, which struggled along on its own, Glacier benefited greatly from its Great Northern connection. The principal problem for both parks was puny federal appropriations, which translated into little or no money for roads and improvements. It was one thing for Washington to create a park, and quite another for it to provide needed funding for such politically weak causes. Hill saw to it that "safe and good" roads were built, an achievement that resulted in automobiles being admitted in 1912; two years later, drivers could penetrate "its very heart." He personally supervised the construction of two lodges and a series of Swiss-style chalets within and adjacent to the park. Visitors, by then, far surpassed Mesa Verde's.[22]

In 1915, Colorado gained its second national park, Rocky Mountain, sixty miles northwest of Denver. Visitors and settlers had been roaming this future park area since the 1860s; eventually, the hamlet of Estes Park had blossomed in the beautiful valley of the same name. By 1911, that little town had become a "big playground," with five large hotels, a like number of golf courses, hundreds of summer homes, and boulevards perfect for "road driving and motoring."

In the mountains to the west, the earlier Leadville excitement had induced prospectors to scratch around the appropriately named Never Summer Range for several seasons. The prospectors naturally thought they had discovered the new bonanza, and they founded several tiny mining camps before concluding that prospects were better elsewhere in the Rockies. By that time, sportsmen and tourists also were beginning to discover the region's bounty and beauty.

Among those arrivals was a small, wiry man, Enos Mills, who had originally hied himself to Colorado to improve his health. He supported himself in the beginning by working in Estes Park hotels and then, in the off-season, at nearby ranches. A dramatic improvement in his health allowed Mills to work with survey parties throughout the West and as a night foreman for Daly in smoky Butte. He never forgot his beloved mountains and returned in the 1890s to homestead in a high valley on the eastern slope of Long's Peak. From there, he became an innkeeper and launched his uncompromising crusade for a national park. He alienated conservationists, civil leaders, and others during his relentless drive; Mills allowed nothing to stop him from attaining his goal. Even some of his neighbors objected, worrying about loss of private property and distrusting Mills's motivations.

Like McClurg and Grinnell before him, Mills spoke, wrote, and lobbied, gaining a reputation as a magazine journalist and self-taught naturalist. He organized mass meetings and petition drives, secured publicity, and pressured for a national park that would include Long's Peak. The park bill was introduced into Congress in 1914. As in the case of Glacier, and Mesa Verde before it, questions were raised about potential costs and the effect on natural resources. Mining and grazing interests managed to force a reduction in the size of its intended area, while the debate centered once more on use versus uselessness. One supporter, Colorado Congressman Edward Taylor, converted from his opposition to forests, observed that the park would be "marvelously beautiful" and, quite simply, had "no value for anything but scenery." When the bill finally passed, it contained, like Glacier's, provisions to allow prospectors, the Reclamation Service, and others to enter and use park resources, just in case some potential had been overlooked.[23]

Mills chaired the dedication ceremonies of the "nation's newest playground" on a rainy September 4, 1915, humbly calling it "the achievement of my life." *The Denver Post* hailed him as the "Father of Rocky Mountain National Park." Mills understood the significance of the occasion, and everyone present had an inkling of what was happening in the Rockies. Perhaps Congressman Taylor, back on Capitol Hill, had seen the future as clearly as anyone:

> The American people have never yet capitalized our scenery and climate, as we should. It is one of our most valuable assets, and these great assets should be realized upon to the fullest extent.[24]

With four national parks, the Rocky Mountains had positioned themselves to capitalize on those very things.

Probably few of the visitors to Estes Park that day realized that only fifty-six years had passed since the Pike's Peak gold rush, and fewer than that since the rush to Virginia City or the building of the Union Pacific. Those fifty-niners, those sixty-eighters, had helped make the park ceremony possible; so had the visitors who crowded together to hear the dedication speeches. The contrast in life-styles and attitudes between those two generations was remarkable, as remarkable as the contrast in speed and comfort between covered wagons and automobiles, which carried them to these mountains. Not to be forgotten, though, was the connection between the two events, a bond as firm as the surrounding granite mountains.

Man and progress had ended the frontier era; man and progress had evolved the old West into the new. The West had grown up. Now man and progress turned to preserving some of the old before it disappeared forever. The West was acquiring a past, complete with its own legends and profit potential.

The passing generation of pioneers—Mills, Grinnell, McClurg, and others—helped to ensure that their world would not be lost. These national parks preserved the vanishing frontier, as nearly as anything could in 1915. The dreams of 1859 had been transmuted into something strangely different from, and yet hauntingly similar to, the goals that a twentieth-century generation had set for itself. In preserving the past, the parks showed to the future that once there had been a Camelot in the Rocky Mountains. Women and men could still keep their dreams in the midst of the progress that was transforming the world around them. The soul of the West lived on.

EPILOGUE

Despite the great race to convert public land to private ownership, well over a third of the land encompassing the Rocky Mountain region remained under federal control by the end of 1915. Neither the miner, farmer, housewife, rancher, railroadman, lumberman, nor city dweller claimed it permanently, although all were willing to exploit whatever natural resources or manmade opportunities might become available.

The foundation blocks of Rocky Mountain development for the remainder of the century were already in place by then—urbanization, tourism, agriculture, federal largess, mining, and business and industry. Even the last great boon to tourism had been discovered: the previously despised and troublesome snow could be a bonanza for skiing. It would be a few more decades, however, before that new mother lode would be exploited to its profitable potential. A few Coloradans and Wyomingites were drilling expectantly for oil (some within view of the 1859 Gold Hill excitement), hinting at the start of another bonanza.

All this development had taken less than sixty years, but abandoned remains already sat forlornly on mountainsides and in homestead valleys. Modern-day westerners casually observed them and then went about the business of expanding their own generation's dream of the future. Their era combined both a dash of the old and a large dose of the new. The grow-or-die philosophy still guided city fathers and chambers of commerce. The exploitation of the Rockies continued relentlessly, as these twentieth-century westerners looked for fresh ways, or retreaded old methods, to make their fortunes. Theirs was still the land of tomorrow.

Theirs was also a deep and intrinsically racist land, a heritage of the class and racial tensions of the previous generations. They did not really want to share their West with newcomers, but the newcomers came anyway, though in smaller numbers now, drawn by their individual dreams. And dreams, not reality, would continue to bring people to the West.

Urbanization, which had been so much a part of the previous century and was ebbing in the 1910s, served as an indicator of current developments and a benchmark for the future. The camps and towns, in welcoming development, organization, and progress, had played a major role in ending the frontier and evolving the old West into the new. Now they represented nostalgia for the old that was gone. The "rural and western spirit" seemed to the townspeople (and Americans in general, nearly 50 percent of whom lived in an urban environment) idyllic, less pressure-filled, and simpler than the life they had created for themselves. They dreamed of a Camelot, not what they saw beyond their town limits—the more primitive life and the poverty (to their way of thinking) of the farm and ranch, the collapse of the mine, and the abandonment of the camp. They mourned the passing of the mythic old West filled with its range wars, gamblers, drunken brawling, easy money, gunfights, and harlots with hearts of gold.[1]

The West was divided against itself, its past challenging its future. Progress and nostalgia made strange bedfellows in the 1910s. Just as the tourists were both pilgrims and shoppers in search of sensations and souvenirs, so were the resident Rocky Mountain westerners. Both groups mixed the sacred with the profane.

Yet the very establishment of those four national parks, which had helped to create Americans' national identity, spoke for something better than the grubby materialism that had sired the westward movement and settlement. Americans would come to love those parks to death, much to the tourist industry's delight and the park purists' dismay. Westerners, too, could be proud of their regional heritage; they did not have to try to outdo the East or emulate it simply because it set the pace for "American civilization." The West now had the right to advance its own claims. Maybe it had not developed into a western culture, perhaps it never would, but others were looking at it and taking away with them what they considered it to be. Their baggage included part myth and part reality.[2]

That mythic West proved to be a great comfort to some people in the years ahead. They might agree with Henry Ford that history was bunk, but there was something comforting to hang on to when thinking about the West of Buffalo Bill, Zane Grey, and Louis L'Amour. That West seemed to be a national possession, much like the Civil War, which did not have to be shared with anyone else. Its experience spoke for all Americans, not just for westerners. At the very least, it spoke for what they wanted to believe about themselves and their aspirations. Its enlargement into a national epic enhanced the lives of believers, who only regretted that they were born too late to have attended the party. They could still be transformed vicariously into the heroic, tough, optimistic, self-reliant, and independent western hero.[3] They could ride those mountains forever while their world raced forward—impersonal, urbanized, and industrialized.

The myth, in a sense, measured what had been lost in culture and freedom in the Rocky Mountains. The epic West celebrated the victories over larger-than-life natural and manmade obstacles, which had disappeared in the shrinking, mechanical world of the twentieth century. The pioneers could achieve personal success and find a meaning for their lives; that opportunity, on such a grand scale, seemed to have evaporated for their descendants.

The mountains were still there, unconquered and eternal. Poet Thomas Hornsby Ferril caught that salient point:

> I have confused these rocks and waters with
> My life, but not unclearly, for I know
> What will be here when I am here no more.[4]

The Rocky Mountains that had loomed so large to Pike and Fremont were still there, offering the same challenges and generating the same emotions. The physical West could still be sampled and savored. It was real, it was mythic, and in it the two Rocky Mountain Wests rode together eternally.

The Rocky Mountains and their natural resources had shaped two generations of Americans. Mining camps nestled in mountain valleys where they would never have appeared except for the mineral treasure box that had been opened. Railroads, which had once climbed the heights to tap the trade and promote settlement, now serviced the local resident and the tourist. Towns grew at the gateways into the far reaches of the Rockies, industry and coal mines developed in and out of the mountains, and agriculture struggled along the foothills and mountain valleys to supply those Rocky Mountain–locked miners and their communities. People and political entities were already lining up to fight over the water that cascaded down the Rockies' slopes. Finally, three states were thriving along the rugged backbone of the continent, where once there had been none.

The mountains' space and distance had impacted the newcomers' thinking; they had adjusted to it, but had never overcome it. A merchant at Silverton and a miner at Butte could not risk forgetting that they lived in the mountains. For the majority, however, the most important matter was what came from that land, not its natural beauty or its spiritual quality.

Yet there were those who were beginning to think of the mountains as something special, much as Pike, Long, and Fremont had done long ago. These had been the health-seekers of years gone by; now tourists came to commune with scenic wonders that lifted them above the mundane world of their everyday lives. For them, the mountains offered a chance for rebirth, renewal, and rest. The mystique of the Rockies had survived the rush of materialism.

In the 1910s, the Rocky Mountain region displayed all the trends and attitudes mentioned above. The result was not an abomination, but the logical outcome of the westward movement. The pioneers had wanted to re-create the world they had left behind. They had achieved that end perhaps better than they had anticipated. The old West would be theirs forever; the new West belonged to their grandchildren.

It would be a true westerner who would capture the essence of the experience of the past sixty years. Born in Denver in 1896, Thomas Hornsby Ferril published his first poem in a newspaper ten years later. He continued to live in Denver and became, within a generation, the region's most respected poet. Time and time again, he wrestled with the changing times, the old and the new, which he had ample opportunity to experience personally. In "Ghost Town," he wrote,

> Dig in the earth for gold while you are young!
>   . . .
> and here they dug the gold and went away,
> Here are the empty houses, hollow mountains.
> Even the rats, the beetles and the cattle
> That used these houses after they were gone
> Are gone; the gold is gone,
> There's nothing here.

The West that had once been young and exciting was gone. Ferril sensed—Ferril knew—that there was more to the story. In a poem entitled "Two Rivers," he mused about Denver and the West. He spoke eloquently for others less gifted and for the pioneers:

> Most of the time these people hardly seemed
> To realize they wanted to be remembered,
> Because the mountains told them not to die.
>
> I wasn't here, yet I remember them,
> That first night long ago, those wagon people
> Who pushed aside enough of the cottonwoods
> To build our city where the blueness rested.
>
> They were with me, they told me afterward,
> When I stood on a splintered wooden viaduct
> Before it changed to steel and I to man.
> They told me while I stared down at the water:
> If you will stay we will not go away.[5]

NOTES

PREFACE

1. Donald Jackson and Mary Lee Spence, eds., *The Expeditions of John Charles Fremont* (Urbana: Univ. of Illinois Press, 1970), 1: 270–71.

2. Reuben G. Thwaites, ed., *Original Journals of the Lewis and Clark Expedition* (New York: Antiquarian Press, 1959), 2: 335, and 5: 199.

3. Donald Jackson, ed., *The Journals of Zebulon Montgomery Pike* (Norman: Univ. of Oklahoma Press, 1966), 1: 350–51. Maxine Benson, ed., *From Pittsburgh to the Rocky Mountains* (Golden: Fulcrum, 1988), iii–x and 224. Edwin James, *Account of an Expedition* (Ann Arbor: Readex Microprint, 1966), 2: 385.

4. J. S. Holliday, ed., *The World Rushed In* (New York: Simon Schuster, 1981), 204–5. Howard L. Scamehorn, ed., *The Buckeye Rovers in the Gold Rush* (Athens: Ohio Univ. Press, 1965), 29–37. Milo M. Quale, ed., *Across the Plains in '49* (New York: Citadel Press, 1966), 54–59.

5. See Patricia N. Limerick, *The Legacy of Conquest* (New York: W. W. Norton, 1987), 25–28, 32, 75, 82, and 99. Earl Pomeroy, *In Search of the Golden West* (New York: Knopf, 1957), 212. Robert G. Athearn, *The Mythic West* (Lawrence: Univ. Press of Kansas, 1986), 10–22, 221–22, 258, and 271. Ray Allen Billington, *America's Frontier Heritage* (New York: Holt, Rinehart and Winston, 1966), 25 and 179, Clark C. Spence, *Montana* (New York: W. W. Norton, 1978), 191–99. Wallace Stegner, "Who Are the Westerners?," *American Heritage* (December 1987), 41. Martin Ridge, "Frederick Jackson Turner, Ray Allen Billington and American Frontier History," *Western Historical Quarterly* (January 1988), 19. William G. Robbins, "The 'Plundered Province' Thesis . . . ," *Pacific Historical Review* (November 1986), 577–80. Marshall Sprague, *The Mountain States* (New York: Time-Life, 1969), 7.

6. Donald Worster, et al., "The Legacy of Conquest by Patricia Nelson Limerick: A Panel of Appraisal," *Western Historical Quarterly* (August 1989), 315. Billington, *America's Frontier Heritage*, 235. See especially Athearn, *Mythic West*, chap. 10 and the epilogue.

7. See: Earl of Dunraven, *The Great Divide* (Lincoln: Univ. of Nebraska Press, 1967), 188 and 190. Louis Simonin, *The Rocky Mountain West of 1867*, trans. Wilson O. Clough (Lincoln: Univ. of Nebraska Press, 1966), 61. Daniel Tuttle, *Reminiscences of a Missionary Bishop* (New York: Thomas Whittaker, 1906), 76. Sprague, *Mountain States*, 6, 7, and 9. Athearn, *Mythic West*, 182. Stegner, "Who Are the Westerners?," 41. David Lavender, *The Rockies* (New York: Harper and Row, 1968), 1–14.

CHAPTER 1

1. Jackson, *Journals of . . . Pike*, 2: 59–60 and 62.

2. LeRoy R. Hafen, ed., *Pike's Peak Gold Rush Guidebooks of 1859* (Glendale, Calif.: Arthur H. Clark, 1941), 34–36. Ovando Hollister, *The Mines of Colorado* (Springfield, Mass.: Samuel Bowles and Co., 1867), 1–8.

3. *Herald of Freedom* (Lawrence, Kansas), May 26 and June 2, 1855. Hafen, *Pike's Peak Gold Rush Guidebooks*, 44–47.

4. Hollister, *Mines of Colorado*, 8–9. LeRoy R. Hafen, ed., *Colorado Gold Rush* (Glendale, Calif.: Arthur H. Clark, 1941), 25–32.

5. *New York Times*, September 20, 23, and 28, and October 15, 1858, February 21, 1859. *Herald of Freedom*, January 15 and 22, 1859. See also Hafen, *Colorado Gold Rush*, 39–57.

6. Gene Gressley, *West by East: The American West in the Gilded Age* (Provo: Brigham Young Univ. Press, 1972), 2.

7. Samuel S. Curtis to Henry, November 22, 1858, Samuel R. Curtis Letters, Yale University. Hollister, *Mines of Colorado*, 9–10 and 16–18.

8. "Letters of a Returned Pike's Peaker," *Colorado Magazine*, May 1947, 126–27. Robert G. Athearn, *The Coloradans* (Albuquerque: Univ. of New Mexico Press, 1976), 12. *Press and Tribune* (Chicago), March 28, 1859.

9. Horace Greeley, *An Overland Journey from New York to San Francisco in the Summer of 1859* (New York: Alfred A. Knopf, 1964), 97 and 195. Harry Faulkner Diary, May 1, 2, 3, 5, 6, 7, 12, 22, and June 14, 1859, Western History Dept., Denver Public Library.

10. Greeley, *Overland Journey*, 106. Thomas Marshall, ed., *Early Records of Gilpin County Colorado, 1859–1861* (Boulder: Univ. of Colorado), 1–18.

11. Marshall, *Early Records*, 40–42 and 129–30. Minutes of Meetings 1859–62, Consolidated Ditch Co., Western Historical Collections, Univ. of Colorado. *Colorado Republican* (Denver), May 25, 1861.

12. *Rocky Mountain News* (Denver), July 18, August 8 and September 19,

1860, and June 5, 1861. *Miners Record* (Tarryall), August 17 and September 14, 1861.

13. Hollister, *Mines of Colorado*, 102–4. Bradford to William, November 21 and December 22, 1859, Robert Bradford Papers, Huntington Library. Henry P. Walker, *The Wagonmasters* (Norman: Univ. of Oklahoma Press, 1966), 179–92. James E. Fell, Jr., *Ores to Metals* (Lincoln: Univ. of Nebraska Press, 1979), 6–10.

14. Faulkner Diary, June 14, 1859.

15. Faulkner Diary, May 11, 1859. Artemus Ward, *The Complete Works of Artemus Ward* (New York: G. W. Dillingham, 1897), 218. Bradford to Waddell, January 18, 1860, Bradford Papers.

16. Faulkner Diary, September 30, 1859.

17. William Pierson to Richard, January 30, 1860, William Pierson Letter, Colorado College.

18. Hollister, *Mines of Colorado*, 108–9.

19. Mallory Letter, July 8, 1860, Samuel Mallory Letters, Western Historical Collections, Univ. of Colorado.

20. *Rocky Mountain News*, September 21, October 4, 29, November 9, December 4, 1860, January 17, 21, March 14, and June 12, 26, 1861. Hollister, *Mines of Colorado*, 129–30.

21. Billington, *America's Frontier Heritage*, 65–66. Howard Lamar, *The Far Southwest 1846–1912* (New Haven: Yale Univ. Press, 1966), 213–17.

22. Kenneth N. Owens, "Patterns and Structure," *Western Historical Quarterly*, October 1970, 375–76. *Rocky Mountain News*, April 19, 24, May 28, August 28, September 11, and November 13, 1861. *Colorado Republican*, July 13, 1861.

23. *Rocky Mountain News*, April 25 and May 1, 1861. Daniel E. Conner, *A Confederate in the Colorado Gold Fields*, ed. Donald J. Berthrong and Odessa Davenport (Norman: Univ. of Oklahoma Press, 1970), 94. Ovando J. Hollister, *Boldly They Rode* (Lakewood, Colo.: Golden Press, 1949), 5. *The War of the Rebellion: A Compilation of the Official Records . . .* (Washington: Government Printing Office, 1881), ser. 1, vol. 3, 496 and 504.

24. *Rocky Mountain News*, October 2, 30, and December 28, 1861. Gilpin Interview, Bancroft Library, 5–6. Hollister, *Boldly They Rode*, 26–36. Thomas L. Karnes, *William Gilpin Western Nationalist* (Austin: Univ. of Texas Press), 275–79.

25. Hollister, *Boldly They Rode*, 45–68. *Rocky Mountain News*, January–April 1862. *Battles and Leaders of the Civil War* (New York: Century Co., 1884), 2: 103–11 and 697–700. See also Robert L. Kerby, *The Confederate Invasion of New Mexico and Arizona* (Los Angeles: Westernlore Press, 1958).

26. Harry Kelsey, Jr., *Frontier Capitalist: The Life of John Evans* (Denver: State Historical Society, 1969), 117–27. *Rocky Mountain News*, May 24 and November 20, 1862. *Tri-Weekly Miner's Register* (Central City), November 5, 1862.

27. Hollister, *Mines of Colorado*, 111–13. *Colorado Mining Life* (Central City),

August 30, 1862. *Rocky Mountain News*, June 28, 1862. *Tri-Weekly Mining Life*, January 15, 27, 1863.

28. Pierson to Richard, January 30, 1860, Pierson Letter.

29. *Rocky Mountain News*, January 8, 1863, April 16 and June 11 and 25, 1863. Thomas Noel, *Denver: Rocky Mountain Gold* (Denver Chamber of Commerce, 1980), 44–54. Kassler to Maria, May 13, 1863, Philip Alexander, "George W. Kassler," *Colorado Magazine*, January 1962, 41. *Weekly Commonwealth* (Denver), April 23, 1863.

30. Bradford to Waddell, November 21, 1859, Bradford Papers.

31. Hollister, *Mines of Colorado*, 122 and 131–34. *Daily Mining Journal*, December 24, 1863, January 2, March 15, and April 5, 20, and 21, 1864. *New York Tribune*, April 6, 7, and 9, 1864. *New York Times*, April 19, 1864.

32. *Rocky Mountain News*, July 6, 1864. *Daily Mining Journal*, May 6 and July 25, 1864. Oscar O. Winther. *The Transportation Frontier* (New York: Holt, Rinehart and Winston, 1964), 1–12. Nathaniel Hill to Wife, June 9, 1864, Hill Letters, Colorado Historical Society.

33. Robert G. Athearn, *Mythic West*, 193. Emma Teller Tyler interview, Western Historical Collections, University of Colorado. Patterson, undated letter, Patterson Collection, Western History Department, Denver Public Library.

CHAPTER 2

1. William Greever, *Bonanza West* (Norman: Univ. of Oklahoma Press), 215–17.

2. Ward, *Complete Works*, 218. Rossiter Raymond, *Statistics of Mines and Mining* (Washington: Government Printing Office, 1870), 253. Rodman Paul, *Mining Frontiers of the Far West* (New York: Holt, Rinehart and Winston, 1963), 140. Greever, *Bonanza West*, 218–19.

3. Greever, *Bonanza West*, 218–19. Muriel Wolle, *The Bonanza Trail* (Bloomington: Indiana Univ. Press, 1953), 179–81. *Montana Post* (Virginia City), October 8, 1864.

4. Helen White, *Ho! for the Gold Fields* (St. Paul: Minnesota Historical Society, 1966), 83. N. H. Webster, "Journal," *Contributions to the Historical Society of Montana*, 3: 322 and 324.

5. James L. Thane, ed., *A Governor's Wife on the Mining Frontier* (Salt Lake City: Univ. of Utah, 1976), 52 and 65. Lucia Park, "The First School in Montana," *Contributions to the Historical Society of Montana*, vol. 5, 189.

6. *Not in Precious Metals Alone* (Helena: Montana Historical Society), 34. Arthur Dickson, ed., *Covered Wagon Days* (Cleveland: Arthur H. Clark, 1929), 170 and 173. Mary Ronan, *Frontier Woman*, ed. H. Merriam (Helena: Univ. of Montana, 1973), 17 and 18. Raymond Settle and Mary Lund, eds., *Overland Days to Montana in 1865* (Glendale, Calif.: Arthur H. Clark, 1971), 248.

7. Sources for the preceding section: Granville Stuart, *Forty Years on the*

Frontier (Cleveland: Arthur H. Clark, 1925), 1: 234 and 257–58. *Not in Precious Metals Alone,* 35 and 39–40. *Montana Post,* September 10, December 31, 1864, December 30, 1865, May 26, and June 2, 1866. Thane, *Governor's Wife,* 17, 65–66, 68, 72, 83, 86, 102, 122, and 134. Elliott West, "Beyond Baby Doe: Child Rearing on the Mining Frontier," *The Women's West* (Norman: Univ. of Oklahoma Press, 1987), 15. Spence, *Montana,* 31–32. Elliott West, *Growing Up with the Country* (Albuquerque: Univ. of New Mexico Press, 1989), 15–16, 79–81, and 150–51.

8. *Montana Post,* October 7 and December 2, 1865, March 17, June 2, and August 25, 1866. Margaret Ronan, "Memoirs of a Frontier Woman, Mary C. Ronan" (Master's thesis, State University of Montana, 1932), 41–43. *Helena Herald,* May 2, September 26, and October 24, 1867.

9. *Helena Herald,* October 3, 1867; see also September 26 and November 14, 1867. *Montana Post,* September 10, November 12, 1864, and September 15, 1866. Spence, *Montana,* 31–32. *Not in Precious Metals Alone,* 40.

10. Stegner, "Who Are the Westerners?," 38–39. John Guice, *The Rocky Mountain Bench* (New Haven: Yale Univ. Press, 1972), 11 and 13–14. Michael Malone and Richard Roeder, *Montana* (Seattle: Univ. of Washington Press), 61–64. Thomas Dimsdale, *The Vigilantes of Montana* (Norman: Univ. of Oklahoma Press, 1953), 14, 256–57, and 266–67. Hubert H. Bancroft, *History of Washington, Idaho and Montana* (San Francisco: History Company, 1890), 641. Nathaniel P. Langford, *Vigilante Days and Ways* (Chicago: A. C. McClurg, 1912), xiii, xv, 22–23, and 537–39. Helen Sanders, ed., *X Beidler: Vigilante* (Norman: Univ. of Oklahoma, 1957), 22 and 32. Thane, *Governor's Wife,* 52 and 54–55. James Thane, ed., "Love from All to All," *Montana,* (Summer 1974), 18. Ronan, *Frontier Woman,* 13 and 19–20. For a defense of Plummer, see R. E. Mather and F. E. Boswell, *Hanging the Sheriff* (Salt Lake City: Univ. of Utah Press, 1987). *Montana Post,* August 27, 1864, and January 5, 1867. Hubert H. Bancroft, *Popular Tribunals* (San Francisco: History Company, 1881), 2: 696–712.

11. Guice, *Rocky Mountain Bench,* 11 and 77. Stuart, *Forty Years,* 1: 270–71. William Farr, ed., "Germans in Montana Gold Camps," *Montana* (Autumn 1982), 61–69. *Not in Precious Metals Alone,* 34–36. Robert Chadwick, "Montana's Silver Mining Era," *Montana* (Spring 1982), 20. John Mullan, *Miners and Travelers' Guide* (New York: William Franklin, 1865), 148. J. Ross Browne and James W. Taylor, *Report upon the Mineral Resources* (Washington: Government Printing Office, 1867), 329. Malone and Roeder, *Montana,* 51–52.

12. Robert Keller, ed., "A Puritan at Alder Gulch," *Montana* (Summer 1986), 69. *Not in Precious Metals Alone,* 35–36.

13. Webster, "Journal," 322–23. George Aux, "Mining in Colorado," Bancroft Library, 5. Thane, *Governor's Wife,* 37. Stuart, *Forty Years,* 1: 212, 216, and 225. Andrew F. Rolle, ed., *The Road to Virginia City* (Norman: Univ. of Oklahoma Press, 1960), 88, 91, and 93. James Denver, letters of February 20, 1867, Papers, Western History Department, Denver Public Library. Spence, *Montana,* 25–26.

14. Clark Spence, *Territorial Politics and Government in Montana* (Urbana:

Univ. of Illinois, 1975), 8–9 and 21–22. Malone and Roeder, *Montana*, 71–72. Robert Fisk to Lizzie, December 6, 1866, *Not in Precious Metals Alone*, 137. Owens, "Patterns and Structure," 377–79 and 380. Bancroft, *History of Washington . . . Montana*, 644. Guice, *Rocky Mountain Bench*, 34–35.

15. Edgerton to Sister, May 21, 1865, in Thane, *Governor's Wife*, 125. *Montana Post*, February 4, 1865, and August 10, 1867. Charles A. Ashley, "Governor James R. Ashley's Biography and Messages," *Contributions to the Historical Society of Montana*, 6: 222.

16. *Rocky Mountain News*, August 17, 1863. Evans to W. P. Dole, August 24, November 11, 1863, John Evans Papers, Colorado Historical Society. *Weekly Commonwealth* (Denver), November 11, 1863.

17. Fosdick to Evans, May 29, 1864, *The War of the Rebellion: A Compilation of the Official Records* (Washington: Government Printing Office, 1891), 34: 206–7. *Rocky Mountain News*, April 20 and September 1864. Sara Hively Journal, June 12, 14, 1864, Western History Department, Denver Public Library. *Weekly Commonwealth*, June 15 and 22, 1864.

18. Much has been written about these events. See: Raymond Carey, "The Puzzle of Sand Creek," *Colorado Magazine* (Fall 1964); *Report of the Joint Special Committee* (Washington: Government Printing Office, 1867); Irving Howbert, *Memories of a Lifetime in the Pike's Peak Region* (New York: Putnam's, 1925); Michael Sievers, "Sands of Sand Creek Historiography," *Colorado Magazine* (Spring 1972); *Rocky Mountain News*, December 1864–July 1865; Kelsey, *Frontier Capitalist*, 137–53.

19. *New York Times*, April 19 and July 12, 1864. *Rocky Mountain News*, April 27, 1864. *Daily Mining Journal* (Black Hawk), April 20, 21, May 26, and June 22, 1864.

20. Hollister, *Mines of Colorado*, 355–58. Hill to Wife, October 3, 1864, N. Hill Letters, Colorado Historical Society. Fell, *Ores to Metals*, 9–25.

21. *Rocky Mountain News*, September 8, 1865, March 4, April 18, July 3, 1867, and November 4, 1868. Fell, *Ores to Metals*, 11–26 and 29.

22. *Rocky Mountain News*, July 2, 1867. Raymond, *Statistics*, 347–49. *American Journal of Mining* (New York), January 8, February 2, 9, 1867, and October 3, 1868. *The Clear Creek Gold and Silver Mining Company* (Philadelphia: H. G. Leisenring, 1866), 4, 7, and 9.

23. For the preceding Montana section, see: Stuart, *Forty Years*, 2: 31; Browne and Taylor, *Report*, 328; Farr, "Germans," 62 and 68; David G. Weaver, "Early Days in Emigrant Gulch," *Contributions to the Historical Society of Montana*, 7: 77, 80–85, 94. Rolle, *Road*, 23 and 107.

24. *Not in Precious Metals Alone*, 29. Green C. Smith, "Second Message," *Contributions to the Historical Society of Montana*, 5: 148. Browne and Taylor, *Report*, 237 and 329–30. William A. Clark, "Centennial Address," *Contributions to the Historical Society of Montana*, 2: 51. Chadwick, "Montana's Silver," 20. Paul, *Mining Frontiers*, 140–41. Greever, *Bonanza West*, 179–80 and 238–40.

25. Rossiter W. Raymond, *Mineral Resources of the States and Territories West of the Rocky Mountains* (Washington: Government Printing Office, 1869), 6.

26. F. M. Thompson, "1865 Report," Franklin Kirkaldie to Family, August 30, 1865, and Thomas W. Harris, Diary, July 2 and 9, 1865, *Not in Precious Metals Alone*, 28, 41, and 92–93. Sidney Edgerton, "First Message to the First Legislative Assembly," *Contributions to the Historical Society of Montana*, 3: 345. *Rocky Mountain News*, 1859–65. Dickson, *Covered Wagon Days*, 174 and 190–91. Alexander McClure, *Three Thousand Miles through the Rocky Mountains* (Philadelphia: J. B. Lippincott, 1869), 263–64. Dick Pace, "Henry Sieben," *Montana* (Winter 1979), 3–5 and 12–13. Gressley, *West by East*, 11.

27. White, *Ho!*, 218–19. Rolle, *Road*, 84, 86, 89, 94–95, 100. Hal Sayre, "Early Central City . . . Reminiscences," *Colorado Magazine* (March 1919), 51. Tuttle, *Reminiscences*, 170 and 413. Simonin, *Rocky Mountain West*, 32–33, 38, and 51. He also thought North America was "the country of the future."

28. Rolle, *Road*, 75, 84, and 94. Tuttle, *Reminiscences*, 170. Dimsdale, *Vigilantes*, 18–19. Ronan, *Frontier Woman*, 9, 17–18, 22, 34, and 40. Ellen C. Pennock, "Incidents in My Life as a Pioneer," *Colorado Magazine* (April 1953), 129. Hill to Wife, July 5, 1864, Hill Letters. *Daily Mining Journal*, November 23, 1864. Amelia Buss, September 16, 1866–September 21, 1867, Diary, Western History Department, Denver Public Library. Fisk, quoted in Paula Petrik, "Mothers and Daughters of Eldorado," *Montana* (Summer 1982), 52–53, 28.

29. McClure, *Three Thousand Miles*, 213. Keller, "Puritan," 69.

CHAPTER 3

1. Ward, *Complete Works*, 217. Mark Twain, *Roughing It* (Hartford: American Publishing Company, 1872), 99, 103, and 105. For earlier immigrants' responses, see Sandra Myres, *Ho for California!* (San Marino: Huntington Library, 1980); Dale Morgan, *Overland in 1846* (Georgetown, Calif.: Talisman Press, 1963), 2 vols.; David Lavender, *Westward Vision* (New York: McGraw-Hill Co., 1963).

2. Twain, *Roughing It*, 98.

3. Robert E. Riegel and Robert G. Athearn, *America Moves West* (New York: Holt, Rinehart and Winston, 1971), 494–96. Winther, *Transportation Frontier*, 99–100. Robert G. Athearn, *Union Pacific Country* (New York: Rand McNally and Co., 1971), 28–33.

4. Twain, *Roughing It*, 59–60.

5. Lewis L. Gould, *Wyoming: A Political History, 1868–1896* (New Haven: Yale Univ. Press, 1968), 4–6. Marshall Sprague, *The Great Gates* (Boston: Little Brown, 1964), 262. T. A. Larson, *History of Wyoming* (Lincoln: Univ. of Nebraska Press, 1965), 36–42. Pomeroy, *In Search*, 65.

6. Campbell, quoted in Larson, *History of Wyoming*, 36.

7. Simonin, *Rocky Mountain West*, 63–65.

8. *Cheyenne Leader*, February 29, 1868. Larson, *History of Wyoming*, 46–47. Samuel A. Bistol, "The Newspaper Press of Wyoming," 1–2, Bancroft Library. Lola Homsher, ed., *South Pass 1868: James Chisholm's Journal of the Wyoming Gold Rush* (Lincoln: Univ. of Nebraska Press, 1960), 30–31.

9. Lyle W. Dorsett, *The Queen City* (Boulder: Pruett Publishing Co., 1977), 21–23. Kelsey, *Frontier Capitalist*, 169–79. Gressley, *West by East*, 12. Robert Perkin, *The First One Hundred Years* (Garden City, N.Y.: Doubleday and Co., 1959), 304–8. Owens, "Patterns and Structure," 391. *Rocky Mountain News* (Denver), June 20, 22, and 24, 1870.

10. *Cheyenne Leader*, February 14, 15, March 2, and May 8, 9, 1868. Larson, *History of Wyoming*, 54–57.

11. Emmett Chisum, "Boom Towns on the Union Pacific," *Annals of Wyoming* (Spring 1981), 7 and 9. Limerick, *Legacy of Conquest*, 77. A. Dudley Gardner and Verla R. Flores, *Forgotten Frontier* (Boulder: Westview Press, 1989), 9–25. *Miners' Monument* (Hanna, Wyo.: privately printed, 1984), 1–2. Rossiter Raymond, *Statistics of Mines and Mining* (Washington: Government Printing Office, 1873), 367.

12. Hubert Howe Bancroft, *History of Nevada, Colorado and Wyoming* (San Francisco: History Co., 1890), 639–40. C. C. Coutant, *The History Wyoming* (Laramie: Chaplin, Spafford & Mathison, 1899), 639–42. Homsher, *South Pass*, 216–18 and 220–22.

13. Raymond, *Statistics* (1870), 336. Coutant, *History of Wyoming*, 638, 650, and 662. Limerick, *Legacy of Conquest*, 86.

14. Coutant, *History of Wyoming*, 659. *Engineering and Mining Journal* (New York), March 7, 149; March 21, 181; and April 18, 1868, 245. Raymond, *Statistics* (1870), 327–28. *Sweetwater Mines* (South Pass, Wyo.), March 21, and July 3, 1868. Homsher, *South Pass*, 4–6, 42–45, 73–75, 81, 89, 100, and 145–46.

15. *Sweetwater Mines*, June 6, 1868 and June 19, 1869. Raymond, *Statistics* (1870), 325, 328, and 337. Raymond, *Statistics* (1873), 327, 375, and 376.

16. Gould, *Wyoming*, 26–27, Larson, *History of Wyoming*, 78–82. Sandra Myres, *Westering Women and the Frontier Experience 1800–1915* (Albuquerque: Univ. of New Mexico Press, 1982), 219–21. T. A. Larson, "Wyoming's Contribution . . . Women's Rights Movement," *Annals of Wyoming* (Spring 1980), 15. Gordon M. Bakken, *Rocky Mountain Constitution Making* (New York: Greenwood Press, 1987), 85 and 87. Guice, *Rocky Mountain Bench*, 131.

17. T. A. Larson, "Esther Morris," *The Reader's Encyclopedia* (New York: Thomas Y. Crowell Company, 1977), 773. Myres, *Westering Women*, 213. Virginia Scharff, "The Case for Domestic Feminism," *Annals of Wyoming* (Fall 1984), 36.

18. Raymond, *Statistics* (1873), 371–72. Raymond, *Statistics* (1870), 312.

19. *Engineering and Mining Journal*, April 16, 244–45; September 5, 147; and October 31, 1868, 276. Raymond, *Mineral Resources*, 146 and 150–51. Raymond, *Statistics* (1870), 253–55, 286, and 306. Michael Malone, *The Battle for Butte* (Seattle: Univ. of Washington, 1981), 6 and 9–10. Bancroft, *History of Washington . . . Montana*, 728. White, *Ho!*, 21.

20. J. H. Goodspeed to Bacon, June 29, 1868, and Mahany to Bacon, May 10, 1869, Bacon Papers, Huntington Library. Fell, *Ores to Metals*, 57–75. Raymond, *Statistics* (1870), 293–94, 339, and 388–91.

21. Raymond, *Mineral Resources*, 139–40.

22. Stuart, *Forty Years*, 2: 31–34. Raymond, *Statistics* (1870) 255 and 281. Frank Hall, *History of Colorado* (Chicago: Blakely Printing Co., 1890), 1: 473–75. *Daily Mining Journal* (Black Hawk), April 26, 1864.

23. Leonard Arrington, *The Changing Economic Structure of the Mountain West* (Logan: Utah State Univ. Press, 1963), 20–21. Gressley, *West by East*, 2–3, 36, and 37. Guice, *Rocky Mountain Bench*, 8.

24. Raymond, *Statistics* (1870), 338.

CHAPTER 4

1. K. Ross Toole, *Montana: An Uncommon Land* (Norman: Univ. of Oklahoma Press, 1959), 99–110. Lavender, *Rockies*, 209–11. Michael P. Malone and Dianne G. Dougherty, "Montana's Political Culture," *Montana* (Winter 1980), 46. Kenneth N. Owens, "The Prizes of Statehood," *Montana* (Autumn 1987), 9. *Rocky Mountain Bench*, 34–35, 39, and 43.

2. Spence, *Territorial Politics*, 74–75. Malone and Dougherty, "Montana's Political Culture," 46. Toole, *Montana*, 110–11.

3. *Rocky Mountain News* (Denver), December 12, 1860 and May 2, 9, and 23, 1866. *Miners' Register* (Central City), September 14, 1864. Percy Fritz, *Colorado* (New York: Prentice-Hall, 1941), 196–99. Athearn, *Coloradans*, 101–2. Lamar, *Far Southwest*, 287–90. Richard Lamm and Duane A. Smith, *Pioneers and Politicians* (Boulder: Pruett, 1984), 29–35. See also Frank Hall, *Colorado* (Chicago: Blakely Printing Co., 1890–91), 2 vols.

4. Gould, *Wyoming*, 15, 48, and 270. Larson, *History of Wyoming*, 120–29.

5. Spence, *Territorial Politics*, 56. Guice, *Rocky Mountain Bench*, 34–35. Richard Roeder, "Electing Montana's Territorial Delegates," *Montana* (Summer 1988), 57–58 and 68. Malone and Dougherty, "Montana's Political Culture," 46.

6. *Rocky Mountain News*, March 22 and July 2, 8, and 26, 1876. *Engineering and Mining Journal* (New York), September 9, 1876, 172. Athearn, *Coloradans*, 104–5. Owens, "Patterns and Structure," 384–85.

7. Gould, *Wyoming*, 15, 48, and 268–69. Larson, *History of Wyoming*, 127–29.

8. Spence, *Territorial Politics*, 3, 159–60, and 310. Malone, *Battle for Butte*, 11–12. Owens, "Patterns and Structure," 387.

9. Howard Lamar, ed., *The Reader's Encyclopedia of the American West* (New York: Thomas Y. Crowell Co., 1977), 190 and 1163–64.

10. Gould, *Wyoming*, 48 and 270. Gressley, *West by East*, 18 and 21. Larson, *History of Wyoming*, 109 and 123–28.

11. Guice, *Rocky Mountain Bench*, 81–95. Larson, *History of Wyoming*, 129–31.

12. Clark C. Spence, "The Territorial Bench in Montana," *Montana* (Winter 1963), 65. Guice, *Rocky Mountain Bench*, 43, 80, and 149–50. Gordon Bakken, *The Development of Law in the Rocky Mountain Frontier* (Westport, Conn.: Greenwood Press, 1983), 121 and 129–30.

13. *International Review* (July 1880), quoted in Billington, *America's Frontier Heritage*, 34.

14. *The Statistics of Population* . . . (Washington: Government Printing Office, 1872), 1: 3 and 195–96.

15. Rossiter Raymond, *Statistics of Mines and Mining* (Washington: Government Printing Office, 1871), 313. Paul, *Mining Frontiers*, 172–75. Guice, *Rocky Mountain Bench*, 117. See also Curtis H. Lindley, *A Treatise on the American Law Relating to Mines and Mineral Lands* . . . (San Francisco: Bancroft-Whitney, 1897), vol. 1. *Reports of the Cases Argued* . . . *Montana Territory* (San Francisco: Bancroft-Whitney Co., 1873), 235–45, 284–86, and 306–11. *A Dictionary of Mining, and Related Terms* (Washington: U.S. Department of the Interior, 1968). Bakken, *Development*, 52–53, 111, and 127. Limerick, *Legacy of Conquest*, 65. Rossiter Raymond, *Statistics of Mines and Mining* (Washington: Government Printing Office, 1872), 453–59.

16. James to Sister, May 26, 1873, Rayner, Letters, Colorado College, Special Collections. *Montana Post* (Virginia City), February 4, 1865, and August 10, 1867. *Sweetwater Mines* (South Pass), April 7, 1869. *Ouray Times*, February 8, 1879. Raymond, *Statistics* (1871), 312.

17. Riegel and Athearn, *America Moves West*, 461–66. Edgar I. Stewart, *Custer's Luck* (Norman: Univ. of Oklahoma Press, 1955), 57–85. Robert G. Athearn, *William Tecumseh Sherman and the Settlement of the West* (Norman: Univ. of Oklahoma Press, 1956), 309–15.

18. *Rocky Mountain News* (Denver), September–October 1879. *Dolores News* (Rico), October 15 and November 1879. *Solid Muldoon* (Ouray), September–October 1879. Marshall Sprague, *Massacre* (Boston: Little, Brown and Company, 1957), 164–68, 226–28, and 307–18.

19. *Butte Miner*, July–September 1877. Athearn, *William Tecumseh Sherman*, 315–22. Rex Myers, "The Settlers and the Nez Perce," *Montana* (Autumn 1977), 20–22, 24, and 27–28. Spence, *Montana*, 54–55.

20. Ronan, *Frontier Woman*, 110.

21. Will to Peggy, September 10, 1880, Jackson Papers, Colorado College, Special Collections.

22. *Proceedings of the Constitutional Convention* (Denver: Smith Brooks Press, 1907), 7–16 and 683–87. Lamar, *Far Southwest*, 290–95.

23. *Proceedings*, 723–37. *Colorado Transcript* (Golden), July 5, 1876. *Rocky Mountain News*, March 22 and July 2 and 26, 1876.

24. Frank Fossett, *Colorado:* . . . (Denver: Daily Tribune Steam Printing House, 1876), 144–45, 147, 438, and 467.

25. *Engineering and Mining Journal*, May 27, 512; June 24, 615; and October 7, 1876, 231. *New York Times*, September 28, 1876, 2.

26. Roeder, "Electing Montana's Territorial Delegates," 64 and 67. Spence, *Territorial Politics*, 290–93, 302, and 307. Bakken, *Rocky Mountain Constitution Making*, 88–91. Malone and Roeder, *Montana*, 85. Malone and Dougherty, "Montana's Political Culture," 46. *Proceedings and Debates*, 1: 78–80, 88, 404, and 575; 2: 866–68.

27. Gould, *Wyoming*, 268 and 270. Gordon M. Bakken, "Voting Patterns in the Wyoming Constitutional Convention," *Annals of Wyoming* (October 1970), 225. Bryant B. Brooks, *Memoirs of Bryant B. Brooks* (Glendale: Arthur H. Clark, 1939), 206–7. Larson, *History of Wyoming*, chap. 9.

28. Larson, *History of Wyoming*, 248–49 and 253–54. Bakken, *Rocky Mountain Constitution Making*, 87–88. P. S. Wilson, "Dictation," Bancroft Library, 6. Bakken, "Voting Patterns," 233.

CHAPTER 5

1. *Engineering and Mining Journal*, May 27, 512; and November 14, 1876, 301. Raymond, *Statistics* (1872), 2, 287–93, and 316–28. Fossett, *Colorado*, 262–68 and 353–65. *Colorado Banner* (Boulder), May 10, 1877. Charles Henderson, *Mining in Colorado* (Washington: Government Printing Office, 1926), 32 and 88–89.

2. Henderson, *Mining in Colorado*, 113, 122, 216, and 245. Robert G. Athearn, *Rebel of the Rockies: A History of the Denver and Rio Grande Western Railroad* (New Haven, Conn.: Yale Univ. Press, 1962), 38–39 and 43–44. *Rocky Mountain News*, May 9, 1874. Rossiter Raymond, *Statistics of Mines and Mining* (Washington: Government Printing Office, 1873), 324. *Engineering and Mining Journal*, May 5, 1877, 291–92.

3. Edward Blair, *Leadville* (Boulder: Pruett Publishing Co., 1980), 27–39. *Rocky Mountain News*, October 31, 1877, and November 22, 1881. *Daily Chronicle* (Leadville), June 7, 1879. Foote to Helena, May 12, 1879, James D. Hague Collection, Huntington Library. *Leslie's Illustrated*, April 12, 1879, 86–87. Ernest Ingersoll, "The Camp of the Carbonates," *Scribner's Monthly* (October 1879), 819–22. Eddie Foy and Alvin F. Harlow, *Clowning through Life* (New York: E. P. Dutton, 1928), 122. William Salter, ed., *Memoirs of Joseph W. Picket* (Burlington: George Ellis, 1880), 125. Athearn, *Mythic West*, 261.

4. *Denver Weekly Times*, October 16, 1878. *Denver Tribune*, December 1, 1878. Sprague, *Great Gates*, 230. Henderson, *Mining in Colorado*, 69, 89–90, and 176.

5. Malone, *Battle for Butte*, 15–16. *Engineering and Mining Journal*, March 3, 140, and April 28, 1877, 272. Michael P. Malone, "Midas of the West," *Montana* (Autumn 1983), 4–6 and 8. Robert Black III, *Railroad Pathfinder* (Evergreen: Cordillera Press, 1988), 91–96.

6. Raymond, *Statistics* (1873), 272. Clark, "Centennial Address," 2: 49–50 and 53.

7. Raymond, *Statistics* (1873), 258, 260, and 278–80. *Engineering and Mining Journal*, September 1, 1877, 163. Malone and Roeder, *Montana*, 60–61. Robert G. Athearn, "Railroad to a Far Off Country," *Montana* (1968), 23.

8. *The Statistics of the Population of the United States . . . , Ninth Census* (Washington: Government Printing Office, 1872), 2: 790. Gould, *Wyoming*, 9–10 and 14–15.

9. *Statistics . . . Ninth Census*, 2: 760, 779–80, and 790. Larson, *History of Wyoming*, 115 and 298–99. William F. Rae, *Westward by Rail* (New York: Promontory, 1974), 92. *Mineral Resources of the United States* (Washington: Government Printing Office, 1888), 212 and 380. *Engineering and Mining Journal*, December 10, 1872, 377.

10. Malone and Roeder, *Montana*, 67–68, discusses frontier shiftiness. Raymond, *Statistics* (1870), 286–87. *Engineering and Mining Journal*, July 9, 1872, 27.

11. Original census returns 1860 and 1870, microfilm copies, Southwest Center, Fort Lewis College. Raymond, *Statistics* (1873), 369. Gordon O. Hendrickson, ed., *Peopling the High Plains* (Cheyenne: Wyoming State Archives, 1977), 175 and 178. John C. Paige, "Country Squires and Laborers," *Peopling the High Plains*, 29. David Kathka, "The Italian Experience in Wyoming," *Peopling the High Plains*, 67–68.

12. Randall E. Rohe, "After the Gold Rush," *Montana* (Autumn 1982), 14 and 15. *Boulder County News*, March 20, April 8, 17, and May 1, 1874. *Engineering and Mining Journal* (New York), April 6, 1878, 240. Rose Hum Lee, *The Growth and Decline of Chinese Communities in the Rocky Mountain Region* (New York: Arno Press, 1978), 71 and 73.

13. Raymond, *Statistics* (1870), 260 and 272. Raymond, *Statistics* (1873), 261, 272, and 292–93.

14. John R. Wunder, "Law and the Chinese in Frontier Montana," *Montana* (Summer 1980), 18 and 20. Swartout, "Kwangtun to Big Sky," *Montana* (Winter 1988), 44, 48, and 49. Spence, *Montana*, 89.

15. *Rocky Mountain News*, July 4, 31, 1880, and December 2, 1881. *Engineering and Mining Journal*, August–September 1880. *Leadville Democrat*, May 27, 1880. *Leadville Weekly Herald*, June 19, 1880.

16. D. M. Rollins to William Jackson, December 15, 1881, Lyman Bass to Palmer, October 26, 1881, and Ed. O. Wolcott to Lyman Bass, November 10, 1881, Jackson, Papers. See also Stanley Dempsey and James E. Fell, Jr., *Mining the Summit: Colorado's Ten Mile District, 1860–1960* (Norman: Univ. of Oklahoma Press, 1986), 116–24.

17. *D&RG Prospectus* (London: n.p., 1881), 4. *Mineral Resources of the United States* (Washington: Government Printing Office, 1888), 60. Henderson, *Mining in Colorado*, 176 and 201. Malcolm J. Rohrbough, *Aspen: The History of a Silver Mining Town, 1879–1893* (New York: 1986), chaps. 9–12. *Rocky Mountain Sun* (Aspen), September 25, 1886, and March 12, 1887.

18. *Colorado Coal and Iron, 1882* (Colorado Springs: Gazette, 1882), 9–11.

19. Rodman Paul, "Colorado as a Pioneer," *Mississippi Valley Historical Review* (June 1960), 43–50. Rodman Paul, *A Victorian Gentlewoman* (San Marino: Huntington Library, 1972), 15–18 and 179–86. Rohrbough, *Aspen,* 118. See also Clark C. Spence, *Mining Engineers and the American West* (New Haven: Yale Univ. Press, 1970); Samuel F. Emmons, *Geology and Mining Industry of Leadville, Colorado* (Washington: Government Printing Office, 1886).

20. Malone, "Midas of the West," 6. Malone, *Battle for Butte,* 21–22.

21. *Engineering and Mining Journal,* July 9, 1881, 19. *Mineral Resources of the United States* (Washington: Government Printing Office, 1884), 224. Malone, *Battle for Butte,* 12–13, 18–19, 24–29, and 30. *Mineral Resources of the United States* (Washington: Government Printing Office, 1886), 211 and 215–16.

22. *Mineral Resources of the United States* (1887), 69. *Mineral Resources of the United States 1889–90* (Washington: Government Printing Office, 1891), 60. Malone, *Battle for Butte,* 34–38. *Engineering and Mining Journal,* August 11, 1888, 114.

23. Malone, *Battle for Butte,* 31. *Engineering and Mining Journal,* November 10, 1888, 388.

24. *Engineering and Mining Journal,* June 30, 385; August 25, 120, and September 8, 1883, 141; and November 10, 1888, 388. *Mineral Resources* (1887), 58–59. Bancroft, *History of Washington . . . Montana,* 739. Malone and Roeder, *Montana,* 144–47. Chadwick, "Montana's Silver," 25. Granite Miners Association, Butte Miners Association, Western Historical Collections, University of Colorado.

25. *Engineering and Mining Journal,* August 27, 1881, 135; June 2, 1888, 404; and June 22, 573; and December 21, 1889, 550. Bancroft, *History of Washington . . . Montana,* 777.

26. *Report of the Mining Industries of the United States* (Washington: Government Printing Office, 1886), 121, 186, and 194–96. *Mineral Resources* (1887), 58–59. *Engineering and Mining Journal,* February 17, 1883, 92; and December 7, 1889, 50.

27. *Mineral Resources* (1887), 212, 216–17, 275, 380, and 381–82. *Mineral Resources* (1883), 61–62 and 85–89. Philip A. Kalisch, "The Woebegone Miners of Wyoming," *Annals of Wyoming* (October 1970), 238–39. *Elk Mountain Pilot* (Crested Butte), April 14, 1881. *Harper's Weekly,* February 16, 1884, 111. James B. Whiteside, "Protecting the Life and Limb of Our Workmen" (Ph.D. diss., University of Colorado, 1986), 2, 11, 16–17, 103, 110, and 117. A. Dudley Gardner and Verla R. Flores, *Forgotten Frontier* (Boulder: Westview Press, 1989), 41–43.

28. ERH to John Willoughby, September 1, 1881, Letter, Mines and Mineral Resources Collection, Colorado College, Special Collections.

CHAPTER 6

1. *The Statistics of Population . . . Ninth Census* (Washington: Government Printing Office, 1872, vol. 1, 3, 95–96, 195–96, and 295–96.

2. Athearn, *Rebel of the Rockies*, 1–21. Marian M. McDonough, ed., "Quest for Health, Not Wealth, 1871," *Montana* (Winter 1964), 31. Marshall Sprague, *Newport in the Rockies* (Chicago: Swallow Press, 1980), 27–67. Gressley, *West by East*, 26.

3. Athearn, *Rebel of the Rockies*, 25–29.

4. *Catalogue of the . . . Colorado College* (St. Louis: McKitterick, 1875), 14 and 15–16.

5. The Palmer quote is found in Athearn, *Rebel of the Rockies*, 27. *Colorado Springs . . .* (Colorado Springs: Tribe and Jefferay, 1879), 5 and 9. McDonough, "Quest," 32. *Wolfe's Mercantile Guide . . . Directory* (Omaha: Omaha Republican, 1878), 258. *Colorado Springs in 1875* (Colorado Springs: M. J. Connor, 1875), 12–13. *Annual Report . . . National Land* (Colorado Springs: Gazette, 1879), 4–5. William Bell, "Address," Colorado College Special Collections, 5. Rayner to Ma, January 5, and April 21, 1872, Rayner Letters, Colorado College Special Collections.

6. H. H., *Colorado Springs* (Boston: Roberts, 1883), 12, 16, 21, and 85. Joseph Gordon and Judith Pickle, eds., *Helen Hunt Jackson's Colorado* (Colorado Springs: Colorado College, 1989), xv–xviii. Isabella Bird, *A Lady's Life in the Rocky Mountains* (Norman: University of Oklahoma, 1960 reprint), 152 and 156.

7. Rayner to Folks, September 27, 1871, Rayner Letters. *Colorado Springs in 1875*, 15. Bell to Jackson, May 1, 1877, William S. Jackson Papers, Colorado College, Special Collections. *The Manitou Mansions* (Colorado Springs: Gazette, 1877), 1 and 2.

8. Agnes W. Spring, *Colorado Charley* (Boulder: Pruett Publishing, 1968), 27 and 54. Bird, *Lady's Life*, 72–73, 102, and 116. Will to Helen, August 26, 1875, W. Jackson Papers.

9. Larson, *History of Wyoming*, 159–60.

10. Athearn, "Railroad," 4. Ray Allen Billington and Martin Ridge, *Westward Expansion* (New York: Macmillan Publishing Co., 1982), 587–88 and 656–57. Toole, *Montana*, 91–92. Winther, *Transportation Frontier*, 58, 100–101, and 109.

11. Stanley R. Davidson and Rex C. Myers, "Terminus Town," *Montana* (Autumn 1980), 23–26.

12. *Not in Precious Metals Alone*, 128. Chadwick, "Montana's Silver," 20–21. Roeder, "Electing Montana's Territorial Delegates," 64. Malone and Roeder, *Montana*, 129. Ronan, *Frontier Woman*, 123.

13. Sprague, *Great Gates*, 241 and 261. Athearn, *Rebel of the Rockies*, 91, 102–27, 134–35, and 162. *Report to the Stockholders of the D&RG* (Colorado Springs: Gazette, 1881), 11–12. William Bell, "Address," 11, Colorado College, Special Collections.

14. Howard Grilerat (?) to Jackson, January 19, 1887, and T. J. Potter to Jackson, May 7, 1887, William S. Jackson Papers, Colorado College, Special Collections. See also Athearn, *Rebel of the Rockies*, 153–60; Paul C. Nagel, "A West that Failed," *Western Historical Quarterly* (October 1987), 403–7.

15. Rohrbough, *Aspen*, 150–59. Dempsey and Fell, *Mining the Summit*, 94–100 and 211–20.

16. Noel, *Denver*, 50–67 and 70–74. Dorsett, *Queen City*, 61–82. Perkin, *First One Hundred Years*, 355–80. Eugene Adams, Lyle Dorsett, and Robert Pulcipher, *The Pioneer Western Bank* (Denver: First Interstate Bank of Denver, 1984), 51–65. Thomas Noel, *Growing through History with Colorado: The Colorado National Banks* (Denver: Colorado National Banks, 1987), 23–32.

17. *Statistics of the Population . . . Tenth Census* (Washington: Government Printing Office, 1883), 250. *Population . . . Twelfth Census* (Washington: Government Printing Office, 1901), pt. 1, 250–51. *Butte Miner*, June 5 and September 11, 1877, and January 8, 1878. Malone, *Battle for Butte*, 57–62. Spence, *Montana*, 39, 81, and 95–96.

18. Noel, *Denver*, 89. Adams, Dorsett, and Pulcipher, *Pioneer Western Bank*, 57–61, 67, and 72. Malone and Roeder, *Montana*, 84–85, 140–41. Malone, *Battle*, 62.

19. Stuart, *Forty Years*, 1: 229. Foy and Harlow, *Clowning through Life*, 184–85 and 187. *Anaconda Standard*, December 15, 1890. Clark, quoted in Donald MacMillan, "A History of the Struggle to Abate Air Pollution from Copper Smelters of the Far West 1885–1933" (Ph.D. diss., University of Montana, 1955), 21. [Charles Harrington], *Summering in Colorado* (Denver: Richards, 1874), 24.

20. *Summering in Colorado*, 24. *Engineering and Mining Journal* (New York), September 23, 1877, 236. Harvey to Family, May 22, 1879, Charles H. Harvey Papers, Library of Congress.

21. *Engineering and Mining Journal*, September 14, 1889, 231. Davidson and Myers, "Terminus Town," 26–28.

22. *The Statistics of Population . . . Ninth Census*, 375. *Colorado Directory 1885* (Chicago: R. L. Polk, 1885), 539, 560, and 566. *Weekly Boomerang* (Laramie), December 6, 1883. Arthur McMillan, "A Young Clergyman Looks at Granite's Glittering Glory," *Montana* (Summer 1964), 63. Anne Ellis, *The Life of an Ordinary Woman* (Lincoln: Univ. of Nebraska Press, 1980), 20–25. Frances Stokes, *My Father Owen Wister* (Laramie: n.p., 1952), 36–37.

23. *Report of the National Land and Improvement Company* (Colorado Springs: Gazette, 1883), 7. Will to Peggy, June 6, 1880, William S. Jackson Papers, Colorado College, Special Collections. *Colorado Springs 1886* (Colorado Springs: Tribe and Jefferay, 1885), 54–55, 157, and 174.

24. Raymond, *Statistics* (1870), 281. Earl of Dunraven, *Great Divide*, 43. Ernest Ingersoll, *Knocking Round the Rockies* (New York: Harper and Brothers, 1883), 127. Bird, *Lady's Life*, 26–27, 188, 190, and 197.

25. H. H., *Bits of Travel* (Boston: Roberts, 1886), 279, 281, 302, and 306. Paul, *Victorian Gentlewoman*, 197–80. Frank Warner, *Montana Territory* (Helena: Fisk Brothers, 1879), 120 and 183–84. J. Poulton, "Notes," Western History Department, Denver Public Library. Raymond, *Statistics* (1873), 357. *Wolfe's Mercantile Guide . . . Directory*, 175–81 and 183. Rae, *Westward by Rail*, 84. Robert Strahorn, *The Hand-Book of Wyoming* (Cheyenne: Knight and Leonard, 1877),

52 and 54. Carroll Van West, ed., "An Account of a Trip through the Yellowstone Valley in 1878," *Montana* (Spring 1986), 32–33.

26. For Helena, see Van West, "Account," 32–33. Michael P. Malone and Richard B. Roeder, "1876 in Montana," *Montana* (Winter 1975), 5. Joan Bishop, "A Season of Trial," *Montana* (1978), 64, 69, and 70–71. Tuttle, *Reminiscences,* 458. For Denver, see Dorsett, *Queen City,* 65–72; and Noel, *Denver,* 44–54. Myron J. Fogde, "Brother Van's Call to Frontier Montana," *Montana* (Autumn 1972), 2, 4, and 5–6. Daniel Tuttle, "Early History of the Episcopal Church in Montana," *Contributions to the Historical Society of Montana,* 5: 320. *Silver World* (Lake City), June 24, 1876. George M. Darley, *Pioneering in the San Juan* (Chicago: H. Revell Co., 1899), 22, 68, 124, and 141–42.

27. Kenneth V. Lottich, ed., "My Trip to Montana Territory, 1879," *Montana* (Winter 1965), 19–22. Ellis, *Life,* 37–55. *Colorado Springs 1886,* 58. Paula Petrik, "If She Be Content," *Western Historical Quarterly* (July 1987), 261–65. Burke to Father, June 21, 1882, "Letters," 9. *Weekly Boomerang,* December 6 and 13, 1883. *Sweetwater Gazette* (Green River), February 10, 1887. Nina Ellis Dosker, "Edwin M. Ellis," *Montana* (Winter 1980), 46. James Spencer, "Montana Memories," *Montana* (Winter 1979), 22. Mrs. M. S. Short, March 15, 1880, quoted in Myron J. Fogde, "The Protestant Minister Faces Frontier Montana," *Montana* (Winter 1965), 29. Ethelbert Talbot, *My People of the Plains* (New York: Harper and Brothers, 1906), 116–17.

28. Petrik, "Mothers and Daughters," 53–54. Ronan, *Frontier Woman,* 76, 78–79, 81, and 83. Bird, *Lady's Life,* 163 and 169. H. H., *Bits of Travel,* 398–406. Will to Helen, August 15, 1875, Jackson Papers, Special Collection, Colorado College.

29. Joseph Carey, "Politics and People," 3–4, Bancroft Library. Bowles to Jackson, March 6, 1876, Jackson Papers. Athearn, *Coloradans,* 163. Carolyn Stefanco, "Networking on the Frontier," *The Women's West* (Norman: University of Oklahoma, 1987), 267–68. Myres, *Westering Women,* 223–24. *Ouray Times,* September 2, 21, and October 29, 1877. Billie B. Jensen, "Colorado Woman Suffrage Campaigns of the 1870s," *Journal of the West* (April 1973), 254–71.

30. Petrik, "Mothers and Daughters," 50. Bird, *Lady's Life,* 67. Rayner to Sister, May 26, 1873, Rayner, Letters. *Montana Post,* May 6, 1865. *Montana Radiator* (Helena), February 24, 1869. Darley, *Pioneering,* 53–57. Augusta Tabor, "Cabin Life in Colorado," 4 and 6–7, Bancroft Library. Elliott West, "Heathens and Angels," *Western Historical Quarterly* (April 1983), 145–52. Frank Young, *Echoes from Arcadia* (Denver: Lanning Brothers, 1903), 113–14.

31. Rex Myers, "An Inning for Sin," *Montana* (Spring 1977), 25, 27, and 29–31. West, "Heathens and Angels," 163–64. Elliott West, "Scarlet West," *Montana* (Spring 1981), 19 and 27. Spence, *Montana,* 30–31. Paula Petrik, "Capitalists with Rooms," *Montana* (Spring 1981), 33 and 38. Lawrence B. DeGraaf, "Race, Sex and Region," *Pacific Historical Review* (May 1980), 304–5. Perkin, *First One Hundred Years,* 371–73. Darley, *Pioneering,* 27–30.

32. Petrik, "Capitalists with Rooms," 34 and 39. West, "Scarlet West," 22–

25 and 27. Anne M. Butler, *Daughters of Joy, Sisters of Misery* (Urbana: Univ. of Illinois Press, 1985), 1–15 and 150–55.

33. Wunder, "Law and the Chinese," 18 and 29–30. *Durango Record,* April 9 and September 3, 1881. Lee, *Growth and Decline,* 104, 152–54, 187–89, 192–93, and 203. Swartout, "Kwangtun," 52.

34. Swartout, "Kwangtun," 46–47, 49–51, and 52. Dorsett, *Queen City,* 101–3. Lee, *Growth and Decline,* 73–75. Larson, *History of Wyoming,* 141–43.

35. Limerick, *Legacy of Conquest,* 278. Myres, *Westering Women,* 85–86. DeGraaf, "Race," 286, 290–91, 297–300, and 312–13.

36. Swartout, "Kwangtun," 53. *Proceedings and Debates of the Constitutional Convention* (Helena: State Publishing, 1921), 60–61. Lee, *Growth and Decline,* 75.

37. *Denver Tribune,* September 5, 1882, and April 8, 1883. Marietta Wetherill, "Interview," University of New Mexico. Alice Cochran, "The Gold Dust," *Montana* (Spring 1970), 59–60 and 65–66. William Kershner, "Early Theatre in Butte," *Montana* (Spring 1988), 31–33. David M. Emmons, *Copper Camp* (New York: Hastings House, 1943), 275 and 277.

CHAPTER 7

1. Tupper to Sister, February 19, 1878, Tupper Papers, Western History Department, Denver Public Library.

2. Spence, *Montana,* 41–43. Maurice Frink, *Cow Country Cavalcade* (Denver: Old West Publishing, 1954), 37–45. Maurice Frink, W. Turrentine Jackson, and Agnes W. Spring, *When Grass Was King* (Boulder: Univ. of Colorado Press, 1956), 59–72. William W. Savage, ed., *Cowboy Life* (Norman: Univ. of Oklahoma Press, 1975), 33–39 and 41–49. Robert G. Athearn, *Westward the Briton* (New York: Charles Scribner's Sons, 1953), 102–15.

3. *Not in Precious Metals Alone,* 91 and 94. Bancroft, *History of Washington . . . Montana,* 734–35. Frink, *When Grass Was King,* 16–32.

4. Harmon R. Mothershead, *The Swan Land and Cattle Company, LTD* (Norman: Univ. of Oklahoma Press, 1971), 44–59. Frink, Jackson, Spring, *When Grass Was King,* 355–80. Larson, *History of Wyoming,* 165–67.

5. Nye, quoted in Billington and Ridge, *Westward Expansion,* 624; see chap. 31 for a general overview of ranching. See also Riegel and Athearn, *America Moves West,* chap. 32.

6. Frink, *When Grass Was King,* 59–92. Wm. Baille Grohman, *Camps in the Rockies* (New York: Charles Scribner's Sons, 1882), 320–21.

7. Frink, *When Grass Was King,* 135–56. Mothershead, *Swan Land,* 60–83.

8. Mothershead, *Swan Land,* 58–59. Larson, *History of Wyoming,* 178–79. Richard Goff and Robert H. McCaffree, *Century in the Saddle* (Denver: Johnson Publishing Company, 1967), 64–82.

9. Bryant B. Brooks, *Memoirs of Bryant B. Brooks* (Glendale: Arthur H. Clark, 1939), 195 and 201. Spence, *Montana,* 50–52. Alvin T. Steinel, *History of Agri-*

culture in Colorado (Fort Collins: State Board of Agriculture, 1926), 139 and 146–50.

10. Frink, *Cow Country Cavalcade*, 57–59. Stanley R. Davison, ed., "We Done our Chores," *Montana* (Winter 1983), 44–46. Barbara F. Rackley, "The Hard Winter of 1886–87," *Montana* (Winter 1971), 53–55 and 59. Spence, *Montana*, 48–49. Stuart, *Forty Years*, 2: 237. Goff and McCaffree, *Century in the Saddle*, 119–24. Frink, *When Grass Was King*, 93–100 and 225–40. Dun report, August 11, 1887, quoted in Mothershead, *Swan Land*, 76–77; see also 71–83.

11. Frink, *Cow Country Cavalcade*, 62–65. Frink, *When Grass Was King*, 100–110 and 259–69. Malone, *Battle for Butte*, 37. Rackley, "Hard Winter," 59. See Mothershead, *Swan Land*, chap. 5.

12. Mari Sandoz, *The Cattlemen* (New York: Hastings House, 1958),360–402. Larson, *History of Wyoming*, 269–79. David Emmons, *Garden in the Grasslands* (Lincoln: Univ. of Nebraska Press, 1971), 192. Asa Mercer, *The Banditti of the Plains* (Norman: Univ. of Oklahoma Press, 1954), xvi–xix and 67–93.

13. Mercer, *Banditti*, xxiv, xxv, and 149. Sandoz, *Cattlemen*, 396–402.

14. Frink, Jackson, and Spring, *When Grass Was King*, 115. Brooks, *Memoirs*, 176.

15. Michael P. Malone and Richard B. Roeder, "1876 in Field and Pasture," *Montana* (Spring 1975), 29–31. J. D. Kirby Diary, April–July 1870, Western History Department, Denver Public Library. Gould, *Wyoming*, 9. *Rocky Mountain Husbandman*, quoted in Frank Grant, "Embattled Voice," *Montana* (Spring 1974), 40.

16. Lamar, quoted from Carl Ubbelohde, Maxine Benson, and Duane A. Smith, *A Colorado History* (Boulder: Pruett Publishing Company, 1988), 203. Clark C. Spence, *The Rainmakers* (Lincoln: Univ. of Nebraska Press, 1980), 6–8. Emmons, *Garden*, 18–24 and 128–35. Steinel, *History of Agriculture*, 245–54.

17. A. E. Blount, "Dictation," 1, Bancroft Library. Ava Betz, *A Prowers County History* (Lamar: Prowers County Historical Society, 1986), 103–8. Gilbert C. Fite, *The Farmers' Frontier* (New York: Holt, Rinehart and Winston, 1966), 123–32. Emmons, *Garden*, 154–61. Steinel, *History of Agriculture*, 254–55.

18. James F. Willard, ed., *The Union Colony* (Boulder: Univ. of Colorado, 1918), x–xxi and 355–70. James F. Willard and Colin Goodykoontz, eds., *Experiments in Colorado Colonization* (Boulder: Univ. of Colorado), xiv–xxxvii and 425–68.

19. *Proceedings of the Constitutional Convention* (Denver: Smith-Brooks Press, 1907), 700–701. Gordon M. Bakken, *The Development of Law on the Rocky Mountain Frontier* (Westport, Conn.: Greenwood Press, 1983), 88–89. Steinel, *History of Agriculture*, 193–94. Robert Dunbar, *Forging New Rights in Western Waters* (Lincoln: Univ. of Nebraska Press, 1983), 86–90. Percy S. Fritz, *Colorado* (New York: Prentice-Hall, 1941), 327–29. Donald J. Pisani, "Enterprise and Equity," *Western Historical Quarterly* (January 1987), 23–30. Ubbelohde, Benson, and Smith, *Colorado History*, 198–200. David Getches, ed., *Water and the American West* (Boulder: Univ. of Colorado, 1988), 1–5.

CHAPTER 8

1. Raymond, *Statistics* (1871), 280. Hiram M. Chittenden, *Yellowstone National Park* (Norman: Univ. of Oklahoma Press, 1964), 81.

2. Lewis W. Selmeier, "First Camera on the Yellowstone," *Montana* (Summer 1972), 43, 35, and 52. Weldon F. Heald, "Thomas Moran," *Montana* (October 1965), 44, 46–47, and 52. Richard A. Bartlett, *Yellowstone: A Wilderness Besieged* (Tucson: Univ. of Arizona Press, 1971), 1–3. Chittenden, *Yellowstone*, 183–84.

3. Bartlett, *Yellowstone*, 213–17. Fogde, "Brother Van's Call," 5. Earl of Dunraven, *Great Divide*, 207, 220, and 237.

4. Strahorn, *Hand-Book*, 121. Van West, "Account," 33.

5. Strahorn, *Hand-Book*, 110–12, 121, 126–27, and 132–43.

6. Rae, *Westward by Rail*, 91 and 93. Bird, *Lady's Life*, 25–26. H. H., *Bits at Home*, 276. H. H., *Colorado Springs*, 17. Ingersoll, *Knocking Round the Rockies*, 194.

7. Rae, *Westward by Rail*, 84–89. Unidentified newspaper articles, 1871 (?), D&RG Scrapbook, Colorado College, Special Collections. H. H., *Colorado Springs*, 21–22. H. H., *Bits of Travel at Home* (Boston: Roberts, 1886), 282. Tupper to Dear Rachie, September 30, 1874, Tupper Letters.

8. Malone and Roeder, *Montana*, 67–68, discusses frontier shiftiness. Raymond, *Statistics* (1870), 286–87. *Engineering and Mining Journal*, July 9, 1872, 27.

9. Louisa L. Koppe, Interview, University of New Mexico, Special Collections. Rae, *Westward by Rail*, 83. Clark, "Centennial," 59. Tupper to My Dear Sister, November 17, 1878, Tupper Papers.

10. Bartlett, *Yellowstone*, 46–47. Margaret A. Cruikshank, "A Lady's Trip to Yellowstone in 1883," ed. Lee H. Wittlesey, *Montana* (Winter 1989), 10–11.

11. Bartlett, *Yellowstone*, 59, 221, 233–40, and 257–59.

12. Lee H. Whittlesey, ed., "In Yellowstone Park, 1886–1889," *Montana* (Winter 1983), 10–11.

13. *Helena Independent*, September 25, 1885. Lawrence R. Borne, *Dude Ranching* (Albuquerque: Univ. of New Mexico Press, 1983), 23–25 and 40–42. Ed to Mother, July 1, 1881, Hayes Papers, Colorado College, Special Collections. Stanley Wood, *Over the Range to the Golden Gate* (Chicago: R. R. Donnellely and Sons, 1889), 13 and 17. Burke to Father, February 15, 1881, "Letters," *Montana* (January 1969), 5. Spencer, "Montana Memories," 23.

CHAPTER 9

1. *Boulder News and Courier*, December 17, 1880, and March 23, 1883. *Boulder Herald*, November 3, 1886. *Speeches on the Coinage of Silver* (Washington: privately printed, 1886), 2: 527, 541, and 543. Gressley, *West by East*, 2–3 and 36. For general coverage of the silver issue, see Gilbert C. Fite and Jim E. Reese, *An Economic History of the United States* (Boston: Houghton Mifflin Co., 1965), 449–54.

2. Robert G. Athearn, *High Country Empire* (Lincoln: Univ. of Nebraska Press, 1960), 198–203. Limerick, *Legacy of Conquest*, 129 and 152.

3. Gressley, *West by East*, 3 and 37. Fite, *Farmer's Frontier*, 172–92 and 218–24. Athearn, *High Country Empire*, 211–15. John D. Hicks, *The Populist Revolt* (Lincoln: Univ. of Nebraska, 1960), chap. 8.

4. Spence, *Montana*, 98–99. Malone and Roeder, *Montana*, 162–63. James E. Wright, *The Politics of Populism* (New Haven: Yale Univ. Press, 1974), 130–40. Hicks, *Populist Revolt*, 238–71. Eugene H. Roseboom, *A History of Presidential Elections* (New York: Macmillan Co., 1958), 298–300. Robert W. Larson, "Populism in the Mountain West," *Western Historical Quarterly* (April 1982), 155–58.

5. Leon W. Fuller, "Colorado's Revolt against Capitalism," *Mississippi Valley Historical Review* (December 1934), 344–47 and 353. Wright, *Politics of Populism*, 146–52. W. H. Harvey, *Coin's Financial School* (Chicago: Coin Publishing Company, 1894), 20, 32, 40, 46, 52, 103, 106–7.

6. *Silver Standard* (Silver Plume, Colo.), June 24, 1893. Tabor speech, January 30, 1890, Box 15, Tabor Collections, Colorado Historical Society. *Engineering and Mining Journal*, January 7, 1; and July 1, 1893, 2. Palmer to Schlesinger, December 15, 1892, Palmer Papers, Colorado College, Special Collections.

7. Larson, *History of Wyoming*, 284–85. Gould, *Wyoming*, 96–97, 194, and 266. Hicks, *Populist Revolt*, 301–9.

8. Carolyn Stefanco, "Networking on the Frontier," *The Women's West* (Norman: Univ. of Oklahoma Press, 1987), 273–74. Carrie C. Catt and Nettie R. Schaler, *Women Suffrage and Politics* (New York: Charles Scribner's Sons, 1926), 118–19. Myres, *Westering Women*, 237. Billie B. Jensen, "Let the Women Vote," *Colorado Magazine* (Winter 1964), 13–25.

9. *Effects of Demonetization of Silver on the Industries of Colorado . . .* (Denver: Smith-Brooks, 1893), 1–33. *Engineering and Mining Journal*, July 22, 1893, 44. Parson to A. Kennedy, September 25, 1893, George Parson Papers, Colorado College, Special Collections.

10. Gould, *Wyoming*, 194. *Helena Weekly Independent*, May 18, 1893. Stone, quoted in Muriel Wolle, *Montana Pay Dirt* (Denver: Sage Books, 1963), 250–51. *Engineering and Mining Journal*, July 8, 38; September 30, 352; and November 11, 1893, 505. Chadwick, "Montana's Silver," 16–17 and 28–31. Malone, *Battle for Butte*, 54–55.

11. Hauser to G. G. Vest, August 12, 1893, and Rollin Hartt to Mother, December 7, 1896, quoted in *Not in Precious Metals Alone*, 133 and 164. Malone, *Battle for Butte*, 54–55.

12. Malone and Roeder, *Montana*, 146. For the crash, see Fite and Reese, *Economic History*, 305–7.

13. The Bryan quote is in Richard B. Morris and William Greenleaf, *The History of a Nation* (Chicago: Rand McNally and Company, 1969), 2: 275. Wolcott to Palmer, October 29, 1893, Palmer Letters. *Engineering and Mining Journal*, July 15, 49 and 66; July 28, 97; August 5, 131; November 4, 485; November 11,

516; and November 18, 1893, 516. Wolcott to Palmer, April 18, 1894, Palmer Letters. Hicks, *Populist Revolt*, 311–17.

14. Thomas H. Carter, "Speech, February 26, 1896," 22, copy in Palmer Collection.

15. *Silverton Standard*, October 10, 1896. *Helena Weekly Independent*, October 8, 1896. *Rocky Mountain News*, July–November 1896. *Cripple Creek Guide*, July 25 and October 17, 1896. Malone and Dougherty, "Montana's Political Culture," 46. Hague to Mary, November 9, 1896, Hague Collection, Huntington Library.

16. Original election returns, Colorado State Archives. Spence, *Montana*, 101. Larson, "Populism in the Mountain West," 149–53 and 164, Malone and Roeder, *Montana*, 162–63. Gould, *Wyoming*, 231, 258–59, and 261. Hicks, *Populist Revolt*, 354–59 and 375–79.

CHAPTER 10

1. Parsons to L. Lefevre, May 22, 1893, Parsons Papers. Henderson, *Mining in Colorado*, 247. *Engineering and Mining Journal*, August 26, 1893, 208.

2. Henderson, *Mining in Colorado*, 56–60 and 246–47. Robert G. Taylor, *Cripple Creek* (Bloomington: Indiana Univ. Publications, 1966), 32–51 and 88–95. Marshall Sprague, *Money Mountain* (Boston: Little, Brown and Co., 1953), 40–47, 111–32, and 208–19. *Engineering and Mining Journal*, September 13, 1896, 241. Frank Waters, *Midas of the Rockies* (Chicago: Sage Books, 1972), 237–41 and 257–67.

3. Hamilton Smith to Hague, May 25, Hague to Smith, June 14, Hague to Smith, June 15, 1895, and Report on the Portland Mine, Hague Collection.

4. Ellsworth Daggett to Hague, December 14, 1895, Hague Collection.

5. Parsons to Bradford, May or June 1894, to J. Caldwell, February 28, 1895, and to West, May 2, 1894, Parsons Papers.

6. Spence, *Montana*, 34–35. Austin Moore, ed., *Souls and Saddlebags* (Denver: Big Mountain Press, 1962), 139–40. Gene M. Gressley, ed., *Bostonians and Bullion* (Lincoln: Univ. of Nebraska Press, 1968), 36–41. *Engineering and Mining Journal*, January 10, 1891, 74: June 23, 591; August 26, 223; September 30, 354; and December 23, 1893, 650; July 4, 15; and August 29, 1896, 193. *Wyoming State Tribune* (Cheyenne), August 10, 1892.

7. Limerick, *Legacy of Conquest*, 113–14. See also Malone, *Battle for Butte*, 217. Malone and Dougherty, "Montana's Political Culture," 46–47. Spence, *Montana*, 100–102.

8. Spence, *Montana*, 95–97. Lavender, *Rockies*, 284–85. Carroll Van West, "Marcus Daly and Montana," *Montana* (Winter 1987), 60–61. Malone, "Midas of the West," 8–9.

9. Spence, *Montana*, 100–101. Susan Leaphart, "Frieda and Belle Gligelman," *Montana* (Summer 1982), 85. Lavender, *Rockies*, 326–27. "Yellowstone Journal," July 25, 1890, Western Historical Collections, University of Colorado.

Not in Precious Metals Alone, 143–44. William Lang, "Spoils of Statehood," *Montana* (Autumn 1987), 34 and 43–45.

10. Malone, "Midas of the West," 9–14. Lavender, *Rockies,* 327–28. Clark, quoted in Spence, *Montana,* 102.

11. *Engineering and Mining Journal* (New York), May 23, 614; and June 13, 1891, 702. Brian Shovers, "The Perils of Working the Butte Underground," *Montana* (Spring 1987), 26. Malone, *Battle for Butte,* 45 and 52–53. Van West, "Marcus Daly," 60–62.

12. *New York Times,* April 28, 1899, 1. *Engineering and Mining Journal,* April 29, 1899, 494. Malone, *Battle for Butte,* 131–32 and 135–39.

13. Spence, *Montana,* 103–5. Malone, *Battle for Butte,* 49–50. Toole, *Montana,* 197–206.

14. *Engineering and Mining Journal,* October 31, 648; and November 14, 1903, 727. Malone, *Battle for Butte,* 42.

15. Toole, *Montana,* 206–10. Spence, *Montana,* 104–6.

16. Malone, *Battle for Butte,* 190, 200, and 210. Spence, *Montana,* 37–38, 96. Malone, "Midas of the West," 2, 8, and 17.

17. Larson, *Wyoming,* 336–37 and 377–78. David Kathka, "The Italian Experience in Wyoming," in Hendrickson, *Peopling the High Plains, 70. Mineral Resources 1901,* 447. *Mineral Resources of the United States* (Washington: Government Printing Office, 1906), 462 and 711. *Mineral Resources of the United States* (Washington: Government Printing Office, 1911), 57. Philip A. Kalisch, "Woebegone Miners," 239–40. James B. Whiteside, "Protecting the Life and Limb of our Workmen" (Ph.D. diss., University of Colorado, 1986), 9–10, 42, 126, and 133–35. Gardner and Flores, *Forgotten Frontier,* 103–16. Edith Erickson, quoted in *Miners' Monument,* 2.

18. Lizzie A. Ewing, "Diary," July 2, 1902, Western History Department, Denver Public Library. Whiteside, "Protecting," 3, 32, and 43. Clark, quoted in Gardner and Flores, *Forgotten Frontiers,* 103; see also 102–16. *Engineering and Mining Journal,* January 4, 1908, 80.

19. Whiteside, "Protecting," 4. Gardner and Flores, *Forgotten Frontier,* 124–26. *Mineral Resources* (1910), 57. Larson, *Wyoming,* 334–35. *Engineering and Mining Journal,* September 22, 1900, 346; January 3, 56; April 18, 590; October 24, 618; November 7, 1903, 715; and January 4, 1908, 6, 30, and 39–40. Joseph E. Toole, *Message of Gov. Joseph K. Toole to the Tenth Legislative Assembly* (Helena: n.p., 1907), 14. Henderson, *Mining in Colorado,* 96–99. *Mineral Resources* (1905), 43, 47, 335–36, and 341.

CHAPTER 11

1. Richard Lingenfelter, *The Hardrock Miners* (Berkeley: Univ. of California Press, 1974), 43–53, 64–65, and 113–15. Ronald C. Brown, *Hard-Rock Miners* (College Station: Texas A&M Univ. Press, 1979), 124 and 145. Mark Wyman,

Hard Rock Epic (Berkeley: Univ. of California Press, 1979), 152, 168, and 179–82.

2. *Engineering and Mining Journal*, February 11, 133; February 25, 1893, 182. Lingenfelter, *Hard-Rock Miners*, 219–25. Vernon Jensen, *Heritage of Conflict* (New York: Greenwood Press, 1969), 54–57. San Juan District Records and Western Federation Constitution 1893, 1895, WFM Archives, Western Historical Collections, University of Colorado.

3. Jensen, *Heritage*, 40–51. Harry to Alice, April 22 and June 6, 1894, Harry J. Newman Papers, Colorado College, Special Collections. Sprague, *Money Mountain*, 133–61. Waters, *Midas of the Rockies*, 143–47. Wright, *Politics of Populism*, 159–62 and 179–80. Interview with Waite, Hagerman Committee, June 2, 1894, Colorado College, Special Collections.

4. Brown, *Hard-Rock Miners*, 147–48. Blair, *Leadville*, 183–99. Carroll D. Wright, *A Report on Labor Disturbances in the State of Colorado . . .* (Washington: Government Printing Office, 1905), 86–101.

5. Wright, *Report*, 106–10. *Engineering and Mining Journal* (New York), July 13, 1901, 47.

6. *Engineering and Mining Journal*, January 18, 117; and Dec. 6, 1902, 761. *Daily Journal* (Telluride), November 20–21, 1902. *American Labor Union Journal* (Butte), December 4, 1902, and April 2, 1903.

7. Jensen, *Heritage of Conflict*, 118–23. Memorandum, November 24, 1903, W. S. Jackson Papers, Colorado College, Special Collections. Sprague, *Money Mountain*, 140–41 and 250–51. Roosevelt to Stewart, October 15, 1903, Philip B. Stewart Collection, Colorado College, Special Collections.

8. Jensen, *Heritage*, 127–39 and 147–54. Elizabeth Jameson, "Imperfect Unions," *Class, Sex and the Woman Worker* (Westport, Conn.: Greenwood Press, 1977), 191. George G. Suggs, Jr., *Colorado's War on Militant Unionism* (Detroit: Wayne State Univ. Press, 1972), 84–117. Wright, *Report*, 112–22 and 147–50.

9. *Miners Magazine* (Butte), November 26 and December 3, 1903. *San Miguel Examiner* (Telluride), March 19, 1904. *Engineering and Mining Journal*, March 31, 531; and May 19, 1904, 820. Suggs, *Colorado's War*, 118–45. Jensen, *Heritage*, 138–44. Gressley, *Bostonians and Bullion*, 92, 98, and 101. Wright, *Report*, 107–9.

10. Suggs, *Colorado's War*, 179 and 180. *Miners Magazine*, December 3, 1903, and January 14, 1904. Gressley, *Bostonians and Bullion*, 101.

11. Ray S. Baker, "The Reign of Lawlessness," *McClure's Magazine* (May 1904), 45–46, 48, and 51–56. Roosevelt to Stewart, August 3, 1904, Stewart Collection.

12. *Mineral Resources of the United States* (Washington: Government Printing Office, 1906), 243. *Engineering and Mining Journal*, January 4, 1908, 31. Malone, *Battle for Butte*, 5–6.

13. Lewis L. Gould, ed., *The Progressive Era* (Syracuse: Syracuse Univ. Press, 1974), 7. Arthur A. Ekirch, Jr., *Progressivism in America* (New York: New Viewpoints, 1974), 40–47.

14. Gardner and Flores, *Forgotten Frontier*, 124–26. Malone and Roeder, *Montana*, 206. Jerry Calvert, "The Rise and Fall of Socialism in a Company Town, 1902–05," *Montana* (Autumn 1986), 2, 4–8, 11–13.

15. *Telluride Journal*, April 9, 1903. *San Miguel Examiner* (Telluride), March 30 and April 6, 1907. Wright, *Politics of Populism*, 232, 248–49, 258–60. Fritz, *Colorado*, 378–79. Suggs, *Colorado's War*, 24–26 and 146–47.

16. Ekirch, *Progressivism*, 43–49.

CHAPTER 12

1. See *Population: Twelfth Census* (Washington: Government Printing Office, 1901), pt. 1, and original 1900 census returns, microfilm copy, Fort Lewis College.

2. Lang, "Spoils of Statehood," 38–39 and 40–43. *Population: Twelfth Census*, pt. 1, 249–51.

3. *Cripple Creek Prospector*, December 8, 1892. Harry to Alice, January 5, and October 26, 1895, March 18, April 20, and 30, and May 3, 1896, to Wife, September 13, 1898, and October 5, 1899, Harry J. Newman Papers, Colorado College, Special Collections. Mariette Wetherill Interview, July 9, 1953, University of New Mexico. *Cripple Creek Crusher*, December 2, 9, 1892, and January 27, 1893. *Cripple Creek Guide*, April 25, May 2, July 18, August 15, 29, and December 19, 26, 1896, and February 20 and March 6 and 13, 1896.

4. *Report of the National Land and Improvement Company* (Colorado Springs: Gazette, 1894), 3. Sprague, *Newport*, 167–69. *Manitou, Colorado's Great Resort* (Denver: n.p., 1897), 10, 13, and 15.

5. Duane A. Smith, "Baseball Champions of Colorado," *Journal of Sport History* (Spring 1977), 51–71. Mark Foster, *The Denver Bears* (Boulder: Pruett Publishing Company, 1983), 10–25.

6. *Denver Times*, November 15, 1904. *Denver Post*, November 17, 1904. William E. Davis, *Glory Colorado!* (Boulder: Pruett Press, 1965), 205–9.

7. *Rocky Mountain News*, November 29, 1905.

8. Gene Fowler, *Timberline* (Garden City, N.Y.: Garden City Books, 1951), 333–36. *Montana* (Helena: Independent Publishing, 1909), 146. *Society Blue Book of Colorado Springs* (Colorado Springs: Blue Book Publishing, 1903), 1–80. Emmons, *Copper Camp*, 24.

9. Bakken, *Development of Law*, 30–32. Susan Armitage, "Through Women's Eyes," *The Women's West* (Norman: Univ. of Oklahoma Press, 1987), 12.

10. Richard B. Roeder, "Crossing the Gender Line," *Montana* (Summer 1982), 64–67 and 70–73. *Cripple Creek–Victor Mining District Directory* (Cripple Creek: Directory Publishing, 1895), 56–63, 159–63, and 225–52. *Cripple Creek Crusher*, February 10, 1893. *Cripple Creek Guide*, September 5 and November 21, 1896. *Cripple Creek District Directory 1900* (Cripple Creek: Gazetteer, 1900), 89–105, 458–92, and 725–62. Myres, *Westering Women*, 238, 250, 264–66, and 268. Elliott

West, "Beyond Baby Doe," *The Women's West* (Norman: Univ. of Oklahoma Press, 1987), 189. Elizabeth Jameson, "Women as Workers," *The Women's West*, 150. Petrik "If She Be Content," 281–85. Ellis, *Life*, 189, 204–5, 230, and 296.

11. Thomas J. Noel, *The City and the Saloon* (Lincoln: Univ. of Nebraska Press, 1982), 111–17. Malone and Roeder, *Montana*, 190. Mary G. Slocum, "Women in Colorado under the Suffrage," *The Outlook* (December 26, 1903), 997–1000. Elizabeth McCracken, "The Women in America—Women's Suffrage in Colorado," *The Outlook* (November 28, 1903), 739, 741, and 744. See also Jameson, "Imperfect Unions," 179–80 and 183–84.

12. Gould, *Progressive Era*, 1–6, 60–61, and 121. Richard Hofstadter, *The Age of Reform, from Bryan to F.D.R.* (London: Jonathan Cape, 1962), 131–37. Gressley, *West by East*, 6. Ekirch, *Progressivism in America*, 3–4, 19–20, and 127–30.

13. Thomas Noel, *Denver* (Denver: Denver Chamber of Commerce, 1980), 96–99.

14. Colin B. Goodykoontz, ed., *Papers of Edward P. Costigan Relating to the Progressive Movement in Colorado* (Boulder: Univ. of Colorado Press, 1941), 4. Ben B. Lindsey and Harvey J. O'Higgins, *The Beast* (New York: Doubleday, Page, 1910), 158–60. Marjorie Hornbein, "Colorado's Amazing Gubernatorial Election Contests of 1904" (Master's thesis, University of Denver, 1967), 37–39.

15. *Weekly Republican* (Denver), October 27, 1904. Hornbein, "Colorado's Amazing Gubernatorial Election," 19–20, 27–36, 63, 70–77, and 245. *Durango Democrat*, March 17–21, 1905. Lindsey and O'Higgins, *Beast*, 185, 206, and 220.

16. Spence, *Montana*, 109–16. Larson, *History of Wyoming*, 322–23. Malone and Roeder, *Montana*, 196–98. Robert A. Harvie and Larry V. Bishop, "Police Reform in Montana, 1890–1918," *Montana* (Spring 1983), 46–50. Malone and Dougherty, "Montana's Political Culture," 49. *Meeker Herald*, March 15, 1913. *Daily Democrat* (Durango), September 3, 1909. Roland L. DeLorme, "Turn-of-the-Century Denver," *Colorado Magazine* (Winter 1968), 10–15. D'Ann Campbell, "Judge Ben Lindsey and the Juvenile Court Movement, 1901–1904," *Arizona and the West* (Spring 1976), 5–20.

17. Roosevelt to Stewart, June 26, 1905, Philip B. Stewart Collection, Colorado College, Special Collections. Larson, *History of Wyoming*, 322–25. William H. Moore, "Progressivism and the Social Gospel in Wyoming," *Western Historical Quarterly* (July 1984), 299–302 and 315–16.

18. Toole, *Montana*, 211–17. Spence, *Montana*, 109–10.

19. *Durango Weekly Democrat*, August 26 and September 16, 1910. Gerald D. Welch, "John F. Shafroth," (Master's thesis, University of Denver, 1962), 16–17, 31–32, 51–52, and 131. E. K. MacColl, "John Franklin Shafroth," *Colorado Magazine* (January 1952), iv–v and 42–44. Duane A. Smith, "Colorado and Judicial Recall," *The American Journal of Legal History* (July 1963), 198–209.

20. Larson, *History of Wyoming*, 318. Loeb to Stewart, March 31, 1901, and Roosevelt to Stewart, November 24, 1902, Stewart Collection.

CHAPTER 13

1. Donald MacMillan, "A History of the Struggle to Abate Air Pollution from Copper Smelters of the Far West, 1885–1933" (Ph.D. diss., University of Montana, 1973), 22. *Engineering and Mining Journal,* December 20, 711; and December 27, 1890, 737; January 24, 112; February 7, 176; August 29, 247; and December 26, 1891, 733. *Anaconda Standard,* November 27 and December 6, 1890.

2. MacMillan, "History of the Struggle," 2, 41, 79–80, and 95. *Engineering and Mining Journal,* January 2, 1892, 58. *Butte City Illustrated,* 81 and 83. William D. Haywood, *Bill Haywood's Book* (London: Martin Lawrence, n.d.), 83.

3. Malone, *Battle for Butte,* 42–44. Larson, *History of Wyoming,* 377. Joseph Petulla, *American Environmentalism* (College Station: Texas A&M Press, 1980), 25. Joseph Petulla, *American Environmental History* (San Francisco: Boyd and Fraser Publishing, 1977), 221–25. G. Michael McCarthy, *Hour of Trial* (Norman: Univ. of Oklahoma Press, 1977), 29–31, 44, and 46.

4. Petulla, *American Environmental History,* 224–25. McCarthy, *Hour of Trial,* 46–48, 51–52, 63–65, and 71.

5. McCarthy, *Hour of Trial,* 77–87, 94–97, and 119.

6. McCarthy, *Hour of Trial,* 182–89. Larson, *History of Wyoming,* 377–78.

7. McCarthy, *Hour of Trial,* 204–8.

8. *Mining and Scientific Press* (San Francisco), 1902. *Engineering and Mining Journal,* 1902–8. MacMillan, "History of the Struggle," 5, 7, 8, 133–37, and 163–80.

9. *Mining and Scientific Press,* April 12, 202–3; and September 13, 1902, 145. *Montana: The Most Productive Ore Center of the Inter-Mountain Region* (Butte: North American Industrial Review, 1904), 8 and 148. MacMillan, "History of the Struggle," 163–80. John Hays Hammond, *The Autobiography of John Hays Hammond* (New York: Arno, 1974), 562–63.

10. *Engineering and Mining Journal,* October 19, 1907, 750; March 26, 1910, 645; and May 6, 1911, 892. MacMillan, "History of the Struggle," 158–60. Spence, *Montana,* 113–14. Michael Malone, "The Collapse of Western Metal Mining," *Pacific Historical Review* (August 1986), 457–58.

11. Petulla, *American Environmental History,* 268–71. Fite, *Farmer's Frontier,* 190. Gould, *Progressive Era,* 117. Barton W. March, *The Uncompahgre Valley and the Gunnison Tunnel* (Montrose: Marsh and Torrence, 1905), 21, 76, and 80. Duane Vandenbusche and Duane A. Smith, *A Land Alone* (Boulder: Pruett Publishing Company, 1981), 186–87. Steinel, *History of Agriculture,* 527–28 and 536–38.

12. Fritz, *Colorado,* 471–73. Bakken, *Development of Law,* 88–89. Robert G. Dunbar, *Foraging New Rights in Western Waters* (Lincoln: Univ. of Nebraska Press, 1983), 77–78 and 134–35.

13. Brooks, *Memoirs,* 225–26. See also Dunbar, *Foraging New Rights,* 105–17.

CHAPTER 14

1. *Engineering and Mining Journal,* July 1, 5–6, and August 10, 1893, 187. *A Week at the Fair* (Chicago: Rand, McNally and Company, 1893), 14–15, 60, 102–3, 201, 203, 217, and 246.

2. Karl Baedeker, ed., *The United States with an Excursion into Mexico* (New York: De Capo Press, 1973), 372–74, 379–87, 391–92, 406–9, 415–16, and 424.

3. W. Thomas White, "Commonwealth or Colony?," *Montana* (Autumn 1988), 12 and 15. Athearn, *Union Pacific Country,* 326–27 and 295–309. Carlos A. Schwantes, "Images of the Wageworkers' Frontier," *Montana* (Autumn 1988), 38 and 40. Moore, *Souls and Saddlebags,* 147. "Yellowstone Journal," July 19, 1890. Gardner S. Turrill, *A Tale of the Yellowstone* (Jefferson, Iowa: G. S. Turrill, 1901), 12–13, 15, 17, 20–22, 31–32, 69, 78, 91, and 99.

4. Clyde A. Milner II, "The Shared Memory of Montana Pioneers," *Montana* (Winter 1987), 3–5 and 9–12. *Durango Herald,* May 7 and 14, 1896. *Lake City Times,* August 18, 1898.

5. *Helena Weekly Independent,* May 9, 1895. Spence, *Montana,* 107–8. Larson, *History of Wyoming,* 310–12. *Rocky Mountain News,* May–August 1898. *Lake City Times,* August 18, 1898.

6. *Weekly Republican* (Denver), October 13, 1898. *Rocky Mountain News* (Denver), October 29, 1899, July 14, 1903, February 13, and March 11, 1906, and January 1, 1918. *Denver Post,* October 28, 1917.

7. Emmons, *Copper Camp,* 253–54. Joseph K. Toole, *Message of Gov. Joseph K. Toole to the Tenth Legislative Assembly* (Helena: n.p., 1907), 20 and 38. T. B. Long, *70 Years a Cowboy* (Regina, Sask.: Western Printers, 1959), 8.

8. *Chicago Tribune,* February 28, 1909. Virginia W. Johnson, "Tough Taft," *Montana* (Autumn 1982), 51–52. Schwantes, "Images," 40. William H. Goetzmann and William N. Goetzmann, *The West of the Imagination* (New York: W. W. Norton and Co., 1986), 287–88. Albert Johannsen, *The House of Beadle and Adams* (Norman: Univ. of Oklahoma Press, 1950), 1: 1–14 and 2: 343–413. James K. Folsom, "Dime Novels," *The Reader's Encyclopedia of the American West* (New York: Thomas Y. Crowell Co., 1977), 303–4. Henry N. Smith, *Virgin Land* (New York: Vintage Books, 1950), 99–114.

9. Norman Forester, ed., *American Poetry and Prose* (Boston: Houghton Mifflin Co., 1957), pt. 1, 340. Smith, *Virgin Land,* 64–74. See also John R. Milton, *The Novel of the American West.*

10. Rodman W. Paul, ed., *A Victorian Gentlewoman in the Far West* (San Marino: Huntington Library, 1972), 1–4. *Colorado: Short Studies of Its Past and Present* (Boulder: Univ. of Colorado, 1927), 164–65. Emmons, *Copper Camp,* 258. Leslie A. Wheeler, "Montana and the Lady Novelist," *Montana* (Winter 1977), 41–43. *Butte Miner,* June 8, 1913. Goetzmann and Goetzmann, *West,* 301 and 314. Earl Pomeroy, *In Search of Golden West* (New York: Knopf, 1957), 107–8. Athearn, *Mythic West,* 46 and 163.

11. Stegner, "Who Are the Westerners?," 39 and 41. *Century Magazine* ar-

ticle, quoted in Athearn, *Mythic West*, 235; see also 163–65. Katharine F. Ellis, "My Lady of the Rocky Mountains," *The Outlook* (February 16, 1907), 365–69. Katharine F. Ellis, "A Fourth of July Celebration in the Rockies," *Outlook* (July 2, 1910), 482–86.

12. Goetzmann and Goetzmann, *West*, 148–57 and 170–88. Phillip D. Thomas, "Bierstadt of Dusseldorf," *Montana* (Spring 1976), 2 and 17. Clarence S. Jackson, *Picture Maker of the Old West* (New York: Charles Scribner's Sons, 1947), 105–23, 189–90, and 302.

13. Spence, *Montana*, 191. Richard B. Roeder, "Charles M. Russell and Modern Times," *Montana* (Summer 1984), 4, 7, and 10–12. Malone and Roeder, *Montana*, 283–84. Goetzmann and Goetzmann, *West*, 237–38 and 261–78.

14. Washington Correspondent to Howbert, October 31, 1901, Irving Howbert Papers, Colorado College, Special Collections.

CHAPTER 15

1. Spence, *Montana*, 132–35. Larson, *History of Wyoming*, 359–65. Toole, *Montana*, 229–35. Athearn, *Mythic West*, 30–32 and 38.

2. Webb, quoted in Athearn, *Mythic West*, 83; see also 34 and 38.

3. Spence, *Montana*, 132–34 and 194. *The Resources . . . Montana* (Helena: Independent Publishing, 1914), 41. *Bulletin*, quoted in Larson, *History of Wyoming*, 365.

4. Elinore P. Stewart, *Letters of a Woman Homesteader* (Boston: Houghton Mifflin, 1914), v–x, 3, 15–18, 207–11, 213, 214–17, and 279. See also her *Letters from an Elk Hunt* (Lincoln: Univ. of Nebraska Press, 1979).

5. Spence, *Rainmakers*, 1–8, 46–51, and 132–36. Limerick, *Legacy of Conquest*, 36 and 42.

6. Malone and Roeder, *Montana*, 180–81. Larson, *History of Wyoming*, 348–50 and 355–56. Petulla, *American Environmental History*, 270–71. Bakken, *Development of Law*, 88–89.

7. Dunbar, *Forging New Rights*, 136–37 and 197. M. Paul Holsinger, "Wyoming v. Colorado Revisited," *Annals of Wyoming* (April 1970), 47–49. Fritz, *Colorado*, 473–74. Larson, *History of Wyoming*, 420. Steinel, *History of Agriculture*, 219–20.

8. Thomas Tonge, *All About Colorado* (Denver: Smith-Brooks, 1913), 25 and 47–48. William L. Hewitt, "Education for Agribusiness," *The Midwest Review* (Spring 1987), 35.

9. Dorsett, *Queen City*, 141–49 and 181–82. Athearn, *Coloradans*, 229–332. Larson, *History of Wyoming*, 408–10. Malone and Roeder, *Montana*, 204–5.

10. Athearn, *Mythic West*, 44–45 and 47. Gressley, *West by East*, 6 and 28. Limerick, *Legacy of Conquest*, 36 and 42.

11. Emmons, *Copper Camp*, 2. *Daily Missoulian* (Missoula), February 17 and 22, 1914. William M. Raine, "Colorado, A National Playground," *The Outing*

Magazine (May 1911), 205–6. Theodore Wiprud, "Butte: a Troubled Labor Paradise," *Montana* (Autumn 1971), 37. Wilkinson, quoted in Jameson, "Women as Workers," 151.

12. Spence, *Montana*, 117–18. Malone and Roeder, *Montana*, 202–4.

13. Barron B. Beshoar, *Hippocrates in a Red Vest* (Palo Alto: American West Publishing Company, 1973), 295–308. James A. Atkins, ed., *Human Relations in Colorado* (Denver: Publishers Press, 1968), 70–75. Whiteside, "Protecting," 9, 32, and 35. Phyllis Smith, *Once a Coal Miner* (Boulder: Pruett Publishing Company, 1989), 103–50. Barron B. Beshoar, *Out of the Depths* (Denver: Golden Bell Press, 1957), chaps. 12–17. Zeese Papanikolas, *Buried Unsung* (Salt Lake City: Univ. of Utah Press, 1982), 207–47.

14. Jensen, *Heritage*, 325–53. Western Federation of Miners Records, Box 1, Western Historical Collections, University of Colorado. Wiprud, "Butte," 34–35. Malone and Roeder, *Montana*, 209–11. Malone, *Battle for Butte*, 209. *Engineering and Mining Journal* (New York), September 5, 446; September 12, 1914, 497 and 502; and January 9, 1915, 110.

15. L. W. Trumbull, *Atlantic City Gold Mining District* (Cheyenne: Bristol, 1914), 73–74, 81, and 87. *Mineral Resources of the United States* (Washington: Government Printing Office, 1916), 355, 577, 580–82, 589, and 597. *Engineering and Mining Journal*, July 2, 37; July 9, 86; August 20, 345 and 354; October 29, 1910, 845; and January 9, 1915, 110. *Elkton Consolidated Mining and Milling Company* (Colorado Springs: n.p., 1913), 1. Henderson, *Mining in Colorado*, 99–101. Michael Malone, "The Collapse of Western Metal Mining," *Pacific Historical Review* (August 1986), 463–64.

16. Victor City Council Minutes, no. 7, 1915, Victor, Colorado. St. Elmo City Records, 1915, Colorado College, Special Collections.

17. *Resources and Opportunities of Montana 1914*, 17, 23, 130, 221, and 225. Tonge, *All About Colorado*, 88 and 95. Edwin Sabin, *The Peaks of the Rockies* (Denver: Carson-Harper, 1911), 2, 4, and 14–18. Thomas J. Noel, "Paving the Way to Colorado," *Journal of the West* (July 1987), 43 and 46.

18. *Union Pacific Outings* (Omaha: Union Pacific, 1910), 7, 12–14, and 19. Borne, *Dude Ranching*, 31–33. Tonge, "All About Colorado," 108. Raine, "Colorado," 202 and 210.

19. Bartlett, *Yellowstone*, 53, 63–66, and 257.

20. Raine, "Colorado," 210–11, 20. *Durango Democrat*, June 19, 1914. *Mesa Verde National Park* (Washington: Government Printing Office, 1915), 5–6 and 28–29.

21. Alfred Runte, *National Parks: The American Experience* (Lincoln: Univ. of Nebraska Press, 1979), 74–75. Madison Grant, *Early History of Glacier National Park Montana* (Washington: Government Printing Office, 1919), 5–6. John Ise, *Our National Park Policy* (Baltimore: Johns Hopkins, 1961), 172–73. George Bird Grinnell, "The Crown of the Continent," *The Century Magazine* (September 1901), 660–61 and 663.

22. Ise, *Our National Park Policy*, 171–77, 179, and 202. Grant, *Early History*,

6–9. *The Resources and Opportunities of Montana*, 228 and 230. Runte, *National Parks*, 76–77 and 94.

23. Raine, "Colorado," 209–10. Edwin J. Foscue and Louis Quam, *Estes Park* (Dallas: Univ. Press, 1949), 43 and 51–52. Ise, *Our National Park Policy*, 212–15. Carl Abbott, "To Arouse Interest in the Outdoors: The Literary Career of Enos Mills," *Montana* (Spring 1981), 3–4, 5, and 9. C. W. Buchholtz, *Rocky Mountain National Park* (Boulder: Colorado Associated Univ. Press, 1983), 122–36. Taylor, quoted in Runte, *National Parks*, 77.

24. Abbott, "To Arouse Interest," 9. Buchholtz, *Rocky Mountain*, 136–37. Runte, *National Parks*, 93.

EPILOGUE

1. Bill Hornby, "History Shows the West Will Grow; Only Quality Is at Issue," *Denver Post*, May 2, 1989. Athearn, *Mythic West*, 61 and 70. Billington, *America's Frontier Heritage*, 45. Stegner, "Who Are the Westerners?," 41. Pomeroy, *In Search*, 212.

2. Runte, *National Parks*, 75. Pomeroy, *In Search*, 213. Stegner, "Who Are the Westerners?," 41. Limerick, *Legacy of Conquest*, 29–30 and 308–10. Robbins, "'Plundered Province,'" 594–96. Athearn, *Mythic West*, 155. See also Bill Hornby, "What to Show Visitors in Denver?," *Denver Post*, August 6, 1987.

3. Athearn, *Mythic West*, 258, 271, and 273. Stegner, "Who Are the Westerners?," 36.

4. Thomas Hornsby Ferril, "Time of Mountains," *Westering* (Boise: Ahashta Press, 1986), 1. See also Howard Lamar's review of Athearn, *Mythic West*, in *Colorado Heritage*, no. 4 (1987), 43.

5. Ferril, "Ghost Town," "Two Rivers," *Westering*, 16 and 42. Jack Kisling, "The Essence of the West," *Denver Post*, March 1, 1987. Bill Hornby, "Tom Ferril's pen is stilled. . . ," *Denver Post*, February 28, 1989.

ESSAY ON BIBLIOGRAPHY

For specific references, the reader is encouraged to check the endnotes. This essay is intended to provide a starting point for launching further investigation of the history of the Rocky Mountain West. The following is a selected bibliography, composed primarily of books, which will lead the reader deeper into the fascinating world of Rocky Mountain history. As for the prospector of 1859 or 1879, there is much to be discovered and mined.

The first stop should be the general histories of the three states. The most recent ones provide not only the latest scholarship, but also bibliographies that cover a variety of topics. For Montana, Clark Spence, *Montana: A Bicentennial History* (New York, 1978), and Michael Malone and Richard B. Roeder, *Montana: A History of Two Centuries* (Seattle, 1976), provide excellent overviews. Slightly older, but still challenging, is K. Ross Toole, *Montana: An Uncommon Land* (Norman, 1959). See also: Michael A. Leeson, ed., *History of Montana* (Chicago, 1885); Merrill G. Burlingame, *The Montana Frontier* (Helena, 1942); and Merrill G. Burlingame and K. Rose Toole, eds., *A History of Montana* (New York, 1957).

Wyoming has two outstanding histories: T. A. Larson, *History of Wyoming* (Lincoln, 1965, 1978), and Lewis L. Gould, *Wyoming A Political History, 1868–1896* (New Haven, 1968). Older histories, such as C. C. Coutant, *The History of Wyoming* (Laramie, 1899), and I. S. Bartlett, ed., *History of Wyoming from Territorial Days to the Present* (Chicago, 1918), offer limited help.

For Colorado, four books provide the general overview: Robert G. Athearn, *The Coloradans* (Albuquerque, 1976); Carl Ubbelohde, Maxine Benson, and Duane A. Smith, *A Colorado History*, 6th ed. (Boulder, 1988), Marshall Sprague, *Colorado: A Bicentennial History* (New York, 1976); and Carl Abbott, Stephen J. Leonard, and David McComb, *Colorado: A History of the Centennial State* (Boulder,

1976, 1982). Among the older, multivolume histories, Frank Hall, *History of the State of Colorado* (Chicago, 1889–95); James Baker and LeRoy Hafen, eds., *History of Colorado* (Denver, 1927); and LeRoy Hafen, ed., *Colorado and Its People* (New York, 1948) stand out.

State historical societies are excellent places in which to dig for a variety of primary sources, including those invaluable local newspapers. The societies also publish historical journals that contain a multitude of articles on nearly every subject imaginable. These are *Montana: The Magazine of Western History* and the earlier *Contributions to the Historical Society of Montana, Annals of Wyoming,* and *The Colorado Magazine* and its descendants, *Colorado Heritage* and *Essays and Monographs in Colorado History.*

Ray Allen Billington and Martin Ridge, *Westward Expansion,* 5th ed. (New York, 1982), and Robert E. Riegel and Robert G. Athearn, *America Moves West,* 5th ed. (New York, 1971), place the Rocky Mountains within the context of the entire West. Robert G. Athearn, *High Country Empire: the High Plains and Rockies* (Lincoln, 1960), and Rodman W. Paul, *The Far West and the Great Plains in Transition* (New York, 1988), narrow the view somewhat; David Lavender, in *The Rockies* (New York, 1968), covers a longer chronological time than this study, and Marshall Sprague is more selective in *The Great Gates: The Story of the Rocky Mountain Passes* (Boston, 1964) and more general in *The Mountain States* (New York, 1969). Hubert Howe Bancroft's multivolume western history series contains a potpourri of information; see especially *History of Nevada, Colorado, and Wyoming* (San Francisco, 1890) and *History of Washington, Idaho and Montana* (San Francisco, 1890). Gene Gressley, *West by East: The American West in the Gilded Age* (Provo, 1972), is a thoughtful and interpretive small volume. Michael P. Malone, ed., *Historians and the American West* (Lincoln, 1983), gives a variety of insights into the subject and its historians. Ray Allen Billington, *America's Frontier Heritage* (New York, 1966), adds further discernment of the engrossing, interpretive history of the West.

Firsthand accounts of the nineteenth- and early twentieth-century Rocky Mountains offer a rare look into a vanished world. There are many, but among the best that do not fit neatly into more specific categories are the following: Isabella L. Bird, *A Lady's Life in the Rocky Mountains* (Norman, 1960 reprint of the 1879 edition); Earl of Dunraven, *The Great Divide* (Lincoln, 1967 reprint of the 1876 edition); Anne Ellis, *The Life of an Ordinary Woman* (Lincoln, 1980 reprint of the 1929 edition); Harriet Backus, *Tomboy Bride* (Boulder, 1969); George M. Darley, *Pioneering in the San Juan* (Chicago, 1899); Gene Gressley, ed., *Bostonians and Bullion: The Journal of Robert Livermore 1892–1915* (Lincoln, 1968); Ernest Ingersoll, *Knocking Round the Rockies* (New York, 1883); Alexander McClure, *Three Thousand Miles through the Rocky Mountains* (Philadelphia, 1869); Rodman W. Paul, ed., *A Victorian Gentlewoman in the Far West: The Reminiscences of Mary Hallock Foote* (San Marino, 1972); Albert Richardson, *Beyond the Mississippi* (Hartford, 1867); Andrew F. Rolle, ed., *The Road to Virginia City; The Diary of James Knox Polk Miller* (Norman, 1960); Mary Ronan, *Frontier Woman: The Story of Mary*

Ronan (Helena, 1973); Louis Simonin, *The Rocky Mountain West in 1867*, trans. Wilson D. Clough (Lincoln, 1966); Elinore Pruitt Stewart, *Letters on an Elk Hunt* (Lincoln, 1979); Granville Stuart, *Forty Years on the Frontier* (Cleveland, 1925); James L. Thane, Jr., ed., *A Governor's Wife on the Mining Frontier: Letters of Mary Edgerton from Montana, 1863–1865* (Salt Lake, 1976); and Daniel Tuttle, *Reminiscences of a Missionary Bishop* (New York, 1906).

Mining played the major role in the territorial and early statehood periods of Colorado and Montana, and in the past generation, it has received long overdue scholarly study. Rodman Paul, *Mining Frontiers of the Far West, 1848–1880* (New York, 1963); William Greever, *The Bonanza West* (Norman, 1963); Duane A. Smith, *Rocky Mountain Mining Camps: The Urban Frontier* (Lincoln, 1967, 1974); and Otis E. Young, Jr., *Western Mining: An Informal Account of Precious Metals . . . to 1893* (Norman, 1970) provide the introduction. James E. Fell, Jr., *Ores to Metals: The Rocky Mountain Smelting Industry* (Lincoln, 1979); Clark C. Spence, *Mining Engineers and the American West: The Lace-Boot Brigade, 1849–1933* (New Haven, 1970); and Spence's *British Investments and the American Mining Frontier, 1860–1901* (Ithaca, 1958) are more specialized studies. Muriel S. Wolle, *The Bonanza Trail* (Bloomington, 1953) and *Montana Pay Dirt* (Denver, 1963), and T. H. Watkins, *Gold and Silver in the West* (Palo Alto, 1971), are more popularly written accounts.

Butte has attracted the most attention in Montana; see Michael P. Malone, *The Battle for Butte: Mining and Politics on the Northern Frontier, 1864–1906* (Seattle, 1981); David M. Emmons, *The Butte Irish: Class and Ethnicity in an American Mining Town, 1875–1925* (Urbana, Ill., 1989), and *Copper Camp* (New York, 1943). Thomas J. Dimsdale, *The Vigilantes of Montana* (Norman, 1953 reprint of the 1866 edition), William J. Trimble, *The Mining Advance into the Inland Empire* (Madison, 1914), and Larry Barsness, *Gold Camp* (New York, 1962), cover the Virginia City excitement. Wyoming's hard-rock industry has received little attention, except for Lola Homsher, ed., *South Pass, 1868: James Chisholm's Journal of the Wyoming Gold Rush* (Lincoln, 1960).

A growing number of books on Colorado mining have touched upon all aspects of this state's significant industry. For example, Duane A. Smith, *Colorado Mining* (Albuquerque, 1977), gives an overview, and Smith's *Song of the Hammer and Drill: The Colorado San Juans, 1860–1914* (Golden, 1982) surveys this important district. Stanley Dempsey and James E. Fell, Jr., *Mining the Summit: Colorado's Ten Mile District, 1860–1960* (Norman, 1986); Marshall Sprague, *Money Mountain: The Story of Cripple Creek Gold* (Boston, 1953); Terry Cox, *Inside the Mountains: A History of Mining Around Central City, Colorado* (Boulder, 1989); Edward Blair, *Leadville: Colorado's Magic City* (Boulder, 1980); Malcolm J. Rohrbrough, *Aspen: The History of a Silver Mining Town, 1879–1893* (New York, 1986); and Duane A. Smith, *Silver Saga: The Story of Caribou, Colorado* (Boulder, 1974) indicate the scope of recent work.

The miners themselves and their unions have attracted increased attention. Mark Wyman, *Hard Rock Epic* (Berkeley, 1979); Ronald C. Brown, *Hard-Rock*

Miners (College Station, 1979); and Richard E. Lingenfelter, *The Hardrock Miners* (Berkeley, 1974) furnish a fine overview. Vernon Jensen, *Heritage of Conflict: Labor Relations in the Nonferrous Metals Industry up to 1930* (New York, 1968), is a more general survey.

Until very recent years, coal mining has generally been ignored; that short-coming is now being rectified. Three recent books—Priscilla Long, *Where the Sun Never Shines: A History of America's Bloody Coal Industry* (New York, 1989); the more specialized study by A. Dudley Gardner and Verla R. Flores, *Forgotten Frontier: A History of Wyoming Coal Mining* (Boulder, 1989), and Phyllis Smith, *Once a Coal Miner: The Story of Colorado's Northern Coal Field* (Boulder, 1989)— are excellent introductions. The Ludlow troubles have attracted many scholars; see George McGovern and Leonard Guttridge, *The Great Coalfield War* (Boston, 1972), and Barron Beshoar, *Out of the Depths* (Denver, 1942).

Scholars of mining should never overlook the host of government publications that are available. From J. Ross Browne and James W. Taylor, *Reports upon the Mineral Resources* (Washington, 1867), and Rossiter Raymond's various vol-umes, *Statistics of Mines and Mining* (Washington, published during the 1870s), through the annual reports on *Mineral Resources of the United States* to more specialized tomes, such as Charles W. Henderson, *Mining in Colorado* (Wash-ington, 1926), all are gold mines of facts and statistics. The same can be said for the state publications—for example, the *Report of the Inspector of Coal Mines for the State of Wyoming* (Cheyenne, published in various years). The census returns, in both their published and original forms, offer a wealth of infor-mation.

Territorial government came on the heels of the miners. Earl Pomeroy, *The Territories and the United States, 1861–1890* (Philadelphia, 1947), furnishes an overview, as do Howard Lamar, *The Far Southwest, 1846–1912: A Territorial History* (New Haven, 1966), and Kenneth Owens, "Patterns and Structure in Western Territorial Politics," *Western Historical Quarterly* (October 1970), 372–92. Specifically for the Rocky Mountains, see Gordon Bakken, *The Development of Law on the Rocky Mountain Frontier: Civil Law and Society, 1850–1912* (Westport, Conn., 1983) and *Rocky Mountain Constitution Making, 1850–1912* (New York, 1987); John Guice, *The Rocky Mountain Bench: The Territorial Supreme Courts of Colorado, Montana and Wyoming, 1861–1890* (New Haven, 1972); and Clark C. Spence, *Territorial Politics and Government in Montana* (Urbana, Ill., 1975). Col-orado and Montana published the proceedings of their constitutional conven-tions in *Proceedings and Debates of the Constitutional Convention* (Helena, 1921) and *Proceedings of the Constitutional Convention* (Denver, 1907).

Politically, the Populist party and the election of 1896 have received the most attention. Thomas Clinch, *Urban Populism and Free Silver in Montana* (Mis-soula, 1970), and James Wright, *The Politics of Populism: Dissent in Colorado* (New Haven, 1974), are excellent.

The army helped to open the Rocky Mountain region, but most of the campaigns were to the east. The Civil War years are examined in Duane A.

Smith, *The Birth of Colorado: A Civil War Perspective* (Norman, 1989); Daniel Ellis Conner described the problems of being a southerner in *A Confederate in the Colorado Gold Fields* (Norman, 1970); and a firsthand account is found in Ovando J. Hollister, *Boldly They Rode: A History of the First Colorado Regiment of Volunteers* (Lakewood, 1949 reprint of the 1863 edition). Robert G. Athearn presents the overview in *William Tecumseh Sherman and the Settlement of the West* (Norman, 1956), as does Robert M. Utley, *The Indian Frontier of the American West, 1846–1890* (Albuquerque, 1984). Edgar I. Stewart, *Custer's Luck* (Norman, 1956), and Robert M. Utley, *Cavalier in Buckskin: George Armstrong Custer and the Western Military Frontier* (Norman, 1988), provide insights into the well-known campaigns and Little Big Horn battle. Old, but still the best on the Ute conflict in western Colorado, is Marshall Sprague, *Massacre: The Tragedy at White River* (Boston, 1957).

Unlike the more glamorous mining industry, agriculture has not earned a great deal of attention in the Rocky Mountain region. Gilbert C. Fite, *The Farmers' Frontier, 1865–1900* (New York, 1966), and John T. Schlebecker, *Whereby We Thrive: A History of American Farming, 1607–1972* (Ames, Iowa, 1975), set the scene. Alvin Steinel, *History of Agriculture in Colorado* (Fort Collins, 1926), is dependable, but slow reading. Elinore Pruitt Stewart, on the other hand, has an exciting narrative: *Letters of a Woman Homesteader* (Boston, 1914).

The cattle frontier lapped around the edges of the mountains and breached some of the high mountain valleys. Maurice Frink, *Cow Country Cavalcade* (Denver, 1954), and Maurice Frink, W. Turrentine Jackson, and Agnes Wright Spring, *When Grass Was King* (Boulder, 1956), trace Colorado and Wyoming developments. Harold Briggs, *Frontier of the Northwest: A History of the Upper Missouri Valley* (New York, 1940), and Michael Kennedy, ed., *Cowboys and Cattlemen* (New York, 1964), introduce Montana. Asa Mercer gives his opinion on the Johnson County War in *The Banditti of the Plains* (Norman, 1954 reprint of the 1894 edition); and Mari Sandoz, *The Cattlemen* (New York, 1958) places it on the larger stage. T. B. Long, *70 Years a Cowboy* (Regina, Sask., 1959), and the previously cited *Forty Years on the Frontier*, by Grenville Stuart, offer participants' views of the Montana cattle industry.

Transportation provided the means to overcome distance and isolation, two major obstacles to settlement. Henry P. Walker, *The Wagonmasters* (Norman, 1966); William E. Lass, *A History of Steamboating on the Upper Missouri* (Lincoln, 1962); and Oscar Winther, *The Transportation Frontier* (New York, 1964), provide the overview. The literature on railroads is extensive. Tivis, E. Wilkins, *Colorado Railroads: Chronological Development* (Boulder, 1974), and Robert M. Ormes, *Railroads and the Rockies: A Record of Lines in and near Colorado* (Denver, 1963), introduce the reader to Colorado. Robert G. Athearn's two books, *Union Pacific Country* (New York, 1971) and *Rebel of the Rockies: A History of the Denver and Rio Grande Western Railroad* (New Haven, 1962), present the history of these significant railroads. Richard C. Overton, *Burlington Route, A History of the Burlington Lines* (New York, 1965), describes Montana's major lines. Robert

Black III, *Railroad Pathfinder: The Life and Times of Edward L. Berthoud* (Evergreen, Colo., 1988); Harry E. Kelsey, Jr., *Frontier Capitalist: The Life of John Evans* (Denver, 1969); and J. B. Hedges, *Henry Villard and the Railways of the Northwest* (New Haven, 1930), tell the story of three railroaders.

Because of its mining birth, much of the history of the Rocky Mountain region is strongly urban. John W. Reps, *Cities of the American West: A History of Frontier Urban Planning* (Princeton, 1979) gives an overview. For a sampling of the mining communities, see the prior section on the mining industry. Denver, as the dominant community, has received the most scholarly attention. Recent studies are Thomas Noel, *Denver: Rocky Mountain Gold* (Denver, 1980); Lyle W. Dorsett, *The Queen City* (Boulder, 1977); Gunther Barth, *Instant Cities: Urbanization and the Rise of San Francisco and Denver* (New York, 1975); and Thomas Noel and Barbara Norgren, *The City Beautiful and Its Architects, 1893–1941* (Denver, 1987). Beyond mining and Denver, urban history is a young Rocky Mountain discipline, with many towns awaiting their Homer. See: Sharon Field, ed., *History of Cheyenne, Wyoming* (Dallas, 1989); Marshall Sprague, *Newport in the Rockies: The Life and Good Times of Colorado Springs* (Chicago, 1980); and Duane A. Smith, *Rocky Mountain Boom Town: A History of Durango, Colorado* (Boulder, 1980, 1986).

Tourism came early to the region and has emerged as an economic pillar. Scholars were somewhat late in examining its significance but have recently worked to overcome this tardiness. The books with which to begin are Earl Pomeroy, *In Search of the Golden West: The Tourist in West America* (New York, 1957), and Robert G. Athearn, *Westward the Briton* (New York, 1953). Lawrence R. Borne, *Dude Ranching* (Albuquerque, 1983), discusses one of the specialized tourist businesses. The national parks have captured most of the attention; see: Richard A. Bartlett, *Yellowstone: A Wilderness Besieged* (Tucson, 1983); Hiram M. Chittenden, *Yellowstone National Park* (Norman, 1964 reprint of the 1895 edition); C. W. Buchholtz, *Rocky Mountain National Park: A History* (Boulder, 1983); and Duane A. Smith, *Mesa Verde National Park: Shadows of the Centuries* (Lawrence, 1988). Glacier still awaits a modern historian, but Madison Grant, *Early History of Glacier National Park Montana* (Washington, 1919), is a starting point. For the general overview, see John Ise, *Our National Park Policy* (Baltimore, 1961), and Alfred Runte, *National Parks: The American Experience* (Lincoln, 1979). Looking at the region through eyes of the nineteenth-century tourist guide, Karl Baedeker, ed., *The United States with an Excursion into Mexico* (New York, 1973 reprint of the 1893 edition), is a fascinating experience.

Conservation, environment, and water are crucial topics that are just beginning to receive attention. Outstanding is Michael McCarthy, *Hour of Trial: The Conservation Conflict in Colorado and the West, 1891–1907* (Norman, 1977). See also David H. Getches, ed., *Water and the American West* (Boulder, 1988); Robert G. Dunbar, *Forging New Rights in Western Waters* (Lincoln, 1983); Roy E. Huffman, *Irrigation Development and Public Water Policy* (New York, 1953); and

Joseph M. Petulla, *American Environmentalism: Values, Tactics, Priorities* (College Station, Tex., 1980).

Susan Armitage and Elizabeth Jameson, *The Women's West* (Norman, 1987), and Sandra Myres, *Westering Women and the Frontier Experience, 1800–1925* (Albuquerque, 1982), are fine introductions to women's experiences in the Rocky Mountains. Elliott West, *Growing Up with the Country: Childhood on the Far Western Frontier* (Albuquerque, 1989), breaks new ground; and Anne Butler, *Daughters of Joy, Sisters of Misery: Prostitutes in the American West, 1865–90* (Urbana, Ill., 1985), sheds new light on an old subject. Check also the listings under firsthand accounts.

Minorities have not received a great deal of attention in the study of Rocky Mountain history. Rose Hum Lee, *The Growth and Decline of Chinese Communities in the Rocky Mountain Region* (New York, 1978), and Glenda Riley, "American Daughters; Black Women in the West,"*Montana* (Spring 1988), 14–27, show there is a rich field to be worked.

The Rocky Mountains in the twentieth century are another area that is begging for scholars to research and to study. Some outstanding books have been published, however, which are excellent guides to follow: Gerald Nash, *The American West in the Twentieth Century* (Albuquerque, 1973, 1977), Robert G. Athearn, *The Mythic West in Twentieth Century America* (Lawrence, 1986), and Patricia N. Limerick, *The Legacy of Conquest: The Unbroken Past of The American West* (New York, 1987). Richard D. Lamm and Michael McCarthy, *The Angry West: A Vulnerable Land and Its Future* (Boston, 1982), is provocative and emotional.

INDEX